s 1980
The Soviet m

Wesley Andrew Fisher

THE SOVIET MARRIAGE MARKET

Mate-Selection in Russia and the USSR

Studies of the Russian Institute  Columbia University

PRAEGER SPECIAL STUDIES • PRAEGER SCIENTIFIC

Library of Congress Cataloging in Publication Data

Fisher, Wesley A
    The Soviet marriage market.

    Bibliography: p.
    Includes index.
    1. Marriage--Russia. 2. Mate selection--
Russia. 3. Marriage age--Russia. I. Title.
HQ785.F52   306.8'0947   78-19737
ISBN 0-03-045346-1

The Russian Institute of Columbia University sponsors the *Studies of the Russian Institute* in the belief that their publication contributes to scholarly research and public understanding. In this way the Institute, while not necessarily endorsing their conclusions, is pleased to make available the results of some of the research conducted under its auspices. A list of the *Studies of the Russian Institute* appears at the back of the book.

Published in 1980 by Praeger Publishers
CBS Educational and Professional Publishing
A Division of CBS, Inc.
521 Fifth Avenue, New York, New York 10017 U.S.A.

© 1980 by Praeger Publishers

0123456789   038   987654321

Printed in the United States of America

To my parents,

with gratitude and affection

ACKNOWLEDGMENTS

My very great intellectual debt to William J. Goode is obvious through-out the pages that follow. I would like in addition to express my gratitude to him for his sponsorship of this project and his personal kindness to me. Robert Lewis was enormously helpful in coping with the difficulties of working with Soviet demographic data, and Peter Juviler's comments on the manuscript were highly useful in improving it. Eugene Litwak, W. Phillips Davison, and Loren Graham also were kind enough to comment.

Mary Ann Miller of Columbia's Lehman Library assisted with the task of locating and searching through literally hundreds and hundreds of Imperial Russian and Soviet statistical compilations. The Department of Social and Economic Affairs of the United Nations and Dr. Murray Feshbach of the Foreign Demographic Analysis Division, U.S. Department of Commerce, kindly allowed me access to their data files.

A Fulbright-Hays Faculty Research Abroad Grant and a fellowship from the International Research and Exchanges Board (IREX) allowed me to spend an academic year in the Soviet Union searching for additional data and discussing my ideas with Soviet colleagues. I am most grateful to the many Soviet scholars in demography, ethnography, and sociology who gave so freely of their time and advice; while not all of my conclusions may be in accordance with their own, I have incorporated many of their criticisms and suggestions into this volume. Ambassador Malcolm Toon graciously permitted me to collect data on Soviet-U.S. marriages on the basis of information in the United States Embassy in Moscow. The assistance of Lawrence Napper of the Consular Section was invaluable in this regard.

John Long, Inna Shalin, St. Claire Blair, Bruce Cooper, and Gosia Brykczynska helped with the manuscript.

I would like to take this opportunity to thank George Fischer, Marshall Shulman, Robert K. Merton, and Allen H. Kassot, who, although they have not had any direct hand in the work on this study as such, encouraged me to develop my interest in Soviet society and Soviet sociology.

Above all I am grateful to my father and mother, a specialist in matrimonial and family law and a marriage and divorce counselor respectively, without whose affectionate support this study never would have been possible.

And then there are my wife Regine and son Maxim.

CONTENTS

95

LIST OF TABLES

Table

Table

xi

Table

Table

Table

Table

Table

Table

1

INTRODUCTION

Attempting to explain family life in terms of the demands of society's economic structure, Marx and Engels essentially employed a market theory of mate-selection. Their conceptualization of mate-selection under capitalism as a market following principles of exchange was quite explicit. They considered that monogamy among the bourgeoisie aided the accumulation of capital by ensuring the orderly transfer of property from father to son. In return for the economic power of their future husbands, women were forced to sell their bodies on a marriage market. The resulting unions among the bourgeoisie were seen as hateful, calculated marriages of convenience or, as Engels put it, the "crassest prostitution—sometimes of both partners, but far more commonly of the woman, who only differs from the ordinary courtesan in that she does not let out her body on piece-work as a wage-worker, but sells it once and for all into slavery" (Engels 1942: 63).

Haggling over dowries and a spirit of exchange typified entrance into marriage, though Engels recognized that the bourgeoisie did not necessarily conceive of themselves as driving a bargain on a market. In Protestant countries, he noted, "the rule is that the son of a bourgeois family is allowed to choose a wife from his own class with more or less freedom; hence there may be a certain element of love in the marriage, as, indeed, in accordance with Protestant hypocrisy, is always assumed, for decency's sake" (Engels 1942: 62-63). He noted that often bourgeois marriage markets were formally free and that to a great extent any man could as a legal matter marry any woman:

> In regard to marriage, the law, even the most advanced, is fully satisfied as soon as the partners have formally recorded that they are entering into the marriage of their own free consent. What goes on in real life behind the juridical scenes, how this free consent comes about—that is not the business of the law and the jurist. And yet the most elementary comparative jurisprudence should

1

show the jurist what this free consent really amounts to. In the
countries where an obligatory share of the paternal inheritance
is secured to the children by law and they cannot therefore be
disinherited—in Germany, in the countries with French law and
elsewhere—the children are obliged to obtain their parents' consent to their marriage. In the countries with English law, where
parental consent to a marriage is not legally required, the parents
on their side have full freedom in testamentary disposal of their
property and can disinherit their children at their pleasure. It is
obvious that, in spite and precisely because of this fact, freedom
of marriage among the classes with something to inherit is in reality
not a whit greater in England and America than it is in France and
Germany. (Engels 1942: 64-65)

Among the proletariat under capitalism, the absence of property supposedly reduced the importance of monetary variables in mate-selection. The
working-class woman's employment in industry and her consequent greater
equality with men removed much of the necessity of her having to sell herself on a marriage market. Instead, personal preference and mutual love predomi-
nated among motives for marriage: "Sex-love in the relationship with a woman
becomes, and can only become, the real rule among the repressed classes, which
means today among the proletariat . . ." (Engels 1942: 63). Economic variables
still played a role in the conclusion of marriage among the working class under
capitalism, however, because of the great poverty of the proletariat. Economic
need, for example, encouraged the worker to marry early in order to protect
himself by having more children to put to work in the sweatshops and mines
(Marx 1906: vol. I, 706).

While Marx's and Engels's conceptualization of mate-selection as a market
is clearest in regard to monetary economic variables, their more general discussion of the nature of the family shows that they also had some sense of the
importance of noneconomic, nonmonetary variables in mate-selection still within a framework of bargaining and exchange. Thus they held that women had
exchanged their socially dominant position in the primitive communistic household for the "right of chastity, of temporary or permanent marriage with one
man only" (Engels 1942: 46). It has been argued that in their discussion of the
family generally, Marx and Engels were moving away from economic determi-
nism toward a multifactor theory (see Geiger 1968: 28-40).

Marx and Engels foresaw that in the future the salutary aspects of mate-
selection among the proletariat would develop further. With abolition of the
private ownership of the means of production, marriage would come to be a
union reflecting free choice between partners without regard to economic considerations. Mate-selection, in other words, would cease to function as a market
in regard to monetary criteria. Indeed, there is reason to suppose that Marx and
Engels envisioned mate-selection in the future as ceasing to function as a market

in any sense whatsoever, not only in regard to monetary considerations, but also nonmonetary ones as well:

> Full freedom of marriage can therefore only be generally established when the abolition of capitalist production and of the property relations created by it has removed all the accompanying economic considerations which still exert such a powerful influence on the choice of a marriage partner. For then there is *no other motive* left except mutual inclination. (Engels 1942: 72, emphasis added)

In view of the importance they placed on economic matters, and in particular on the abolition of private property, the elimination in the future of a market structure to mate-selection simply is clearest in Marx's and Engels's thought as regards economic criteria. To the extent that they saw economic inequality as the source of other types of inequality relevant to marriage markets, however, Marx and Engels also believed that in the future there would be no market structure to mate-selection in any sense whatsoever. Certainly their conception of what life under communism would be like—no differences between physical and mental labor, between town and country, and so on—implies an end to all inequalities relevant to mate-selection. Love alone, love "by its nature exclusive" and of long duration, would be the basis for marriage. The only "exchange" would be love for love. While in view of discussions of affection-liking as a means of social control (Goode 1973) it may be objected that this in itself forms a type of market structure, it is clear that Marx and Engels desired to do away with any and all exchange, bargaining, or haggling in the process of courtship. The pattern of who would marry whom in the future was expected to approach something close to random mating on the basis of emotional attraction.

The Bolsheviks readily adopted Marx's and Engels's conceptions of mate-selection, particularly their views on the market nature of bourgeois marriage and the elimination of economic criteria for marriage under socialism. "Under capitalism," Nadezhda Krupskaia declared "marriage is a business deal. There are the advantages of marrying a rich man or a rich woman, of marrying a man of position or the daughter of a minister; getting a housewife or a breadwinner, and so forth" (Krupskaia 1957: 179). With the Revolution all that changed. Wrote Alexandra Kollontai:

> The Communist system will help to clear married life from its undercurrent of material calculations and profit. Previously if a man was about to get married he would calculate and count whether he could afford a wife and how far that would prove profitable for him. A girl, before marrying, would work out what her husband could offer her.
>
> The Communist society approaches the working woman and the working man and says to them: "You are young, you love each

other. Everyone has the right to happiness. Therefore live your life. Do not flee happiness. Do not fear marriage, even though marriage was truly a chain for the working man and woman of capitalist society."

On the ruins of the former family we shall soon see a new form rising which will involve altogether different relations between men and women and which will *be a union of affection and comrade-ship, a union of two equal members of the communist society, both of them free, both of them independent, both of them workers. . . .* Marriage will be purified of all its material elements, of all money calculations, which constitute a hideous blemish on family life in our days. Marriage is henceforth to be transformed into a sub-lime union of two souls in love with each other, each having faith in the other. . . . (translated in Schlesinger 1949: 56-58, 66-68, emphasis in original)

The repudiation of older forms of mate-selection and the attempt through legislation and other means to create new systems of courtship struck a major sympathetic chord not only among Russian Marxists but also among the general population (see Chapter 2).

Today Marx's and Engels's images of a marriage market under capitalism and the absence or gradual disappearance of any such market under socialism are with some modifications the dominant theoretical conceptions of Soviet sociology regarding courtship and mate-selection. Thus Soviet sociologists approve market and exchange theories of mate-selection proposed by Western sociologists as accurate descriptions of social relations under capitalism, although such theories are said to shock Soviet sensitivities. In a recent monograph on the family, Minsk sociologist Nikolai Iurkevich states:

> The trade jargon alone in which bourgeois sociologists talk about marriage stuns the Soviet reader. "Dreaming," writes one of the most well-known American sociologists of the family C. Kirkpatrick in a textbook for students, "is less effective than realistically going out into the market of dates, engagements and marriage with eyes opened wide for a good deal for the right price." Goode stresses that groom and bride do not at all have to be at the same level in all respects. On the contrary, he says, it seems probable that be-tween them there have to be a sufficient number of valued different characteristics that become the object of trade. (Iurkevich 1970: 84)

In like manner the best-known of Soviet family sociologists, Anatolii Kharchev, cites Western discussions to the effect that love is not a sufficiently hopeful basis for forming a family as evidence not only of the calculation involved in mate-selection in the capitalist world, but also of the encouragement of such calculation in the writings of Western "bourgeois" sociologists (Kharchev 1969: 107).

Contemporary Soviet authors recognize that romantic love exists in the West primarily as the result of the ideology of individualism, but such love is considered to be generally unattached to marriage: it is the basis for sexual liaisons rather than for the unification of families (Kharchev 1969: 107). Recently it has been admitted that the basis for marriage has been changing from a material to a spiritual one in the West, but it is said to be doing so more slowly than in the USSR (Riurikov 1975). At the same time, Soviet condemnation of mate-selection under capitalism is in some ways even stronger than Marx's and Engels's. Robert Winch's theory of complementary needs, for example, has been rejected on the ground that it implies a psychological basis, or love, for choosing a spouse under capitalism. In other words, it is not considered enough to say that within a small pool of eligibles love prevails as a motive: under capitalism calculation is held to extend to the psychological motivation itself (Golofast 1971: 154). Even Engels believed that love occurred within a small pool of eligibles (see Engels 1942: 62-63). Similarly, although it is accepted that the proletariat is freer than the bourgeoisie in mate-selection under capitalism, William J. Goode's observation that families higher in the social structure grant less freedom in courtship than families lower down (consonant with Marx's and Engels's own observations) has been partially repudiated on the ground that public opinion and often legal structures control interracial and interreligious marriages throughout the entire social structure of capitalist countries (Kharchev 1969: 110).

In discussion of mate-selection in their own society, Soviet sociologists have moved beyond the simplistic notion that the establishment of a socialist state automatically means an end to economic variables in mate-selection. A marriage market based on economic considerations is held to have disappeared in the USSR, but it is recognized that monetary considerations sometimes may play a role in the marital decisions of particular individuals:

> In our society marriage as a rule is concluded for love and mutual desire. The liquidation of private ownership of the means of production carried with it the disappearance of a class of people who had at their disposal enormous unearned income. Socialist society has its stratification which cannot be said not to have an influence on the area of relations we are studying [marriage]; but in any case, an honest Soviet person disposes only of what he has earned. This by itself has undermined any basis for bargaining upon entrance into marriage. Women have received in socialist society a right equal to that of men to work and to income. Moreover, this right is not only written in the law, but is carried out in practice. The necessity for women to sell themselves has been removed by this. The liquidation of private property and the liberation of women have created condi-

tions under which material calculation, as a general rule, no longer determines mate-selection. (Iurkevich 1970a: 91)

In a recent book on family theory, Kharchev states:

> The experience of development of the family in the socialist countries bears witness to the fact that the opinion according to which the destruction of private property and provision of occupational employment of women on equal conditions with men automatically takes care of new relations between the sexes must be recognized as somewhat simplifying real processes. In the first place, socialism does not guarantee either society as a whole or separate families protection from temporary material difficulties. As a result, the possibility of appearance of utilitarian views, condemned by communist morality but not entirely uprooted, towards marriage and sexual ties generally is preserved, although to an incomparably smaller degree than formerly.
>
> In the second place, the factual situation where a person believes that he/she loves another person and has the moral right to enter with him/her into close relations and formalize a marriage, and that where a person really experiences love including its higher aspects such as exclusivity and altruism, are by far not identical. And if in the second case a socialist marriage is truly the opposite of one under private property relations and really corresponds to the ideal, in the first this opposition and correspondence are primarily formal ones (Kharchev 1974a: 9-10)

Although mention is made of some economic functions of the family in the future as continuing so as to help in the labor education of children, ties between husband and wife are to be entirely on a moral basis (Kharchev 1967: 18-19). The lingering economic aspects of marriage referred to in the above quotations are to disappear entirely with the development of communism:

> In the preparation for and contraction of marriage the main changes will be the complete elimination of economic or other attendant motives in selecting a mate and further enrichment of the moral and aesthetic content of relations between the sexes. . . . Distribution according to needs and the elimination of survivals of property instincts in people will exclude the possibility of marriages of economic convenience or for any other reason than personal inclination. Correspondingly, to an even greater degree than under socialism, marriage will be between persons of more or less the same age. Late marriages will also evidently die out. That will be because for one thing the well-being of a family will not depend on the need to complete an education, acquire a trade or profession or the other circumstances that often prevent a first deep love from being consummated by marriage. Then too, improved methods of education will reduce

and perhaps destroy altogether the gap that now exists between the sexual and moral coming of age of youth. (Kharchev undated: 54)

As pointed out above, Marx and Engels were against a market system of mate-selection not only so far as monetary variables were concerned, but also in regard to nonmonetary variables. Given the predominance of Marxism-Leninism in Soviet social science, it is understandable that most Soviet discussions of the applicable variables in mate-selection would center on questions of economics, but it is clear from a number of Soviet writings on courtship that calculation of any sort regarding any criteria whatsoever in the choice of a mate as opposed to "pure" emotional attraction or love is of questionable legitimacy. Thus in discussion of the possibility of establishing marriage bureaus in the USSR (on the issue of marriage bureaus and computer matchmaking, see Chapter 2), the idea of people applying to such a bureau to find a spouse even though they are not concerned with property or economic matters as such—instead want to find someone of a particular age, who lives in a particular place, who has or does not have children, for example—has been condemned as involving calculation (Vorozheikin 1971: 101-2). To the extent that condemnation of a market in mate-selection in any regard whatsoever has entered Soviet social values, it has been noted that there are a large number of casual marriages where people "pride themselves on their lack of calculation" (Vishnevskii 1975a).

Spontaneous entrance into marriage without calculation may be admirable from the standpoint of Marxism-Leninism, but as a practical matter it has had the effect of creating a large number of marriages that have not been sufficiently considered. Lack of forethought and consideration in marital choice is said to be a major source of divorce in the USSR (Kharchev 1969: 111). As a result, a number of authors recently have advocated more careful consideration in making one's marital choice, claiming that while economic criteria should not come into play, nonetheless a certain amount of calculation regarding nonmonetary matters is necessary:

> A significant category of people who retain a view of love as a "judgment" by this understand calculation in the worst meaning of the word. It stands to reason that everyone entering into marriage counts on something: the advantages of family over single life, the warmth of conjugal relations, the fact that with a loved one it is easier to go through life. This moral type of calculation finds its reflection in everyday and entirely justified desires to see one's companion in life sufficiently cultured and educated, having a specialty and skill or achieving them, knowing how to take care of himself/herself and future children through conscientious work, striving for fidelity and love and friendship with parents, etc. One should not enter into marriage "banging one's head" or as if jumping into the unknown. But all this in no way signifies that the calculation is of the naked advantages of marriage. (Laptenok 1967: 136)

Similar points have been made in articles with titles such as "Love Alone?" (Riurikov 1974) and "Love by Calculation?" (Vishnevskii 1975a). In other words, it is now sometimes claimed that a market system in some respects exists or should exist in the USSR regarding nonmonetary variables, but that economic considerations as such in mate-selection essentially have been removed from Soviet courtship.

Soviet denial of a market structure to mate-selection in the USSR is intriguing in light of the movement in recent years in Western social theory to explanations of social behavior, and of mate-selection in particular, in exchange and market terms both as regards monetary and nonmonetary variables (Goode 1956; 1962; 1963; 1964: 31-43; 1974; Burr 1973: 71-102; Becker 1973; 1974; Freiden 1974; Preston and Richards 1975; Santos 1975; Sawhill 1977; and others). In Goode's writings the process of mate-selection in all societies is conceptualized as a market system, with different societies varying as to who is doing the bargaining and controls the market, the rules of exchange, and the relative evaluation of different qualities. As potential mates find their approximate level on the market through bargaining processes, there is a press toward homogamous marriages (Goode 1964: 32-33). Love, in this conception, is a universal human potential that constitutes a threat to the marriage market and through it to the stratification system of a society, and is therefore generally controlled. Societies such as the Soviet Union and the United States that have institutionalized romantic love complexes nonetheless control love by permitting freedom of courtship only within small pools of eligibles (Goode 1959; 1964: 39-40).

Gary S. Becker's attempt to apply economic theories of optimal decision making to mate-selection carries the analogy with commodity markets to the extreme by monetizing nonmonetary variables: that is to say, in Becker's conception persons are assumed to be trying to maximize their total "income" through marriage, and traits such as education and caring or loving that are not directly economic in character are given a money equivalent. While the objection has been raised that exchanges regarding nonmonetary variables do not operate in the same fashion as those regarding monetary ones (Goode 1974), Becker's formulations regarding the effect of specifically economic considerations per se on entrance into marriage have received some confirmation (Freiden 1974; Santos 1975; Sawhill 1977: 119. See also Farkas 1976).

In particular, Becker notes that persons must allocate their time between market work and housework. Assuming that men and women are equally efficient at housework, then the gain from marrying is greater the larger the difference between the market wages of men and women, since the partner receiving the lesser market wage is more likely to specialize in housework and the total income of both husband and wife is as a result greater than what it would be were they to remain single. If, as is usually the case, the man's income exceeds that of the woman's, then the man as husband will specialize in market production while the wife concentrates her time in the home. An attempt to test this hypothesis regarding relative wages has shown that a larger proportion of females are married in U.S. states that have higher wage rates of males relative to wage rates of females (Freiden 1974; Santos, 1975). Becker extends the same sort of analysis to traits other than income, hypothesizing that like will marry like except in those traits that are close substitutes in household production (Becker 1973).

Becker's foray into treating love in economic terms would horrify Soviet Marxists. On the one hand, he considers love simply to another nonmarketable household commodity. As such, it does not alter the argument regarding attempts to maximize total "income" and the gain from marrying as opposed to remaining single depending on other factors such as relative difference in wage rates, as described above. Love in this sense increases the chances of persons being married to each other in an optimal sorting but does not override economic considerations. On the other hand, Becker considers love to be essentially "caring," by which is meant concern for the other person, or, translated into economic terms, the dependence of a person's utility level on the consumption of a potential spouse as well as on that person's own consumption. Caring between two persons increases their chances of being married to each other since it raises total "income" available to the parties by reducing the need for policing a mate from appropriating more output than mandated by the equilibrium in the marriage market, and also by making part of their household output a family commodity that is consumed by both: that is, in caring the income of a person is the sum of the couple's consumption, not of a single person's alone (Becker 1974: S14-S15).

Mutual and full caring by both parties might be taken as a definition of love. Becker argues that were such mutual and full caring to prevail throughout society in all matings, there would be a positive correlation between the proportion married and wage rates—that is, the less the differential between wage rates of men and women, the more the marriage—or in other words the opposite of what is to be expected if men and women pursue their own utility alone. This is because were mutual and full caring to be characteristic of all marriages, the output of marriages would not be divisible between mates but would be a family commodity. What is basically being said is that each spouse, under conditions of mutual and full caring, tries to produce as much as possible for the other, wants the other to consume as much as possible, and there is no way to divide up what they are doing for each other. Under such conditions the income of each mate equals the output of the marriage as a whole, and the combinations that result through competition on the market will tend to be between men and women of the same wage levels—that is, given full and mutual caring, the gain from marriage compared to remaining single is greatest the higher the potential mate's wages, but since everyone is in competition the optimal sorting leads to a positive correlation between the wage rates of mates, or wage homogamy (Becker 1974: S12-S17).

The Soviet denial of any market structure to courtship and marriage in the USSR provides a challenge to this development in Western sociology and economics toward viewing mate-selection as a market system. If Soviet mate-selection in fact does not conform to a market model, study of it is of importance in possibly providing clues to the need for alteration in or abandonment of such market theories. Goode's broad comparative study (Goode 1963) raises a strong suspicion that market theories of mate-selection are valid for the Soviet Union as well, but he specifically omitted coverage of the USSR and there has been as yet no real attempt to fill the gap on the basis of empirical evidence. Even were there no Soviet ideological denial of a market structure, it would still be important to test such theories further on a comparative basis.

The position of Soviet sociologists should not be dismissed out of hand as wishful idealism, however, since there are a number of features of Soviet society that do challenge the market conception of mate-selection. In the first place, the Soviet ideological commitment to love as the basis for marriage is more explicit and officially codified than in other societies. Love as a value is specifically propagandized and cultivated by communist morality. Although ideology clearly has been a major factor in family changes throughout the world (Goode 1963), in few societies has there been such extensive propagation by the state of love as the basis for marriage and hatred for marriages of calculation. This point has been stressed by Kharchev in discussion of Goode's observations concerning the convergence of world family patterns (Kharchev 1969: 108-9).* To the extent that this aspect of Marxist-Leninist ideology has entered popular conceptions of morality (see Chapter 2), it presumably serves to reduce the motivation to use marriage as a vehicle for social mobility. Even the flat ideological assertions that marriages of calculation no longer exist in the USSR, even though unproven or untrue, function as self-fulfilling prophecies that reduce the number of such marriages (Geiger 1968: 109-10).

In the second place, as regards the specifically economic aspects of mate-selection, the historically greater employment of women in the Soviet labor force and the provision of social welfare imply that individuals may indeed be more able to be economically independent than in many nonsocialist societies, and in consequence be less reliant on marriage for their economic existence. While this is the position of the official ideology, it is interesting to note that popular commentary in the Soviet press also takes this position. An article entitled "Only Romeo!," for example, argues that the achievement by women of relative equality and self-sufficiency in the outside world—including even the economic feasibility of raising a child alone—means women now want "only

---

*The heavy emphasis in the Soviet school curriculum on the classics of nineteenth-century Russian literature also serves to cultivate love as a value. As a character in a recent Soviet novel puts it, ". . . we give too much significance to love. It's aristocratic literature that taught us to do so . . ." (Kron 1977: 32).

Romeo," only a love relationship in marriage, and are uninterested in marriage's other advantages (Iunina 1971). In this connection, in the United States the greater participation of women in the labor force in recent years has reduced rates of entrance into marriage (Carter and Glick 1976: 392-93), but the USSR proudly points to supposedly high marriage rates even in its official statistical publications. That marriage may not be an economic necessity is not the same thing as saying it is not economically desirable.

Third, there are a number of ways in which it is more difficult to utilize socially the characteristics of one's spouse in the Soviet Union than in other countries. The status characteristics of a husband are not easily convertible into the status characteristics of his wife, and vice versa, as a result of several structural features. While the wealth of a spouse may be enjoyed directly by an individual, it is difficult for the latter to use that wealth to enhance, say, an occupational career, since unlike the U.S. economy the state-owned Soviet economy does not permit the investment of private funds into business ventures. Because of the bureaucratic structure of the Soviet economy, it is of little direct use to marry above oneself unless the spouse or the spouse's family are in the same bureaucratic hierarchy as the individual. While there is some advantage in terms of prestige, power, and access to material goods in marrying someone who is well known or who is the child of successful parents, a man who, for example, works in heavy industry whose prospective bride is the daughter of persons powerful in the Ministry of Culture would find it relatively difficult to convert the status of his wife's parents into advantages for himself since his promotions depend on persons in his particular ministry or sector of the economy. His wife's parents' influence perhaps can be used indirectly to influence his promotions, but the conversion of their status into his has to be considerably more devious than in the United States, where in many cases the money of a wife's family may directly assist in a son-in-law's career. The difficulty of using a spouse's status to promote one's own occupational career is supported by antinepotism laws in the Soviet Union that make it difficult to use relatives of any sort, and spouses in particular, in immediate job situations. The argument may not hold, however, for the very top political circles of Soviet society that are less bureaucratically divided (Fischer 1968)—the careers of Adzhubei and Gvishiani, sons-in-law of Khrushchev and Kosygin respectively, come to mind.

In a far greater number of contexts than in the West, the status of one's spouse is simply unknown. In contrast to the extensive Western press coverage of the wives and husbands of political leaders and other public personalities, the characteristics of the spouses of public figures in the Soviet Union are typically unknown both to the Soviet population and to the rest of the world.* It is sometimes argued that the secretiveness surrounding the family life of the

*A rare exception in recent years was the distribution by the official Soviet press agency Tass of a portrait and brief article about the wife of President Leonid I. Brezhnev,

Soviet elite is an attempt to hide the extent to which kinship ties and connections in fact affect the composition of the ruling groups. This argument can be turned around, however, to say that it is precisely to reduce the effect of kinship on achievement that secrecy is maintained. A variant hypothesis is that the wives who stand behind the elite figures typically have aided their husbands' careers by taking charge of all household duties and do not work, and their nonemployment would be a source of embarrassment to the regime if known (Geiger 1968: 150; for discussion of the kinship ties of the Soviet elite, see Matthews 1978).

The lack of publicity surrounding spouses applies to all of Soviet society, however. The media do not usually report on the family life of anyone, not only that of the elite, since family life is considered to be the private affair of individuals and not of newsworthy interest. Although the personnel departments of factories and institutions presumably know the marital status of workers and employees, they would not necessarily know more than what is inserted into the internal passport at the time of marriage: the spouse's name, date of birth, and the date of the registration of the marriage. In addition, wives and husbands are not invited to each other's place of work. In other words, couples are not seen together at public affairs, nor are their relationships publicized, and this is in keeping with the Soviet commitment to individual achievement.*

Even in casual informal relations between people, it is more difficult to utilize the social standing of a wife or husband than in the United States since among those not well acquainted the marital status of an individual often is not known. Soviet forms of address contain no clues as to marital status, and often husbands and wives retain separate last names. According to the laws of all the Union republics of the USSR, it is possible to take one family name for both husband and wife—either that of the husband or that of the wife—or to retain family names held prior to marriage. (In addition, the codes of the Ukraine, Byelorussia, Azerbaidzhan, Georgia, Moldavia, and Tadzhikistan permit the use of a hyphenated double name for both bride and groom upon marriage.) While the tradition of taking the husband's name remains very strong, particularly in rural areas, the available information indicates that somewhat more than one-fourth of the couples in the larger cities retain separate names, as seen in Table 1.1 (Nikonov 1974: 230-32).

In this regard it is interesting to note that it is considered improper in the Soviet Union for men and women when meeting to give their last name, let alone

---

on the occasion of her seventieth birthday. The press release was given to foreign correspondents and contained very little information on Mrs. Brezhnev (*New York Times* 1977).

*A recent article in the Soviet Union's main military daily *Krasnaia zvezda* sharply castigates servicemen's wives for interceding in their husbands' behalf in cases of promotion not only on grounds of individual achievement, but also because such attempts sometimes have revealed knowledge of military matters the wives "have no business possessing" (Khorev 1979).

TABLE 1.1

Choice of Last Name upon Marriage: Sverdlovsk Region of Moscow, City of Ulianovsk, and 11 Areas of Ulianovsk Oblast, 1971 (per 1,000 Couples)

Family Name Chosen	Sverdlovsk Region of Moscow	City of Ulianovsk	Ulianovsk Oblast	
			Worker Settlements	Rural Areas
Groom's last name	724	984	986	996
Bride's last name	8	1	–	–
Retained names held prior to marriage	268	15	14	4

Source: Niokonov 1974: 230–32.

advertise their social position. The closest thing to a Soviet Emily Post, a book entitled *Soviet Etiquette*, has this to say:

> Becoming acquainted at dances, at a party or at someone's home, it is improper to give your last name but is enough to give your first names or first names and patronymic. Women younger than 20 years of age can limit themselves to their first name, even to a nickname: Tania, Katia, Valia. It is immodest upon becoming acquainted with a woman to stress your high position at work, to inform her of your academic degree, title, etc. (Verb 1971: 112)

Obviously over time such characteristics are found out, and even upon first meeting there are nonverbal cues that may be seized on, but such norms reduce the extent to which individuals are identified with their spouses, as well as the social space between people.

In a number of ways the legal structure of the Soviet Union helps to prevent marriage from taking the form of a market transaction. This is most obvious in laws directed against unions that closely fit Engels's description of bourgeois marriage under capitalism as a form of prostitution. Thus payment of a bride-price and taking advantage of a woman's economic or occupational dependence to compel sexual intercourse or the satisfaction of sexual desires in any other form are crimes in the USSR, and such acts are prosecuted. Article 232 of the RSFSR Criminal Code provides for a year's confinement or correctional tasks plus confiscation of the payment as a punishment for parents, kin, or relatives by marriage of a bride who accept a bride-price for her of money, cattle, or other property. The groom, his parents, kin, and relatives by marriage who pay the bride-price can receive correctional tasks up to one year or censure. Similar provisions exist in the criminal codes of the Kirgiz, Tadzhik, Armenian, and Turkmen republics (*Ugolovnoe Zakonadatel'stvo Soiuza SSR i soiuznykh respublik* 1963: relevant codes; Juviler 1977). Under article 118 of the RSFSR Criminal Code, men who take advantage of a woman's economic or occupational depenence on them to compel sexual relations can be punished with up to three years confinement. Some inconsistency among the codes of the various Union republics exists on this point: the Kazakh, Latvian, and Estonian codes do not offer such protection for women (Ivanov 1973: 100; Juviler 1977).

It is interesting to note that there are no criminal provisions against the payment of dowries, nor are men equally protected against the use of their possible dependence on women to compel them into sexual relations. Marxism generally has paid much more attention to the protection of women and children than it has to men, and this bias toward women shows up in Soviet legislation and in Soviet research on the family as well (for the latter point, see Fisher and Khotin 1977). The general moral tenor of such laws is clear, however.

The 1918 Family Code attempted to abolish marriages of calculation by proclaiming that marriage did not establish community of property and also by declaring invalid any agreement by husband and wife intended to restrict the property rights of either party. While this decree was primarily motivated by the desire to abolish marriage for money, it soon became clear that the law failed to protect women from exploitation after marriage, particularly upon divorce. Many married women could not or would not work, particularly given the lack of child-care facilities, and under the law goods and property acquired after marriage could be interpreted as the legal property of the husband alone. As a result, in 1926 property acquired after marriage was made community property of the spouses, and such is the law in effect today (Geiger 1968: 49-50; Kodeks o brake i sem'e RSFSR 1975: article 20). Although article 21 of the Russian Federation Family Code provides in the case of division of property equal shares for husband and wife, the fact that courts have the right to affect this distribution means that the actual share of property that a spouse is entitled to is unknown until the actual division. This fact has been interpreted by a legal expert as lessening the likelihood of entering marriage for money (Orlova 1971: 62).

The tax structure of the Soviet Union does favor marriage to some extent. From age 18—that is to say, from the age at which in most of the Union republics he has the right to marry—to age 50, a man is taxed for childlessness, and childless married women are also taxed. The amounts involved are not very great, however (Beliavskii and Finn 1973: 22-23). Fees to register a marriage are insignificant: the basic cost is 1.50 rubles, or only about one one-hundredth of the average monthly wage (Pétrakova 1972: 97). Very recently marriage insurance policies have appeared in the USSR that provide the beneficiary with a sum of money upon marriage, but it is unclear how widespread a practice this is ("Marriage Insurance" 1977).

Less radical perhaps in comparison to the legal structures of other countries, but still in keeping with the conception of marriage as a free union rather than an economic contract, are the strong Soviet legal provisions for the conditions of entrance into marriage, in particular for the mutual free consent of the parties. Not only can marriages that have been concluded without the consent of the parties be declared invalid, but also according to article 233 of the RSFSR Criminal Code, all persons involved in compelling a woman to enter into marriage, trying to prevent her marrying, or abducting her for the purposes of having her marry can be deprived of their freedom for up to two years. Similar provisions are in the criminal codes of Uzbekistan, Kirgizia, Kazakhstan, Tadzhikistan, Armenia, Turkmenia, and Azerbaidzhan (*Ugolovnoe Zakonadatel'stvo Soiuza SSR i soiuznykh respublik* 1963: relevant codes; Juviler 1977). The conception that it be the free will of the parties to enter into marriage carries over into the rationale for insisting that they be of marriageable age (usually 18— see Chapter 5) and of sound mind (Orlova 1971: 47-53). Free will in consenting to enter into marriage is often interpreted as being "mature" free will, or in other words, a will that society can and should to some extent influence (Vorozheikin 1972: 99).

Freedom to enter into marriage is supported not only by the Soviet legal apparatus but also by the civic activity of various organizations and by the press. Thus from time to time Soviet newspapers publish approving accounts of instances where parents have been prevented from stopping marriages their children wished to contract. *Izvestiia*, for example, has supported an employee of a Bureau of Registration of Acts of Civil Status (ZAGS) who was mistakenly fired for registering a marriage that a groom's father opposed (Kotelevskaia 1968), and has praised the members of a Zhensovet or Women's Committee for interfering in a situation where the well-to-do parents of a bride had tried to prevent her marriage to the son of a cleaning woman (Shtan'ko 1967). Press support of community interference in the continuation of "outmoded" local marriage customs is especially strong in regard to continuing parental control of marriages in Central Asia. An article in *Pravda*, for example, praised the expulsion from the Communist Party of an official of the Turkmen Central Statistical Administration who had forced his son to marry a stranger (Esenov 1975; for discussion of kin control over mate-selection, see Chapter 2).

Although the legal right to marry is considered to belong to all Soviet citizens without exception (Vorozheikin 1972: 109), there is some evidence that at the very top and bottom of the political hierarchy this right is abrogated. A number of instances of forced marriage for political reasons among the elite of the society have been reported (see, for example, Alliluyeva 1967. Marriages of major cultural figures such as Sholokhov and Shostakovich supposedly also have occurred in this manner.) While some instances of marriages involving prisoners are known, Solzhenitsyn has compared the separation of lovers in labor camps to the practices of nineteenth-century landowners without whose permission marriage between serfs was not possible (Solzhenitsyn 1975: 150, 238-39, 241).

In addition to the conditions that those entering into marriage be of marriageable age and of sound mind, persons marrying are not permitted to be related in direct line of descent, or to be full or half brothers and sisters, or to be adoptor and adoptee. These restrictions are based primarily on biological arguments. The restrictions on incestuous marriages are considered to be absolutely minimal so as to give the greatest amount of freedom of choice of mate to those marrying (Vorozheikin 1972: 116-27). Although it is not specifically stated in the family codes, Soviet marriage law is interpreted as authorizing only marriages to a member of the opposite sex: homosexual marriages are dismissed as "immoral" and "against human nature" (Vorozheikin 1972: 115-16).

The only other legal restriction on marriage is that it not be concluded with a person who is already married. Such a marriage can be declared invalid and, under article 201 of the RSFSR Criminal Code concerning violation of acts of registration of civil status, can be punished. Similar laws exist in other Union republics. Under article 235 bigamy and polygyny are crimes with risks of deprivation of freedom or correctional tasks up to one year. This latter provision is primarily directed against the traditionally polygynous Moslem areas of the country, and hence there is no crime of polygyny in the criminal codes of the Ukrainian, Byelorussian, Lithuanian, Latvian, Estonian, and Moldavian republics (Ivanov 1973: 204; Orlova 1971: 54-55; Juviler 1977).

From the formal legal standpoint, Soviet mate-selection is quite free: the basic restrictions are that marriage can be legally contracted only with someone of marriageable age of the opposite sex, who is not a close relative, who is of sound mind and consents to the marriage, and who is not already married. These are quite minimal restrictions. Restrictive laws of other countries, such as the former antimiscegenation laws of the United States, are cited with great disfavor (see, for example, Kharchev 1964: 191). The few legal restrictions on entrance into marriage that do exist in the USSR have changed little over the years. Under Stalin, a law prohibiting marriage to foreigners was passed in 1947 and then rescinded in 1953. In many ways Soviet legal protection of freedom of courtship extends only to marriages between Soviet citizens (see Chapter 7).

Formal legal protection does not mean that mate-selection even within the Soviet Union is actually free (the extent to which it is or is not is discussed at length in the chapters that follow). It should be noted, however, that in contrast to Western countries, laws regarding freedom of mate-selection are actively implemented by state and community authorities.

Insofar as the Soviet regime is committed to the reduction of inequalities among the population, official sponsorship of an emotional basis for marriage and elimination of a market structure to mate-selection is a way of reducing social inequality that is at times perhaps easier to implement than directly reducing inequality in income, political power, or the content of jobs. It is claimed that "everyone is equally talented when it comes to love" (Riurikov 1974) and that "when two people love they are both equal and worthy of each other" (Leonidova 1972). Marriages between persons differing greatly in socioeconomic status are therefore seen as not only a consequence of or indication of a lack of calculation in the decision to marry and the general homogenization of the population, but also as a cause of further equalization. Because of the Marxist insistence on the primacy of economic factors, this conception of mate-selection as an independent variable in reducing inequality is implicit rather than explicit in most Soviet discussions. A Western observer has claimed that the communist insistence on monogamy and dislike of sexual freedom is an attempt to equalize Soviet society. He argues that since sexual attractiveness is unequally distributed, sexual freedom inevitably means sexual competition. Emphasis on love in marriage and on marriage itself ensures that everyone experiences sex and love to some degree and is a means of controlling the inequalities that would result from such open competition (Gilder 1974).

In some ways elimination of a market structure to mate-selection meshes well with the Soviet political system. To the extent that the regime is still committed to change (see Hough 1972), a solely emotional basis for marriage is desirable in that it maintains a fluidity of relationships and does not allow interests to become entrenched. It has been noted that in the West the prevalence of a love pattern in marriage is connected to the existence of a strong parent-child tie that must be broken in order to enter into marriage (Goode 1964: 39). To the extent that the Soviet government has tried to make a radical break with the past, love as a basis for marriage is helpful to the aims of the regime.

The close emotional bond between the couple that results may not be so liked by political authorities, however, since it forms the basis of potential opposition. In this regard it is interesting to note that anti-utopian novels critical of the totalitarian aspects of Soviet society, such as Zamiatin's *We* and Orwell's *1984*, typically involve a love affair that provides the basis for opposition to the strict political regime (Zamiatin 1924; Orwell 1949). At the very least romantic involvements "represent potentially competing forms of social relations which may remove the individual from the realm of politicized or public preoccupations and activities, or reduce his concern with them" (Hollander 1973: 287). Officially, no contradiction between romantic love and society is said to exist. In contrast to Western culture, the fulfillment of love is claimed to be entirely possible within the context of Soviet society, and the tragic loves of the past converted into "working" Tristans and Isoldes, Romeos and Juliets (Marcuse 1961: 228-29).

As a practical matter, however, the very hostility of the Soviet regime to competing social relations sponsors close love ties: "The very qualities of human intimacy and intensity are, in part, a kind of overcompensation at the family and precinct level for studied inhumanity at higher, more official levels" (Billington 1967: 70). The Leninist fear of spontaneity that leads to attempts to make control and calculation pervasive throughout much of Soviet life sparks the opposite reaction when it comes to intimate personal relations. This phenomenon has been observed many times by journalists and travelers (for example, Smith 1976). "It is among the seeming paradoxes of Soviet life that in a regimented and closely supervised society friendships may flourish in greater depth and intensity than in a much more free, unorganized, and permissive society like the American one" (Hollander 1973: 287).

The possible inapplicability of a market model to Soviet mate-selection can be further seen in the fact that in a society where an individual's personal decisions carry relatively little weight, great calculation concerning any one particular decision is not to be expected. It might even be said that in terms of the important things in life, Soviet citizens' decision whom to marry is virtually the only major choice they make in their lifetime. This is of course an exaggeration, but it contains some truth in a land where persons are given very little choice throughout their lives from the type of toothpaste they use to the political regime under which they live. The freedom to decide whom to marry thus occurs in a context in which personal decision making is not developed, and there is some indication that many people in the Soviet Union would just as soon have even this decision made for them. Much of the popular support for the use of computers in matchmaking comes from a desire to be told what to do—scientifically, of course (Kon 1976). The transference of market decision making from economic goods to mate-selection is thus arguably less plausible in a nonmarket economy.

There are thus a plethora of reasons, both legal and structural, why mate-selection in Soviet society conceivably may not fit market theories of marriage very well. Obviously, market factors are at work in Soviet society generally to some extent, and on an a priori basis it would not be reasonable to expect that Soviet society has moved from a market structure of mate-selection all the way to a pure romantic love complex. Just as state socialist systems have been observed to have reduced the effect of market factors in stratification, however (Parkin 1971), the various features of Soviet society discussed above may very well have reduced the effect of market factors in mate-selection in the USSR.

The present volume undertakes to analyze the available empirical evidence so as to determine what marital patterns prevail in the USSR and the extent to which there is or is not a Soviet marriage market. Emphasis is on the era since World War II, although where possible discussion of the evolution of contemporary patterns since the nineteenth century is included. Regional and nationality variations are taken into account, but in view of the greater availability of information concerning the Western parts of the USSR, somewhat more attention is paid to developments in the Slavic and Baltic regions, in particular to central Russia. As is unfortunately inevitable in a study of Soviet society, many of the conclusions reached are based on evidence that is less adequate than would be desirable and must remain tentative. It is believed, however, that the study is quite complete in its coverage of the available data.

The following chapter examines the extent to which the Soviet population has adopted the Marxist-Leninist ideology concerning entrance into marriage as its own, and then goes on to look at who currently controls the transactions in mate-selection and some of the processes leading up to the final choice of a spouse. In Chapter 3 data on rates of entrance into marriage are assembled, followed by analysis in Chapter 4 of the changing marital status of the Soviet population. In attempting to explain many of the regional and nationality variations in marital status noted in that chapter, Becker's hypotheses regarding relative wage rates and the gain to marriage are then tested. Chapters 5, 6, and 7 look at those characteristics of husbands and wives for which information is available—age, occupation and education, and ethnic identity—and try to determine the degree of homogamy versus heterogamy in those characteristics. Finally, Chapter 8 sifts the evidence to come to a number of conclusions regarding the applicability of market theories to Soviet mate-selection, and the consequences of marriage patterns in the USSR for the nature of Soviet marriage, Soviet society, and the individual.

2

COURTSHIP

If there were no market structure to mate-selection whatsoever, those entering into marriage would select their future partners without regard to socially defined criteria, and presumably no one would be able to say why a particular person was chosen rather than some other: the fact of attraction would be sufficient. No one except the future husband and wife would have any influence or control over the choice or, moreover, any interest in seeing a particular choice made or not made. Time being less necessary to come to a decision to marry with no considerations other than love, the length of courtship would be short. In addition, weddings, and other rituals presumably would reflect the private and personal decision of the parties and the lack of any market structure.

The present chapter examines the extent to which the various peoples of the USSR have adopted the ideological stance of the Soviet regime regarding mate-selection and criteria of mate-selection. The evidence regarding the extent to which Soviet courtship is now a self-selection system is sifted, followed by discussion of current courtship practices. Some observations on the nature of wedding rituals in the USSR conclude the analysis of the processes leading to the final assortment of mates.

POPULAR ATTITUDES TOWARD MATE-SELECTION AND CRITERIA OF MATE-SELECTION

Romantic conceptions of love and belief in love are widespread throughout Soviet society. The majority of the Soviet population has by now accepted the ideological principle that marriage should be contracted only out of love; but as with other areas of the ideology, this idea is accepted more in the abstract than in concrete reference to one's own fate.

Not only do most people in the USSR agree that love in a general sense exists, but they tend to believe in the possibility of a "grand" love, a "great" love. In Table 2.1 are presented the responses of some 15,000 persons surveyed in various areas of central Russia and the Tatar ASSR in 1968-71 concerning beliefs in love. The overwhelming majority of respondents were ready to say that real "great" love exists or to admit that they earlier believed in its existence but are now disillusioned. Evidently belief in romantic love at least at some point in the life cycle is extremely widespread in a society that only a century ago Sir Donald Mackenzie Wallace characterized as evidencing little romance or sentimentality regarding family relations among the peasant majority (Wallace 1912: 91).

As can be seen from Table 2.1, the young and those currently in occupations that involve more contact with the ideology are a little more likely to believe that "great" love exists. Students in higher education and secondary-school teachers are somewhat more likely to be romantic than manual workers or engineering personnel. Seventy-five to 85 percent of all groups, however, believe at some time in their lives in "great" love, which implies that indoctrination with romantic conceptions is highly successful at young ages, followed by some rejection of romantic ideas in later life. Such belief in an aspect of the ideology in early years followed by disillusionment is similar to the situation regarding the career aspirations and expectations of Soviet youth (Yanowitch and Dodge 1968). The importance of exposure to the ideology is perhaps also shown by the fact that of the manual workers surveyed, those in the Moscow area were more likely to value love than were workers elsewhere (Fainburg 1972: 6).

When asked whether in principle marriage should be based on love, a very substantial proportion of the population parrots back the official ideology. Thus when asked "Do you believe in principle that marriage should only be concluded on the basis of love?," 94 percent of a sample of 271 workers, engineers, doctors, and librarians in Minsk in the late 1960s answered affirmatively (Iurkevich 1970a: 95, and 1970b: 101). Similar belief in love as the basis of marriage as an ideal matter was shown in Anatolii Kharchev's study of 500 couples in the Leningrad Palace of Weddings in 1962. In answer to the question "What is in your opinion the main condition for a stable and happy marriage?," 76.2 percent claimed love or love and common views, trust, sincerity, friendship, and the like; 13.2 percent claimed equal rights and mutual respect; 4 percent love and housing conditions; 1.6 percent love and material goods; 0.6 percent presence of children; 0.2 percent "realistic views of life;" and 4.2 percent gave no answer (Kharchev 1964: 179). When asked to rank in order of importance the reasons for establishing a family, eighth-graders and graduating secondary-school students in the Estonian SSR in the late 1960s generally ranked "being together with a person one loves" highest (see Table 2.2).

Belief in love as the basis of marriage is connected to other value orientations. The choice is not simply love versus material calculations as constantly juxtaposed in Soviet ideology, but rather a notion that if one marries not for

TABLE 2.1

Evaluation by Various Social Groups of the Role and Place of Love in Life: Respondents in Central Russia and Tatar ASSR, 1968–72* (percent)

Attitude to Love	Manual Workers	Engineering technical personnel	White-collar workers in industrial enterprises	Personnel in scientific research institutes construction bureaus, planning organizations	Secondary-school teachers	Students in higher education	First-year higher education students	Fourth- and Fifth-year higher education students
Believe that real, great love exists	69.1	72.5	68.0	67.0	82.6	78.4	79.5	77.2
Earlier believed that great love exists but are now disillusioned	11.9	12.1	18.0	8.6	—	4.8	3.4	6.1
Talk, books, films about great love seem exaggerated: it's all simpler	8.8	9.2	7.4	10.7	—	9.0	9.0	9.0
One can be close to someone, but it is all simple and routine—talk about love is a cover, fog, illusion	6.4	4.4	3.4	3.4	7.9	2.6	2.0	3.2

All talk of love is made up, artificial. Do not feel a need for some sort of closeness, etc.	2.5	0.8	2.0	1.5	3.6	1.2	2.0	0.6
Attitude to love is not contained in above possible answers	1.3	1.0	1.2	8.8	5.9	4.0	4.1	3.9
Total	100.0	100.0	100.0	100.0	100.0	100.0	100.0	100.0
N	7,510	2,947	696	713	619	1,580		

*Respondents are workers, engineering-technical personnel, and employees in 12 industrial enterprises in Moscow, Perm, Podmoskov'e, and Perm Oblast; secondary-school teachers in Bugul'm and Al'met'evsk and corresponding rural regions of the Tatar ASSR; and students of Perm Polytechnical Institute and Perm State University.

TABLE 2.2

The Aim of Setting up a Family: Graduating Secondary-School Students and Students in the Eighth Grade, Estonian SSR, 1965–70*

| | Graduating secondary-school students | | | | | Eighth-graders | |
| | Tartu 1965 | Nôo 1966 | Nôo 1967 | Tallinn 1970 | | Tallinn 1970 | |
				Girls	Boys	Girls	Boys
Be together with the person one loves	1	1	1	1	2	1	4
Settle down	2	2	2	2	1	2	1
Bring up children	3	3	3	3	3	3	7
Not to remain alone	4	4	4	4	4	4	3
Have intimate relations officially registered	5	5	5	6	6	5	6
Get freedom from parental guardianship	6	6	7	5	7	7	2
Not to remain unmarried (a bachelor, a spinster)	7	7	6	7	5	6	5

*Reasons for setting up a family ranked in order of choice.
Source: Koemets 1972:53.

love that other psychological motives should nonetheless be most important. Thus when the Minsk sample (N = 221) was asked "If for some reason there was no basis to hope rationally to marry for love, which of the motives listed below would be sufficient in your opinion?," 86 percent answered congeniality, friendship, or respect (Iurkevich 1970a: 95). There is some evidence that belief in love tends to be accompanied by other approved Soviet values. Those in a 1966-67 study in Perm who claimed to have married for love were more likely to value such things as a clear conscience and satisfaction with work, while those who claimed that they had entered marriage as a matter of calculation were more likely to be oriented to promotion in their careers, "getting ahead," and material security (Fainburg 1970: 73-75).

Moving from commitment to abstract ideal values to the motives that Soviet citizens claim as the reasons they entered their own marriages, it seems likely that at the time of their weddings the vast majority of couples believe that they are marrying for love. In surveys of newlyweds in Palaces of Weddings and registration bureaus, virtually all couples claim they are marrying for love (see, for example, Kharchev and Emel'ianova 1970: 63). Among couples already married much depends on the wording of the question. Asked whether they had entered marriage because of love, because everyone does so, or because of some sort of calculation, some 70 to 80 percent of married respondents in Fainburg's sample of 15,000 in central Russia and the Tatar ASSR claimed that they had entered marriage because of love. Students in higher education were particularly likely to claim love as the reason they had married (see Table 2.3. The results presented there are virtually the same as those obtained by the same researcher in 1966-67 with smaller samples: see Fainburg 1970.) This study has been interpreted to mean that about one-fourth of Soviet couples marry for reasons other than love (Riurikov 1974). What it does show is that when confronted with a choice of responses directly ideological in nature, very few people in the Soviet Union are willing to say that they entered into their marriage through some sort of calculation. A somewhat larger percentage are willing to say that they married "because everyone does so."

Open-ended questions concerning the marriage motives of those already married for some time tend to elicit love as an answer in fewer cases than do closed-ended questions, although the majority of men and women still claim that they married for psychological rather than material or other reasons. Tables 2.4 through 2.7 present the results of studies of marriage motives in various regions of the USSR: among manual workers in Minsk, young couples in Leningrad, families with children in Moscow, and in a sample of married Kirgiz men and women. As already stated, a majority of couples believe that they married because of love or other psychological reasons. This conclusion also holds true for a survey of collective farmers in Byelorussia (Kolokol'nikov 1976: 80). It is particularly interesting to note that the sample of Kirgiz men and women does not differ substantially in this respect from the samples in the Slavic areas of the country—evidently the ideology of love as the basis for marriage has penetrated

TABLE 2.3

Evaluation by Various Social Groups of Love as a Factor in Their
Own Marriages: Currently Married Respondents in Central
Russia and Tatar ASSR, 1968–71 (percent)

	Entered marriage because of love	Entered marriage "because everyone does so"	Entered marriage through calculation*	Total
Manual workers	79.3	15.2	5.5	100.0 (5,137)
Engineering-technical personnel	83.7	13.2	3.1	100.0 (2,487)
White-collar workers in industrial enterprises	79.5	16.8	3.7	100.0 (466)
Personnel in scientific research institutes, construction bureaus, planning organizations	74.0	16.1	9.9	100.0 (379)
Secondary-school teachers	72.0	21.7	6.3	100.0 (547)
Students in higher education	92.2	3.9	3.9	100.0 (288)

*"had to do so . . . difficult conditions; at that time there was simply no possibility of thinking about feelings."

N's are approximate. See Table 2.1 for geographic locations.

Source: Fainburg 1972.

even the Moslem Central Asian areas of the country. Studies of newlyweds in the Buryat ASSR and Dagestan ASSR also confirm the acceptance of the ideology by the nonSlavic population. (See Khitynov 1974: 15; Agaev 1972: 8.)

Judging by these various surveys, women tend to be more romantic than men and to claim love as the reason for having married more than their husbands do. This is in accordance with the findings by sex regarding Estonian students' views of the reasons for establishing a family (Table 2.2). Men are more likely to

TABLE 2.4

Marriage Motives of Manual Workers in Three Industrial Plants:
Minsk, Byelorussian SSR, 1969 (percent)

"What caused you to marry? If there were several causes, indicate one that you consider the main cause."	Men	Women
Love	47.9	57.4
Congeniality	16.7	16.6
Attempt to get rid of loneliness	12.6	6.8
Got "carried away" for a short time	5.5	4.1
Desire to improve material position	4.6	3.6
Necessity (birth of child, pregnancy)	3.8	1.7
Irresponsibility	3.5	4.5
Other	2.5	1.8
No answer	3.3	3.5
Total	100.0	100.0
N	365	612

Source: Iurkevich 1970a:97.

TABLE 2.5

Marriage Motives of Young Couples Married 5–6 Years:
Leningrad, Early 1970s (percent)

Motive for entrance into marriage	Men	Women
Love	39.1	49.5
Common interests, views	26.1	28.5
Feeling of loneliness	14.1	4.7
Chance	4.0	2.4
Feeling of empathy	7.4	3.1
Material well-being of future spouse	–	3.1
Housing conditions of future spouse	2.0	1.2
Probability of imminent birth of child	6.7	4.3
Other motives	0.6	3.1
Total	100.0	100.0

N is unclear.
Source: Golod 1975:132.

TABLE 2.6

Marriage Motives: Nuclear Families in Two New Microdistricts
of Moscow, 1972–74

Marriage motives	Percent	N
Mutual respect, friendship, affection	38	191
Community of interests, aims	41	205
Aspiration for harmonious life in a family	64	320
Wish to have children	70	350
Yearning to get rid of loneliness	6.8	34
Material considerations	6.4	32
Other motives	4.0	20

Number of actual respondents was 470 but total of answers exceeds that since some respondents named several motives. Families have children, but unclear whether husband or wife is answering and under what circumstances.

Source: Iankova 1974.

TABLE 2.7

Marriage Motives: Kirgiz in Kirgiz SSR, 1972
(percent)

Love	57.1
Common interests	14.9
"Simply liked each other"	7.4
Partner's physical attractiveness	5.2
Spouse's position, job	3.5
Material calculation	5.2
Fear of remaining single	1.4
Parental insistence	3.5
Other	1.9
Total	100.0

*Does not add due to rounding.
N = 577 men and women, stratified random sample.
Source: Achylova 1972:8.

feel that they entered a shotgun marriage, that they had to marry because they had fathered an illegitimate child.

There is evidence that those with higher education and more exposure to the ideology are more likely to claim that they married for love in answer to open-ended as well as closed-ended questions. The pilot study for the Minsk survey consisted primarily of respondents who were white-collar employees with some amount of higher education. Seventy percent of them (N = 253) claimed that they had married for love as opposed to only 47.9 percent and 57.4 percent of men and women respectively among manual workers in factories in the eventual study itself (see Table 2.4. Iurkevich 1970a: 96).

It is important to distinguish ideals regarding family patterns from actual behavior. Much of the Soviet population's adoption of the ideal of love as a basis for marriage is adoption only in terms of voiced attitudes. As will be seen, many other factors come into play in mate-selection in the USSR than love and romantic attachment alone. At least one Soviet article has recognized that the responses favoring love in such surveys as those reviewed above are ideological in nature rather than a statement of personal conviction ("60,000,000 semei" 1970), and there is evidence of a certain cynicism on the part of the Soviet population toward the value of love as a basis for relations between men and women. In a recent Soviet joke, for example, a prostitute is asked whether she gave her services for love or money. "For love, of course," she answers. "How can you call $3.00 money?" (Many prostitutes work for foreign currency.)

It would be a mistake, however, to dismiss the verbal acceptance by the Soviet population of a romantic basis for marriage, as is implicitly done in arguments that the emergence in the USSR of romantic criteria of mate-selection is unlikely since the society is still not free from material want (see Hollander 1973: 257). The fact that the Soviet population says it believes in romantic love to the extent that it does, even if such statements are only superficial voicing of what is ideologically and politically acceptable, arguably serves to reduce the number of marriages made for economic and other reasons unconnected to love. (The importance of popular acceptance of official ideology in this area in the USSR will be returned to in Chapter 8.)

Soviet ideology also has had a clear effect on the criteria that people use in selecting a mate. Surveys that have asked what people are looking for in a future spouse uniformly have found characteristics such as "loving" or psychological traits to be chosen first among traits desirable in a spouse. Choices further down the list tend to vary depending on the sex of the respondent, but it is striking how low nationality, occupation, and financial status tend to be among attributes considered salient.

In Table 2.8 are the rankings that graduating secondary-school students and eighth-graders in the Estonian SSR gave various traits that they felt to be desirable in a future spouse. In Table 2.9 are scaled the traits that students in the first and fourth years of Tartu State University felt were desirable in an ideal mate. For all these Estonian groups for both sexes, the relations between the

TABLE 2.8

Criteria for Choosing One's Spouse Ranked in Order of Importance by Secondary-School Graduating Students and Eighth-Graders: Estonian SSR, 1965–70

| Criteria | Graduating secondary-school students | | | | | Eighth-Graders | |
	Tartu 1965	Nôo 1966	Nôo 1967	Tallinn 1970 Girls	Tallinn 1970 Boys	Tallinn 1970 Girls	Tallinn 1970 Boys
He (she) loves you	1	1	3	1	1	1	1
I love him (her)	2	2	1	2	2	2	2
Character	3	3	2	3	3	3	4
Education	4	5	5	4	6	5	5
Health	5	6	6	5	7	6	7
Appearance	6	4	4	6	4	4	3
Nationality	7	7	7	7	5	7	6
Profession	8	8	8	8	9	8	8
Financial status	9	9	9	9	8	9	9

*N is unclear.
Source: Koemets 1972: 54.

TABLE 2.9

Scale of Importance of Various Factors in the Image of an Ideal Mate Held by Students in the First and Fourth Year of Tartu State University, 1971

Girls		Boys
	− 1	
Mutual relations Character		
	− 2	
		Mutual relations Character
	− 3	
		Appearance
	− 4	
Education Habits		Habits
	− 5	
Appearance		
		Education Age
Age	− 6	
Nationality		Nationality
Financial status		Financial status
N = 218		N = 149

Source: Kóppel and Tiit 1972:80.

respondent and future spouse are the most important consideration; that is to say, whether the future spouse loves the respondent and whether the respondent loves the future spouse are considered to be the most important criteria in mate-selection. Very important also is the character or personality of the future spouse. Beyond mutual love and the character of the ideal mate, however, there is a split to some extent in the criteria used by men and women. In what looks very much like a typical Western market exchange, the Estonian men tend to give more importance to appearance as a criterion in choosing a future wife, whereas women are somewhat more likely to place importance on the education of a future husband. There is thus an asymmetry in the criteria used by men and women, with men tending to favor "typically feminine" traits as elsewhere in the world, and women tending to place somewhat more emphasis on the education—and perhaps therefore future occupation—of their desired mates. It is remarkable, however, that the occupation as such, financial status, and nationality of the future spouse are considered to be highly unimportant by both men and women. It thus would seem that the ideology has had quite an effect on attitudes in underplaying these characteristics. (For discussion of attitudes toward nationality in marriage, see Chapter 7.)

Elsewhere in the Baltics, a poll of women students in Vilnius State University in the fall of 1973 found the trait considered to be most important in a future husband to be intelligentnost', or essentially "being cultured." The second most important trait was that a future husband treat a woman as a friend equal in all ways to him, and the third was that a future husband have a caring attitude toward his family and children. Other traits mentioned were belief in self, love of work, sobriety, sense of humor, and a striving for all-around perfection. These Lithuanian female students thought the ability to understand a husband was the most important attribute of a wife. The emphasis on psychological characteristics and on relationships was considered by the researcher to be evidence of change in the concept of manly strength from physical or economic prowess to essentially intellectual strength (Solov'ev 1973: 13).

Studies elsewhere in the USSR show generally similar results. A thousand students in the second year of higher education and in specialized academic institutions in Simferopol in 1975 were asked to name the three main traits that attract them in a future spouse. Men named love for husband and children first, then fidelity, then ability to run a household and create a comfortable home. Women named "loving" and "a good family man" as the most desirable attributes in a husband, then named a series of character traits. As in the case of the Estonian students, women were somewhat more likely to desire education in a future husband than men were to desire education in a future wife, and also as in the Estonian case, men tended to place more importance on appearance than did women (Ermishin 1976). Women workers in a textile factory in Minsk chose devotion and industriousness as the qualities most desirable in a husband and also thought that the same qualities were most desirable in a wife (N = 500. Bangerskaia 1975). In like manner, 50 women who had been married for some time who were interviewed in Leningrad in the late 1960s claimed to have valued primarily intelligence and "seriousness" in their husbands prior to entrance into marriage (Kharchev and Emel'ianova 1970: 63).

On the other hand, while in those areas of the USSR traditionally lacking in development of a love complex, voiced criteria of mate-selection now are less concentrated on economic matters, less stress is placed on the psychological characteristics of the spouse. Thus in a survey of rural Kirgizia in the early 1970s only 9.7 percent of the respondents thought the material well-being of the family of bride or groom to be most important, but only somewhat over a quarter of the sample emphasized the character of the future spouse while fully 56 percent thought the spouse's appearance was most important. (N = 430. Achylova 1972: 10.)

At least in voiced attitudes most of the Soviet population agrees with the official ideology and believes that the most important criteria in mate-selection are the psychological characteristics of the future spouse. The acceptance of the ideology is clearest regarding those traits most desired and those most disregarded. Thus most important among the criteria of mate-selection are love and the psychological characteristics of the future spouse, while at the other end of the scale, the financial status of the spouse is most underplayed. In between, the effect of the ideology is not quite so clear. Beauty and personal appearance, for example, are disliked as criteria of prestige and of mate-selection by the official moralists of Soviet society, and for many years the evil heroines of socialist realism were presented as very attractive while the good women were portrayed as plain and unconcerned with their looks (Hollander 1973: 240-41). Notwithstanding this official line, however, Soviet men still place importance on the appearance of their future wives.

Similarly, the importance given to education among attributes of an ideal mate cannot be explained simply by the contribution of education to psychological and personal characteristics as has been argued by Soviet writers (Kuznetsova 1973: 13; see also Chapter 6), but is connected to the role of education in advancement in social status in a bureaucratic society such as the USSR. From time to time there is recognition in the Soviet press of the extent to which the use of education as a criterion in mate-selection represents a desire to advance in social status rather than a concern for the personal characteristics of the spouse. In a letter to the editors of *Sovetskaia kul'tura*, a young male metalworker in love with a student complained:

When she and I were among her comrades she would tell them that I was also a student at another institute. I found it unpleasant that she seemed to be ashamed of me, even though, frankly speaking, I did not feel any sense of inferiority when I was among students. Their conversations and interests were not alien to me. In Tonia's opinion, however, my lack of a student's identification card practically compromised her. She said, "It doesn't matter which one, but you should graduate from an institute."

In conclusion, despite my regrets, I had to break with the girl I loved. My entry into a higher school kept being delayed, and her demand became a burden.

I am now 26 years old; I am a student in a correspondence course, married and raising one son. It would seem that it is long past time to forget the sad story, but I am continually reminded of it by the conversations of my fellow workers and fellow students. Many of them do not hide the fact that they entered higher school not out of any sense of vocation, but rather for calculating reasons. They do care what sort of specialists they become; they are concerned with their "future position in society." They are not attracted to people in workers' occupations. If one of them marries, the first thing he or she reports is not what sort of person his or her spouse is, but rather who he or she is. If he is an engineer, that means the marriage is a successful one. If not, the person has made a stupid mistake. ("Not Simply Love" 1976)

Although no surveys have asked questions regarding attitudes toward the class origins of a potential spouse, it is clear that the class background of a future wife or husband is often taken into account even when the couple themselves are essentially similar in their own education and general socioeconomic status. Two recent popular Soviet plays have revolved around the question of parental opposition to marriages between couples of varying social origins, even though in both instances the would-be bride and groom are essentially similar in all other characteristics, in particular in education. In Vladimir Konstantinov's and Boris Ratser's play *Unequal Marriage*, the son of a well-known philologist falls in love with the daughter of a house painter, and the parents of both conspire to separate the couple. "We are not the right color," the house painter says (see the description of this play in Saikowski 1970). Similarly, in Mikhail Roshchin's play *Valentin and Valentina*, the daughter of an aristocratic family falls in love with the son of a female railroad attendant who warns her son, "She is not a proper match for you." (Roshchin 1971. See also Kaiser 1976: 38-40.) As is to be expected given the constrictions of socialist realism, the two plays end happily for the couples involved, but the point is that class origin is still maintained as a criterion in mate-selection, at least where parents are concerned.

There is little attention paid in Soviet writings to the extent to which men take the occupation of their future mates into account in choosing a wife. Although it is clear that women's occupations are important in actual behavior of mate-selection (see Chapters 4 and 6), there is almost no discussion of the matter except perhaps for claims that "the girl with the job has not lost her appeal" (*Soviet Life* 1973). From indications in the surveys discussed above and other evidence available, it is clear that a man's occupation is a considerably more important criterion in mate-selection than a woman's occupation, notwithstanding the great participation of women in the Soviet labor force. A content analysis of descriptions of marriage and love in two popular youth magazines, *Iunost'* and *Sel'skaia molodezh'*, found that in only 8.6 percent of the stories did the authors give no information concerning the professions of the male characters, whereas in the case of women the percentage was fully 48.2 percent. In other words, in Soviet discussions of marriage and love it is impossible to imagine a man without an occupation, but it is possible to imagine a woman without one (Semenov 1973: 170). In like manner it is claimed that a woman still "wants to see in a man a being of a somewhat higher order in level of knowledge, professional and career achievement than she herself" (Kuznetsova 1973).

Of interest is the veritable absence today of open discussion of political criteria in mate-selection. While in earlier more turbulent times the suitability of a mate was seen as in part resulting from proper political views—heroes of the socialist-realist novels of the Stalin era, such as Korchagin in Nikolai Ostrovskii's novel, *How the Steel Was Tempered* (Ostrovskii 1936), would throw over potential mates for their lack of true communist views—politics no longer seems to be a major consideration when courtship is discussed. This is not to say that political attitudes do not play a role in mate-selection or a role in people's decisions to marry, but in terms of their predominance among criteria of mate-selection and in public discussion of mate-selection they seem to have fallen by the wayside. Certainly no published mention is made of the idea that a future husband or wife should be a member of the Komsomol or Communist Party. To some extent this may be because such criteria as education may be assumed to include such political matters.

The gist of the above discussion is that on the level of voiced attitudes the Soviet population has to a very great extent accepted official Marxist-Leninist ideology concerning motives for mate-selection and criteria of mate-selection. As will be seen, a marriage market exists in the Soviet Union in many ways similar to marriage markets elsewhere, but the point here is that Soviets do not consciously feel themselves to be driving a bargain: although bargains are struck, people do not think of themselves as bargaining. Although such a split between consciousness and behavior is typical of other courtship systems as well (Goode 1964: 32), it is arguable that in the Soviet case the greater elaboration and rigidity of ideology has meant that those entering marriage are even less aware of a market structure to courtship than persons in other countries with institutionalized romantic love complexes. Additional evidence that this is so may be found in Soviet practices of almost casual entrance into marriage and the decline of such institutions as engagements (see the section below on duration of courtship).

The counterargument is that in a system where ideology concerning mate-selection is so rigid and codified and comparisons are constantly made between the hideous bourgeois past, when "marriages of calculation" were supposedly rampant, and the good socialist present when love prevails, the population is repeatedly reminded that calculation in mate-selection is in fact possible. The constant assertions that marriages in the Soviet Union are not based on considerations other than love bring to mind the idea that perhaps it would indeed be possible to marry for reasons other than love.

That this is so in a sizable minority of cases can be seen from the prevalence of so-called fictitious marriages: marriages that have been legally contracted but are not consummated or at least where the parties have no intention of establishing a family. The distinction between fictitious marriages and marriages of calculation often is not very sharp. Under Soviet law fictitious marriages may be recognized as invalid (Kodeks o brake i sem'e RSFSR, 1975: article 43). Under article 20 of the RSFSR Criminal Code it is possible to punish the parties to such marriages with up to a year of corrective labor at their place of work for violating the rules for registering acts of civil status, and further criminal punishment for such persons has been urged (Feofanov 1971). Thus often it is not enough simply to register a marriage to gain the desired calculated end, but a pretense at conjugal relations must be made or actual marital relations established to fool the neighbors and the authorities. Examination of different sorts of fictitious marriages serves as a way of understanding the various self-interested motivations Soviet couples may have in entering marriage.

Fictitious marriages are nothing new in Russia: they have their origins in the practices of the revolutionaries of the 1860s and 1870s who would marry so that the women involved could obtain separate passports to go abroad (Elnett 1926: 83; see also Stites 1978: 91, 132). A number of regulations in contemporary Soviet life have spawned several sorts of fictitious marriages. The most frequent types are marriages contracted to gain living space and/or obtain residence permits to live in the larger cities. It is not permitted to bring a member of the opposite sex into your room or apartment to live with you if you are not registered as married, nor is it possible to live with someone in one of the larger cities if that person does not have the appropriate residence permit. While such restrictions can be breached where separate apartments or private houses are concerned, the shortage of housing means that neighbors in already overcrowded communal apartments take a definite interest in the matter. Thus from the standpoint of obtaining housing and living in the major cities, there is a definite incentive to register marriages.

Many such marriages are, of course, not strictly speaking fictitious marriages: given the difficulties of finding places for sexual contact outside of marriage, many young people marry for lack of privacy in the overcrowded apartments they share with parents and others ("The Young Marrieds" 1964). In studies of marriage motives in Perm, the percentage of those claiming to have entered their marriages "by calculation" was twice as high among those who at the time of the survey were living in their own house as among those who were living in communal apartments (Fainburg 1970: 71).

From time to time the Soviet press reports trials of those who have entered into fictitious marriages to obtain housing or residence permits. Usually such matters find their way into the courts because of the interest of some third party in having the marriage declared fictitious. Thus *Pravda* has reported the case of a Kiev woman doctor who in order to remain in Kiev and obtain housing arranged to marry one of her patients fictitiously, but made the mistake of using a man who already had a wife (Shatunovskii 1969). At times the relationships can become quite complicated. *Izvestiia* reported a case involving a man who after hatching several fictitious marriages for himself, proceeded to run a kind of marriage bureau for such marriages:

> Everything began back in 1962 when Baku resident Leonid Kazakevich decided to move to Moscow. He could not live at the Kursk Rail-

road Station or Vnukovo Airport, nor could he obtain a residence permit. At this point Leonid Kazakevich hatched the idea of a phony marriage. He registered his marriage with one Marina and was subsequently assigned living quarters, even though he and his fake wife had blithely separated. True, he had provided the woman with a Volga automobile as her part of the deal.

Leonid decided to recover his expenses, using the same methods on the seas of matrimony. He proceeded to enter into fictitious wedlock with women named Liuba, Natasha and Margarita. In return for permits to take up residence at his address, Kazakevich received up to 1,000 rubles from his brides. He even wanted to legitimately marry Margarita, "for she's a very nice person, and my wife and I no longer see eye to eye." Financial plans vanquished tender affection, however.

In addition to his own numerous fictitious marriages, Kazakevich became responsible for uniting ten couples in return for some 7,300 rubles and was eventually sentenced for dishonest matchmaking (Feofanov 1971).

Many fictitious marriages for residence permits or housing are simply indispensable for persons who have been transferred to major cities for jobs but are unable to obtain housing for one reason or another (Beliavskii and Finn 1973: 77-83). They also are common among students who are trying to escape government reassignment to the provinces upon graduation and wish to stay in the larger cities (Feofanov 1971; Smith 1976: 9). The prices paid for the privilege of entering into such marriages vary, but the general black market price seems to range from about 1,000 to 2,000 rubles, or in other words, it costs about a year's average salary to enter into such marriages.

About the same amount of money purchases a fictitious marriage to Jews, through whom it is possible to leave the country. Presumably at least some marriages to foreigners also are fictitious and are contracted solely to leave the country. (For further discussion of intercitizenship marriages and emigration, see Chapter 7.) Another type of fictitious marriage involving travel abroad is that between persons who have the opportunity to travel for one reason or another and find that because they are unmarried the state is unwilling to let them go. It is rare that both husband and wife are allowed abroad together, presumably so as to ensure that the spouse will behave abroad and return to the USSR.

Another type of fictitious marriage occurs in order to save one's reputation in the eyes of relatives and close friends because of pregnancy. Such marriages were especially frequent during the period from 1944 to 1968, when a factual state of discrimination against illegitimate children existed as a result of then prevailing Soviet law. Thus in 1955 a woman's letter introduced into a divorce case in Minsk read:

I need a father for my daughter, be it only in documents. . . . I am agreeable to the conclusion of a marriage with anyone regardless of age, position or appearance. To the person with whom I conclude a marriage and who will adopt my daughter, I can provide a large reward and promise full peace and quiet. That is, depending on his desire, I will immediately hide myself so that it will *never* be remembered that I exist. (Iurkevich 1970a: 100)

In view of the continuing problems of illegitimate children even since legal changes in 1968 (Madison 1977), it is likely that fictitious marriages to avoid discrimination against out-of-wedlock children still exist. As indicated in the tables above, a certain proportion of Soviet marriages are considered by those in them to be shotgun marriages.

As in other societies, of course, marriages or promises of marriage are sometimes used to entice persons into things they would not otherwise do. Thus a 1968 *Izvestiia* article recounted how an athletic coach enticed women champion rowers from Saratov to join his team in Kiev by promising to marry them (Proletkin 1968).

Many of the above fictitious marriages are just one end of a spectrum that includes marriages for love that also may include some of these calculating motives. By making various social benefits dependent on the marital status of the parties involved, the Soviet regime sponsors the abuse of possibilities for marrying. While such abuses exist in other countries—such as fictitious marriages to immigrate into the United States, to dodge taxes, and the like—the plethora of such regulations in a bureaucratic, rule-ridden society makes the likelihood of such marriages perhaps greater than in the West. Over time as housing becomes more available, conditions improve, standards of living in various parts of the country become more equal, and foreign travel becomes freer for couples, it can be expected that the number of such marriages will decrease. Up to now, however, these types of arrangements are indicative of ways in which the Soviet Union has sponsored marriages of calculation rather than sought structurally to destroy the possibility for them, even if unintentionally.

CONTROL OF TRANSACTIONS IN MATE-SELECTION

Parental control over mate-selection historically was extensive throughout all the various geographic regions that now comprise the USSR. Among the Russian peasantry until the end of the nineteenth century, marriages were concluded primarily according to parental choice and economic considerations played the major role. The main goal was to find a bride who would be a good worker, and the feelings of young people usually were not taken into consideration to any great extent. (For discussion of reasons for such economic considerations in marriage, see Chapter 4.) As a result there was a frequent practice of elopement or what was alternatively known as samokhodka, ubeg, or samokrutka, a pattern according to which the couple would be married in secret and then after some time would return to the parents to ask for their blessing and forgiveness (Aleksandrov et al. 1964: 469).

Marriages were arranged through the use of matchmakers or svaty, usually elder relatives of the groom who would visit the bride's family at night so as not to be seen, and the marriage arrangements had very definite elements of purchase and sale. Grooms throughout Russia generally paid a kladka or contribution to the expenses of the wedding and the bride's clothes (this has been claimed to be a survival of a bride-price, see Aleksandrov et al. 1964: 470), and in return the size of the bride's dowry was determined. Typically there also was inspection of the groom's house.

In addition to the actual economic contract between the parties, many customs in the traditional Russian peasant wedding ritual were of a somewhat mercenary nature. Thus when the groom's party would set out for the wedding, the bride's relatives would set up various obstacles that the best man then had to buy off with gifts of wine and sweets. Also, the place next to the bride was sold to the best man by the bride's younger brother. In some areas of Russia the bride was ritually purchased from the bridesmaids (Aleksandrov et al. 1964: 469-72; Dunn and Dunn 1967: 96-99).

By the end of the nineteenth century and beginning of the twentieth, matches began to be made more often with the consent of the parties involved. Although parental consent and matchmaking continued, they tended to take on somewhat more of a ritualistic aspect, and the traditional ways in which young people might meet each other increased in importance. Young people would meet in winter at so-called posidelki or sit-downs, spinning-bees. The girls of a village would gather, after which the boys of the village, sometimes within specific age-groups, would arrive to sing and dance with them. To some extent there were aspects of village endogamy, since only those who were residents of the village had the right to sit-down, even though those from other villages attended. In summertime the posidelka was replaced by the gulianie or walk, stroll. These often took the form of a kind of mass outing at which prospective brides and grooms and their parents could have a look at one another (Dunn and Dunn 1967: 23-24).

Although courtship in the towns also included parental consent and matchmaking, there existed something more of a love pattern. Young workers or members of the merchant class would meet at evening parties, at gulianiia, or, very frequently, in church. Indeed, by the turn of the century priests were complaining that the churches were being turned into meetinghouses for young people (Zhirnova 1975). Although selection might be made by the couple themselves, an official agreement or ritual matchmaking persisted even where the matchmaker had not actually done anything. In the towns relatives were sometimes replaced by fellow workers or professional women matchmakers (svakhi) in the bargaining process. As in the countryside a dowry generally was provided by the bride's side, and the groom had to pay everything necessary for the bride's wedding dress. Urban wedding ceremonies also contained the same elements of purchase of the bride as among the peasantry (Aleksandrov et al. 1964: 476).

In general, the same patterns characterized the Ukrainian and Byelorussian areas of the country, but it would seem that something more of a love pattern was institutionalized in the rural regions of those areas than was the case in central Russia. Although the consent of those entering marriage was not necessary to conclude a marriage among either the Ukrainians or Byelorussians, as a factual matter it generally was taken into account. The consent of parents was, however, necessary. As among the Russians the groom would send emissaries to conclude an agreement with the parents of the bride, and as among the Russians a dowry generally was provided, though the latter was of less importance in urban areas (Aleksandrov et al. 1964: 688, 692, 867, 870).

In the Baltic areas of the country youth historically had more of a say in the selection process. This was particularly the case in the Protestant regions. Thus following confirmation Estonian youth would become acquainted at work and in leisure activities. In contrast, the role of parents, particularly the father, in Latvia and Lithuania seems to have been somewhat greater in concluding marriages. While in Estonia the ability of a wife to be a good worker was important, economic considerations seem to have been somewhat more of a concern in Latvia and Lithuania. Throughout the Baltics the tradition of having a matchmaker sent by the groom to conclude all agreements existed, as well as wedding customs similar to those in Slavic areas in which the bride was "bought." As in much of Western Europe the bride had the right of control over the dowry she brought to her marriage (Belitser et al. 1964: 73-76, 173-75, 280-82).

In the Caucasus and Central Asia the role of parents in mate-selection was considerably greater historically than in the Slavic and Baltic areas, particularly among Moslem peoples. Daughters often were given into marriage while still children, and rarely were the wishes of the future partners taken into account. Thus even at the beginning of the twentieth century Armenians

> did not pay any attention whatsoever to the mutual consent of those entering into marriage and even thought that it was ill-mannered for young people to be interested in this question or to express their desire. The choice was made by their parents—when choosing a girl they looked at her mother, when choosing a boy at his father. (Lalaian 1906, cited in Ter-Sarkisiants 1972: 126)

In Central Asia a girl's father decided whom and when she would marry, and in many respects the marriage of a Central Asian girl was a forced marriage (Massell 1974: 111). Primarily an economic transaction between two families negotiated by the fathers, courtship in many parts of these areas involved open haggling over the bride-price or kalym. Exorbitant kalym often led to marriage by abduction (Luzbetak 1951: 76-99; Massell 1974: 112-14). In some areas of the Caucasus by the beginning of the twentieth century, purchase of brides had fallen by the wayside, but haggling for dowries remained (Ter-Sarkisiants 1972: 137-38).

Soviet laws and changes in the socioeconomic structure of the USSR have brought about a situation whereby the majority of brides and grooms now enter into marriage by mutual consent. Although it seems clear that most couples do now enter into marriage of their own free will—to compel persons to marry against their will is a crime in Soviet law (see Chapter 1)—parents and kin still play a large role in the decision to marry. Such authority of parents in mate-selection varies by geographic region along the lines historically existing before the Revolution: although it has been reduced throughout the entire USSR, kin control of mate-selection remains greater in the Caucasus and Central Asia.

The continuing participation of parents in the marital choices of their children in the Slavic areas is connected to a large extent to the problems of the housing shortage and the fact that most newlyweds anticipate living with one or the other set of parents after marriage. Of the 500 couples interviewed in 1962 at the Leningrad Palace of Weddings, 79.6 percent asked the consent of their parents to their marriage, while some 38 percent of all couples expected to live with their parents immediately after marriage (Kharchev 1964: 180). Among women interviewed in the same location in the late 1960s, over three-fourths had introduced their future spouses to their parents, while over 50 percent of them were helped financially by their parents and lived with their parents immediately after marriage (Kharchev and Emel'ianova 1970: 62). Ninety-three percent of the parents of a sample of rural Byelorussian couples surveyed in the early 1970s knew of the young people's decision, and 79.6 percent approved of it (Kolokol'nikov 1976: 81). While these have been the only surveys that have asked a question concerning parental consent directly, it is clear that the same relationship with parents must be true for other areas of the country. Thus over half the newlyweds in Kiev in 1970 intended to live with one or the other set of parents after marrying, and over two-thirds of the brides and over half the grooms were receiving material help from their parents as of the time of entrance into marriage (Chuiko 1975: 89-90). It is hard to see how under such circumstances newlyweds could avoid taking into account the opinions of their parents or of others with whom they plan to live.

Since parents are less likely than those actually entering into marriage to stress the psychological characteristics of a potential spouse among criteria of mate-selection, the fact that so many newlyweds live with their parents decreases the chances that couples will enter into marriage as a result of love. Couples interviewed in Perm in 1966-67 were less likely to say that they had married for love if they were living with their parents (Fainburg 1970: 71).

It is interesting to note that where Soviet parents have disapproved of their children's marital choices, it has been overwhelmingly the groom's parents who have been dissatisfied. Among Kharchev's 1962 sample of Leningrad couples, the parents who objected to their children's marriage were all parents of the groom (Kharchev 1964: 186), and in the study of women in

Leningrad as of the late 1960s, 12 percent of the bride's parents objected to her marriage, whereas 28 percent of the groom's parents objected to his (Kharchev and Emel'ianova 1970: 62). From time to time the Soviet press prints articles attacking parents for interfering in their children's choice of a spouse, and in almost all cases these are instances of parents of the groom objecting to their son's marriage. Very rarely does an article appear concerning objections by the parents of the bride. Such articles concern, for example, a father's maneuvers in trying to get a ZAGS registration worker fired for registering the marriage of his son (Kotelevskaia 1968), or a young student's refusal to stand up to the objections of his father to his marriage where the father had been newly chosen first secretary of the Party Raikom and felt snobbish toward his daughter-in-law (Chachin 1971). In general discussions of parental opposition to the choice of a spouse, the examples used are almost exclusively that of opposition by the grooms' parents (see Ovchinnikova 1970).

The explanation as to why the concern of grooms' parents would be greater than the concern of brides' is to be found in the far greater value of men than of women in the Soviet marriage market. As will be further discussed in Chapter 3, the great shortage of men in the postwar era has meant that it has been much harder for women to find husbands than for men to find wives, and presumably the parents of brides have been more ready to settle for anyone their daughter could get. A common attitude in Soviet society is that if a woman is single she is to be pitied, and it is usually thought that a single woman is unable to find a mate while a bachelor is thought to be single by choice (Svetlanova 1969). Comparison of the two Leningrad surveys gives some reason to suppose that the objections of grooms' parents have become more vociferous over the years: that is to say, there is some evidence that as the sex ratio has normalized and the value of men on the Soviet marriage market has fallen, parents used to the idea that a man can acquire pretty much anyone he wants have more and more objected to their sons' choices of brides.

While parental consent still is frequently sought in the USSR, mates are now generally found outside the home. In the European areas of the country very few now meet through parents and other relatives: only 3.3 percent of the Leningrad couples interviewed in 1962 and only 2 percent of the women interviewed in Leningrad in the late 1960s had met through relatives (Kharchev 1964: 197; Kharchev and Emel'ianova 1970: 62). Kin are more likely to have introduced newlyweds to each other in the areas in which parental control over mate-selection was traditionally very strong, such as the Caucasus and Central Asia. It would seem, however, that as of the present time only a minority of couples even in these areas now meet through parents and other relatives. Thus in a survey done of couples in rural Kirgizia in the early 1970s, only 23.2 percent had met through parents and relatives, and only 15.8 percent of those working in urban industry had so met (Achylova 1972: 8-9).

In urban areas throughout the country something close to 40 percent of couples now meet through school or work. In studies in Leningrad, Kiev, and

Frunze, 17.5 percent, 15.7 percent, and 18.4 percent respectively of couples met in school; 21 percent, 22.1 percent, and 22 percent respectively met at work. A growing number meet at places of leisure, such as the cinema, clubs, and the like; such places accounted for 27.2 percent of Leningrad couples in 1962, 21.6 percent of newlyweds in Kiev in 1970, and even 20.1 percent of couples in rural Kirgizia in the early 1970s. A small but growing proportion meet by accident on the street or in other locations (Kharchev 1964: 197; Chuiko 1975: 98; Achylova 1972: 8-9).

In Table 2.10 are presented the places of meeting of newlyweds in Kiev in 1970 by level of education. Those with incomplete higher or higher education are more likely to have met in school than those with only secondary or incomplete secondary education, while the latter are more likely to have met at work. It is primarily those with secondary education who meet in places of leisure. The proportion of those meeting on the street decreases with more education. These relationships provide some support for the idea that those higher up in the society are more concerned with their choice of spouse and are less likely to meet randomly.

Although self-selection has become the norm throughout the USSR even in those areas that traditionally had strong kin control over marriage and/or formal matchmaking, it is interesting to note that matchmaking still persists in certain groups and is widely practiced as a ritual matter in weddings. While any matchmaking that does not take into account the consent of the parties is strongly condemned and punished by political authorities (see Chapter 1), matchmaking with the consent of the parties still exists in several settings where partners have been unable to find mates with specific desirable characteristics, although it is subject to government harassment. Attempts sometimes are made to put matchmakers on trial, but matchmaking as such is not a crime under Soviet law as long as there is mutual consent of the parties. (For a description of such a case see Beliavskii and Finn 1973: 42-48.) Campaigns have been held against the practice of matchmaking in Jewish synagogues (Shabad 1962). Matchmaking has remained a part of rural wedding ceremonies in most areas of the USSR, but now has a humorous character and generally is limited to the details of the wedding arrangements (Aleksandrov et al. 1964: 491; Pushkareva and Shmeleva 1959; Ter-Sarkisiants 1972: 128; and others).

Of interest is the fact that although matchmaking and arranged marriages have declined, popular demand has increased for such things as marriage bureaus, compatibility services, and computer matchmaking. The poor sex ratios after the war and the fact that women often tend to be concentrated in industries such as textiles where they have little chance of meeting men, while "bachelor cities" with disproportionate numbers of men abound in the far north and at construction sites (Perevedentsev 1977), has meant that many people, particularly those in the older ages, have found themselves lonely and unable to find a mate in a society where close personal relations play a great role in people's lives. In the period immediately following the war, the flight of young women from the

TABLE 2.10

Place of Acquaintanceship by Education: Brides and Grooms in Kiev, 1970 (percent)

Place of meeting	Incomplete secondary	Secondary (general and specialized)	Incomplete higher	Higher
Grooms				
At work	25.7	22.8	17.4	22.8
Leisure	16.8	25.9	16.4	20.7
School	8.0	10.5	34.7	13.5
Vacation	7.1	7.6	7.3	11.4
Lived in same house	8.8	8.4	4.6	6.3
Lived on same street	7.2	8.0	3.8	7.2
On the street	7.1	3.6	4.2	2.1
Other	16.8	12.4	10.4	13.9
No answer	2.5	0.8	1.2	2.1
Total	100.0	100.0	100.0	100.0
Brides				
At work	31.5	25.6	13.0	16.5
Leisure	13.5	26.2	17.0	9.2
School	13.5	9.1	34.2	23.6
Vacation	5.9	7.9	10.5	12.7
Lived in same house	4.7	7.0	5.7	10.9
Lived on same street	4.7	5.9	3.6	5.5
On the street	7.6	5.2	3.3	1.8
Other	14.0	12.1	11.9	16.5
No answer	4.6	1.0	0.8	3.3
Total	100.0	100.0	100.0	100.0

N = 1,000 grooms and 1,000 brides.
Source: Chuilo 1975:101.

countryside to the cities in search of husbands was a common occurrence. With normalization of the sex ratio, such mobility in search of a mate ceased to be so prevalent. As of 1959 Khrushchev announced that it had more or less ended ("Farms Cultivate Love, Khrushchev Declares" 1959), but the problem still continues to some extent. Thus complaints are raised from time to time in the press regarding labor turnover among women workers in textile towns ("The Young Women Are Leaving Krasavino" 1975). There also has been a high labor turnover among rural women schoolteachers (Perevedentsev 1971a).

In like manner there are a limited number of places where young people can spend their free time and meet each other. The number of ways to spend leisure time is not well developed in the Soviet Union and a source of complaint in the Soviet press. Clubs, films, and concerts are claimed by young people to be too structured and uninteresting to provide a place to meet, while bars, cafes, and the like are insufficient in number and provide little opportunity for private conversation (Fisher 1974). As a result, dance halls and something akin to the old narodnoe gulianie prevail in many towns. A few years ago a 100-meter strip on Kirov Street in Astrakhan became the object of much discussion since crowds of young people were gathering to meet there, and a by-product of this custom was drunkenness, fistfights, and the like (Vyzhutovich 1975). Such difficulties also are noted at dance halls. In keeping with the general concept of order in Soviet life, along with recognition of the need for such meeting places, suggestions are made regarding the ways in which they should be organized. Thus in spite of young people's desire to meet in unstructured places, suggestions are made that "the dancers themselves could be made responsible for keeping order at the dances: the dance hall could become a dance club with its own rules and *aktiv . . .*" (Briman 1975).

As of the late 1960s public demand for marriage bureaus and electronic matchmaking began to grow quite strong in the USSR. From 1969 to 1971 a debate raged on the pages of *Literaturnaia gazeta* concerning the advisability of such services. One of the first of the articles to appear bemoaned the plight of single women in the USSR and advocated the use of computers for finding single women husbands:

> . . . and so a husband must be found for Galochka. Traditional matchmaking techniques are brought into play with the approval of public opinion. Valya and Vanya meet at the home of someone who invited them for that purpose. But mention computers as a possible aid to finding a marriage partner—God forbid! Public opinion doesn't approve. Computers cannot make decisions, but they can take account of a person's requirements and help two compatible people to meet. The conservatism of public opinion must be overcome. Who knows, computers may help lower the divorce rate. (Svetlanova 1969)

Five articles and a vast number of letters to the editor followed. Academician A. Berg, chairman of the Scientific Council on Cybernetics of the USSR Academy of Sciences, endorsed the use of computers for matchmaking in an article entitled "Concerning Love Machines and Oracles," claiming that the only thing a computer would do would be to reduce the unlikeliness of a man living in Moscow becoming acquainted with a possible wife living somewhere in Vladivostok (Berg 1970). In the scholarly press as well, marriage bureaus and even newspapers in which persons could advertise for desired partners were advocated (Kharchev and Emel'ianova 1970: 62).

The final article in the debate in *Literaturnaia gazeta* was entitled "Acquaintanceships and Weddings," and was written by sociologist Vladimir Shliapentokh. Shliapentokh noted that over 75 percent of those who had written letters to *Literaturnaia gazeta* were in favor of marriage bureaus and almost half of them voiced a personal interest in using such marriage bureaus. Women aged 30 to 50 were most in favor while young students did not think that they personally needed such services. Only the elderly, those over 60 years of age, were highly opposed to such matchmaking. Educated urban dwellers were more agreeable to the idea of matchmaking by computer than those with less education and those from rural areas. Those writing letters expressed the view that matchmaking by computer would be a tremendous help to women living in predominantly female textile towns and to men living in predominantly male mining towns in Siberia, and stressed the difficulty of meeting people in contemporary urban settings (Shliapentokh 1971).

Six days after Shliapentokh's article appeared, *Pravda* published an article that ended all discussion of computer dating. *Pravda*'s main point of contention with Shliapentokh's article was that there was no mention of love:

> What did this "analysis" offer those who are burdened with loneliness and dream of finding happiness in marriage? Nothing less than an omnipotent, super-efficient, "electronic matchmaker"—a "marriage bureau" employing the latest equipment. . . . Could this learned sociologist, and with him the editors of the newspaper, really believe that the public activeness of Soviet people can find worthy application in fussing over the arrangement of a marriage bureau with an electronic matchmaker ejecting a mechanical list of the virtues of an optimal partner?
> Incredible!
> *Literaturnaia gazeta*'s discussion, useful in intent, about marriage and the family can hardly be said to have culminated in the best way. *Literaturnaia* should have hardly used its columns to propagate an idea alien to our Soviet moral outlook, the idea of arranging a marriage and family by calculation even if electronic calculation. ("Marriages Arranged by Electronic Matchmaker" 1971)

It seems clear that what was objectionable in the proposal of marriage bureaus to Soviet officialdom was not so much the use of new techniques for letting people become acquainted but rather the fact that any questionnaire designed for purposes of establishing some compatibility of partners would have to take into account characteristics and traits that are alien to the conception of romantic love and lack of calculation in marriage. A number of the articles published by *Literaturnaia gazeta* had dealt with the question of what should be contained in such a questionnaire. In describing the beginnings of a family service in Tartu, Estonia, one author had indeed gone so far as to argue that the more questions placed into a questionnaire for such computer matchmaking the better, including such things as living conditions and property status—things clearly not supposed to be taken into account when marrying in the USSR (Voina 1970).

For several years after the *Pravda* article there was little open discussion of such compatibility services. At the same time a certain amount of premarital counseling became available in Leningrad and in some cities of the Baltic republics, but was not officially sponsored nor part of the economic plan (see Danilov 1972; Verb 1975). In the summer of 1974, however, *Literaturnaia gazeta* again picked up the topic with an article by Iurii Riurikov that advocated a kind of compatibility service that would be both a consultation service for married couples and also a bureau through which it would be possible to meet persons of the opposite sex (Riurikov 1974). Debates similar to that in *Literaturnaia gazeta* began to appear on the pages of *Moskovskii komsomolets* and *Nedelia* with the participation of such scholars as S. I. Golod and I. S. Kon. Perhaps as a result of the *Pravda* response to the older *Literaturnaia gazeta* debate, the accent in the discussion began to be less on the prognosis of compatibility and love than simply on the use of computers and "get-acquainted services" for introducing people to each other (see, for example, Kon 1976).

In November 1976, *Literaturnaia gazeta* decided to run as an experiment two marriage notices in response to pressure by readers for some service of this sort. The notices, which evidently were fictitious, read as follows:

Single man, age 48, height 166 cm., education in the humanities, homebody, would like to meet blonde woman under 35 who loves the theater and symphonic music. Moscow, No. 1.
    Divorced woman, age 32, height 162 cm., has 6-year-old child, construction technician, wants to meet man who loves sports, is cheerful and doesn't drink. Voronezh, No. 2. ("Let's Get Acquainted" 1976)

The response to the notices, so out of the ordinary in Soviet life, was tremendous. The newspaper received some 10,000 letters, over 99 percent of which were in favor of establishing get-acquainted services, more than in the 1969-70 debate. Shliapentokh was asked to analyze the letters and carry out a survey of 1,600 subscribers to *Literaturnaia gazeta*. He found that only 20 percent of the letters were from men, an indication of the advantageous position of Soviet men in finding marriage partners (see below), and that respondents to the survey would have preferred the notices to contain more information on personal character traits. Preference was expressed for get-acquainted clubs over such notices or computer matchmaking or, in other words, for services that would involve face-to-face contact (Shliapentokh 1977).

One of the main reactions to the publication of the notices, however, was fatigue with the whole debate. As one woman put it, the discussion "began when my daughter was only 24. Now she is 32, and I don't know if I'll live to see the end of the debate or until my nice, well-educated daughter meets a proper man" ("Get Acquainted!" 1976). Clubs for those over 30 years of age and so-called friendship clubs have been formed in the last few years in Leningrad, Kiev, Taganrog, Rostov-on-Don, Tashkent, Ust Ilim, Lipetsk, Tomsk, Barnaul, Krasnodar, Minsk, Poltava, Novosibirsk, and other cities. Most importantly, the Bureau of the Moscow City Party Committee and the Moscow City Soviet Executive Committee adopted a resolution at the very end of 1977 to stimulate population growth in Moscow that included the organization of a get-acquainted service (Malinovskii 1976; Radzinskii 1977; "First Steps toward Family Service" 1977; " 'He,' 'She' and 'They' " 1978; Fedoseeva 1978; Mushkina 1978). While such services are still considered to be troublesome from aesthetic and moral points of view, they seem to have been accepted now as necessary (Radzinskii 1977; Rubinov 1978). Indeed, there now is some discussion of organizing singles vacation hotels, tour groups, and parties ("The Family and Its Members" 1978).

Public demand for new forms of courtship has been sufficiently great as to change official attitudes. It seems likely, however, that development of such services will be slow, and it remains to be seen to what extent the Soviet population actually will use them.

Reduction in the authority of parents and control of kin over the mate choices of their children generally is associated with a reduction in the importance of dowry and bride-price systems, since such investments cannot be protected (Goode 1963: 34). While the practice of paying dowries and bride-prices has been greatly reduced and indeed eliminated in many areas of the USSR— payment of a bride-price is a criminal act under article 232 of the RSFSR Criminal Code (see Chapter 1)—such customs are still common in the Soviet Union, particularly in Central Asia. This continued existence of dowries and bride-prices is perhaps not surprising in view of the continued importance of parental approval of marriages, if not full control over mate-selection as discussed above.

A Turkmen poetess, Esenova, recently complained that convictions in the Turkmen SSR for payment of kalym total only three or four per year, "when we all know that many more instances of bride purchase occur." Evidently there is a great deal of concealment before the authorities and participation in, or at least overlooking of, the practice by many party and government officials. The size of kalym varies greatly: recent reported cases range from 250 rubles plus seven suits of clothes and 16 pieces of fabric, to a full 16,000 rubles plus 100 oriental gowns and some poultry. The size of kalym depends on the status and value both of the bride and her family, with an uneducated girl reportedly valued more highly than an educated one since girls with university education are considered to know too much and would not submit to their husbands as obedient servants. (For discussion of the relevance of relative education of husband and wife to marital status, see Chapter 4.) Families with many sons claim to spend their lives in poverty trying to save money for kalym. It is unclear just how widespread the practice of kalym is, but it seems to be generally approved in Central Asia on the ground that the custom gives newlyweds a start in life since in-laws repay them part of the kalym in necessary household furnishings (Esenova 1974; Esenov 1977; Murtazakulov 1975).

The amounts of money involved in kalym have been increasing over the years. In the mid-1960s they began to soar. Thus a hospital attendant near Dushanbe who paid some 500 rubles for his bride in 1966 complained, "They used to be cheaper. My brother Safar a few years ago paid only 250. Now for some reason or other they would not take less than 500 rubles" (quoted in Lorince, 1966: 869; see also Urusova 1973). It seems likely that this raise in bride-prices is partly due to greater affluence and partly due to changes in the sex ratio. As the sex ratio has normalized in the Moslem areas of Central Asia and the Caucasus, the supply of brides relative to grooms has become less plentiful, and the price for brides therefore has increased.

The effect of changing sex ratios also is visible as regards the size of dowries. Just as the closing of nunneries in the sixteenth and seventeenth centuries in England increased the number of women available for marriage among the English nobility, thereby increasing the size of dowries (Stone 1961), so too there is evidence that dowries in postwar Armenia increased in comparison with their prewar levels (Ter-Sarkisiants 1972: 137-38). Ethnographic reports of rural Latvia and central Russia in the 1950s and early 1960s reported the custom of giving a dowry as still very much in effect (Belitser et al. 1964: 177; Kushner 1958: 227), as might be expected given the great shortage of eligible men in those areas (see Chapters 3 and 4).

In spite of general ideological agreement that self-selection should be the basis of marriage, considerable parental and kin participation in the decision to marry has remained in postwar Soviet Union, particularly in those rural areas where parental control of mate-selection historically was very strong. Continuing parental influence in mate-selection is not the result of tradition alone, however. Poor housing conditions that have meant that newlyweds generally have had to live with their parents, the poor sex ratios following the war and the consequent difficulties in finding a partner, and the economic utility in the countryside of adding a new member to the family all have helped to maintain some parental authority in courtship. (For further discussion of effects of the sex ratio and the economic utility of new family members, see Chapters 3 and 4.)

DURATION OF COURTSHIP

Under the different kin-controlled courtship systems of the nineteenth century, the length of time a couple might know each other prior to marriage varied greatly, and in many instances the couple did not know each other at all prior to their wedding ceremony. There was generally a period of time, however, between the agreement to a marriage contract and the actual entering into that contract that was marked by a formal betrothal ceremony.

Among the Russian peasantry in the nineteenth century, a preliminary betrothal ceremony, called a malyi zapoi or small drinking bout, followed the agreement to a marriage, and during it the details of the timing of the wedding and the dowry were decided. Following inspection of the groom's house, the rukobit'e (handclapping) or bol'shoi zapoi (large drinking bout) was held in the bride's home, after which it was difficult to withdraw from the arrangement (Aleksandrov et al. 1964: 469-70). Among the upper classes a pomolvka or formal betrothal generally preceded the wedding by over a year (Kharchev 1964: 206). Similar engagement periods prevailed in other areas of the country. (For the history of Russian betrothal and wedding rituals, see Chistova and Bernshtam 1978.)

With the decline in matchmaking, kin-selection, and the various formalities surrounding marriage, these formal periods of time prior to the wedding disappeared, particularly in urban areas. By the 1960s ceremonies such as the rukobit'e were rare in the Russian countryside (Dunn and Dunn 1967: 100), while the very word pomolvka had left the Russian vocabulary.

Prior to the 1968 change in marriage and family laws, a couple could register their union within a few days after making application. As a practical matter, after the establishment of new wedding ceremonies in 1959, demand for the new Palaces of Weddings and the time involved in preparing for more elaborate ceremonies than the simple signing of registration books created a factual period of waiting of one month between the filing of application for and actual registration of marriage (Kulaeva 1974). The observation that many divorcing couples had known each other for only a short time prior to registering their marraige led to a series of suggestions in formulating the new Fundamentals of Family Law in 1968 that a required period of time between the application for registration and the actual registration of a marriage be introduced. There were proposals to make this a formal engagement whereby public announcement of the intention to marry would be made (for example, see Iurkevich 1965: 35). It was not considered possible to define the juridical rights between the parties prior to marriage, however, and since the traditional pomolvka had not carried with it legal consequences, legal requirements were limited to an obligatory period of one month between the application for registration and the registration of a marriage (Orlova 1971: 41-44).

At the present time marriages in the RSFSR and elsewhere must be preceded by an obligatory one-month waiting time that can be extended up to three months or can be reduced for pressing reasons such as pregnancy of the bride (Kodeks o brake i sem'e RSFSR 1975: article 14). Although the same waiting period is a legal requirement throughout the USSR, as a practical matter waiting periods tend to be somewhat shorter in the RSFSR and Byelorussia. According to the practice of these two republics, the head of the ZAGS Registration Bureau can in exceptional cases reduce the length of the waiting period, whereas in the Ukraine and elsewhere this is possible only through application to the ispolkom of the local Soviet (Orlova 1971: 41; Solov'ev 1974).

Control over the length of this obligatory waiting period permits government authorities to interfere to some extent in mate-selection. While the waiting period may be shortened where, for example, a Soviet citizen must go abroad and has as a practical matter known his future bride for a long period of time, the waiting period also may be extended where officials feel that the marriage should either be given greater consideration or if possible prevented—for example, where the groom is about to leave for military service or in the case of marriages between foreigners and Soviet citizens (Kulaeva 1974; Beliavskii and Finn 1973: 62-69).

Suggestions for extension of the obligatory waiting period to six months or more continue to be made in the interests of preventing casual marriages that have little chance of lasting. Since the obligatory waiting period is not quite the same as an engagement in which the couple announce publicly that they are to be married—and parents often do not know that their children have filed for registration of marriage—proposals for a ritual betrothal ceremony and reinstitution of the pomolvka, including formal announcements in newspapers, also continue to be made (see, for example, "Are Betrothals Necessary Today?" 1968; Solov'ev 1974; Kulaeva 1974; Meliksetian 1978).

The concern over the length of time that a couple has known each other prior to marriage and the attempt to legislate a kind of engagement period are interesting in view of the fact that long engagement periods are typically associated with calculation—that is to say, long engagements usually occur where there is concern with the attachment of two families and the intermeshing of fortunes rather than with romantic love. One indication of this is that engagements tend to be longer among the upper classes of society (Goode 1964: 81) as was the case in prerevolutionary Russia. From this perspective the very haste of Soviet young people to marry decried by social observers is, if anything, evidence that romantic love matches are coming to be the norm in Soviet society.

The available evidence indicates that not only has the formal engagement period fallen out of general use in the USSR, but also the period of acquaintanceship of couples has been growing less over the years. Whereas in 1962 17.8 percent of Leningrad couples registering had known each other for less than a year—a percentage considered too large even at that time—by 1972 a quarter of all newlyweds had known each other for less than a year (Kharchev 1964: 205; Atarov 1972). Among newlyweds in Kiev in 1970, 24.3 percent had known each other less than a year (Chuiko 1975: 102). In areas of the country where long periods of acquaintanceship between couples prior to marriage historically were not prevalent, the percentage of newlyweds who have not known each other for very long is even greater: almost half of all couples in the Kirgiz SSR had known each other for less than a year (Achylova 1972: 9-10).

There are several reasons for the brevity of premarital acquaintance. The entire push of the ideology is toward romantic liaisons that do not require much consideration, and with the greater ease of divorce since 1965 and the general protection of spouses under Soviet law, it is unclear that much is to be gained from taking time to make a decision to marry. It has been argued that the USSR as an underdeveloped country lacks a long-term time perspective (Gerschenkron 1975). In a nation in which personal decisions generally make little difference, all decisions including the one to marry have less importance, and people therefore enter into such unions more casually. In addition, in the Central Asian areas of the country, some part of the short duration of premarital acquaintanceship is to be explained by the persistence of matchmaking customs: in a survey of the Kirgiz kolkhoz peasantry, 15.8 percent of couples had never met prior to marriage (Achylova 1972: 9-10).

As in other societies, those closer to the top of Soviet society tend to know each other longer prior to marriage than those below them since there is more for them to consider in the investment. In Table 2.11 are presented data on the length of acquaintanceship of newlyweds in Kiev in 1970 by their social origin. As can be seen from the table, there is a tendency for those from the families of employees—such as white-collar workers—to have known each other somewhat longer than those from manual-worker or collective-farmer families. At the same time, those from collective-farmer families are somewhat more likely to have been acquainted since childhood because of the geographic distribution of the potential mates with whom they come in contact.

A certain proportion of couples are filtered out by the obligatory legal waiting period, which because of waiting lines at Palaces of Weddings tends as a practical matter to be three months for most first marriages ("Waiting Line for the Wedding" 1976). The percentage of couples failing to appear to register their marriages, the no-shows, varies from 10 percent in Leningrad and Vilnius to 11 percent or 12 percent in Moscow, to 14 percent in Minsk, and 15 percent in Kiev (Solov'ev 1974; Chumakova 1974: 121). An analysis of 146 no-shows in the Vilnius Civil Registry Office showed that about one-fourth of such couples were from different class backgrounds and over one-third were of different nationalities. (Discussion of the relative importance of nationality and class origin in marriage can be found in Chapters 6, 7, and 8.) In about one-fourth of the couples the potential bride was older than her groom, a figure larger than the overall percentage of marriages in which the wife is older than the husband (this is around 10 percent—see Chapter 5 below). Thirty percent of the parents of the couples disapproved of their children's marriages, another 20 percent were indifferent, and it must be supposed that the parental attitude had a great deal to do with the breakup of the engagement—43 percent of the couples shared living quarters with their parents. In answer to the question "Why didn't you go through with the marriage?," 73 couples interviewed answered: spiritual incompatibility 25.9 percent; housing difficulties 17.2 percent; parents' negative attitude 14.2 percent; forced separation 13.4 percent; deception 10.1 percent;

TABLE 2.11

Length of Acquaintanceship by Social Origin: Brides and Grooms in Kiev, 1970

Length of acquaintanceship	Grooms			Brides		
	Collective farmers	Workers	Employees	Collective farmers	Workers	Employees
A few days	–	0.7	0.5	1.7	–	0.3
Up to 1 year	29.1	24.9	21.8	19.6	24.7	23.5
1–3 years	51.4	46.2	44.7	63.2	46.4	42.6
3–10 years	17.4	27.9	31.1	13.2	27.6	31.5
Acquainted since childhood	2.1	0.1	1.6	2.3	0.3	1.6
No answer	–	0.2	0.3	–	1.0	0.5
Total	100.0	100.0	100.0	100.0	100.0	100.0

N = 1,000 grooms and 1,000 brides.
Source: Chuiko 1975:103.

physical incompatibility 7.3 percent; and sudden illness 2.6 percent (Solov'ev 1974; 1977: 105-7).

In connection with broken engagements, it should be noted that the institution of an obligatory period of waiting between application for registration of a marriage and the actual registration has created a number of fictitious engagements. In these engagements couples apply to register a marriage so as to have access to the special stores for newlyweds that are accessible only by ticket from the ZAGS Registration Bureau.

As regards the duration of courtship, the Soviet Union is in some respects moving away from its commitment to romantic love free from calculation. The interest of Soviet authorities in the stability of marriages and in increased fertility in recent years has brought about a sort of compromise with romantic conceptions. Soviet practice regarding engagements now works against love at first sight.

A NOTE ON SOVIET WEDDING RITUALS

In examining the question of whether a marriage-market model fits Soviet mate-selection, wedding rituals are of interest because they are the final conclusion of a bargain between the parties and often are accompanied by gift giving, banquets, and the like in which parents and other relatives may have an interest.

Many of the traditional wedding rituals in the territory that is now the USSR did not require the consent of the parties and therefore coincided well with kin control over mate-selection. Although in the Russian Orthodox wedding ceremony the priest questions the groom and bride regarding their willingness to marry, this part of the ritual dates only from the seventeenth century and is not an integral part of the service:

> These questions, which are not a part of the original Orthodox crowning service and which do not exist in the Greek *Euchologia* [Service Book], were introduced in the famous *Trebnik* of the Metropolitan of Kiev, Peter Moghila (seventeenth century). They are directly inspired by the Latin marriage rite, where the "consent" of the bridal pair is seen as the essential "formula" of marriage, whose "ministers" are the bridegroom and the bride themselves. In Orthodoxy, however . . . the meaning of the marriage crowning is to integrate the bridal pair into the very Mystery of Christ's love for the Church: their "consent" is doubtlessly required as a condition, but it is not the very *content* of the sacrament. (Meyendorf 1975: 38-39, emphasis in original)

With the change from religious celebration of marriage to civil registration in 1917, the mutual consent of the parties became a legal necessity and a major part of the ritual of registering a marriage. In the early period after the Bolshevik

Revolution, a couple who signed a statement saying that it was their voluntary intention to marry and that there were no legal impediments to the marriage simply received a certificate of marriage. As of the 1926 code, an official of the registrar's office would read the conditions for legal marriage and warn the couple against any false statements. The couple then signed their names in the register and entries were made in their passports regarding the names and date of birth of their spouses and the date and place of the registration of the marriage. No ceremony or witnesses were required (Mace and Mace 1963: 143-47). In basic outline these legal requirements for registration have remained the minimum ceremony legally necessary to the present day. Soviet law stresses the voluntariness of entrance into marriage and this is reflected in the ritual (see Vorozheikin 1972: 97-108).

The lack of ceremony in such official proceedings, the often lugubrious surroundings of registration offices, and the unpleasantness of registering a marriage at the same office in which deaths also are registered led to inclusion of a provision in the 1944 code for the elaboration of ceremony in the registration of marriages. In the aftermath of the war, wedding rituals of different ethnic groups throughout the Soviet Union were the main topic of study in family research, to a great extent because of the demand for ritual, particularly after the catastrophe (Fisher and Khotin 1977). As of 1959, a Palace of Weddings was opened in Leningrad in the former home of Prince Andrei Romanov, a cousin of the last czar. Such special buildings have since been set aside throughout the country, even in remote regions, to provide attractive surroundings for a new secular marriage ceremony introduced as of that time. Special courses have been established for the directors of local registry bureaus to teach them the correct ceremonial atmosphere for weddings (Mace and Mace 1963: 155; Powell 1975: 75).

One motivation for the establishment of such wedding ceremonies and Palaces of Weddings has been to wean young people away from elaborate and attractive religious ceremonies. To a great extent, this effort has been successful. As can be seen from Tables 2.12 and 2.13, although even as of the late 1950s only a minority of weddings were celebrated religiously, there has been a dramatic decrease in the percent of such weddings since the introduction of new rituals. Reluctance to abandon religious ritual is greater in the Moslem republics of Central Asia (Powell 1975: 80), and rural areas of the country are more likely than urban areas to continue religious weddings. A survey of Tatars in West Siberia from 1969 to 1971 found that while 11 percent (N = 1,133) of Tatars in the city of Tomsk had religious weddings, 25.8 percent (N = 1,479) of those in rural locations had them (Tomilov 1972. On religiosity and weddings, see also section on seasonality of marriage in Chapter 3.)

The majority of marriages are now registered with the new Soviet ceremonies. It is claimed that 80 to 90 percent of all marriages in Krasnodar and Maritime territories, the Tatar ASSR, the Komi ASSR, and Volgograd, Gorky, Tambov and Yaroslavl provinces are now registered with the new ceremonies,

TABLE 2.12

Weddings Marked by Religious Ceremonies as Percentage of All
Weddings: Postwar USSR
(percent)

Geographic location and year	
Drogobycha, Ukrainian SSR, 1960	50
Riazan, 1960	15
Penza, 1962	6.4
Mari ASSR, 1963	4.3
Tallin, 1963	3.2
Tartu, 1963	4
Odessa, 1964	14.5
Komi ASSR, 1964	0.2
Yakabpilskii Raion, Latvian SSR, 1964	7
Lithuanian SSR, 1966	33
Mari ASSR, 1966	1.5
Yaroslavl Oblast, 1969	0.16
Kiev Oblast, 1974	1

Sources: Powell 1975:81; Vasil'evskaia 1972:57; Boev and Urgrinovich 1975; Kapto
1975; Nekhoroshkov 1971:11.

TABLE 2.13

Weddings Marked by Religious Ceremonies as Percentage of
All Weddings: Estonian SSR, 1957–75, Selected Years
(percent)

Year	
1957	29.8
1958	28.0
1959	25.6
1960	18.0
1961	13.6
1962	9.1
1963	6.7
1965	3.4
1970	2.7
1975	2.5

Sources: Powell 1975:81; Andrianov and Belov 1976.

while fully 90 to 100 percent of all marriages in Moscow and Moscow Oblast, Astrakhan, and Briansk Oblast are so celebrated (Stepin 1975). To some extent these figures may be inflated due to the desire of local registry officials to fulfill quotas, but it seems clear that a very large part of the population has adopted the new ceremonies.

In these new ceremonies the Soviet government has retained the element of mutual consent, but the elaborateness of ritual and the entrance of the state into what is supposed to be a personal matter have made the conclusion of marriage less a celebration of a personal emotional event and more of a public contract. In addition, there has been a move toward larger wedding parties, greater expense, and a type of meshchanstvo or petty-bourgeois conspicuous consumption that has been typical of Soviet life since the war.

The basic ceremony is similar to many Western ones, although there are many local ethnic and geographic variations. Below is a description of how the wedding is supposed to be performed in Leningrad according to the book *Soviet Etiquette*.

> The wedding clothes of the bride and groom correspond to the traditional models valid throughout Europe. The groom is usually in a black suit, white shirt, black or colored tie and black shoes, the bride in a white or pink dress and white shoes. On her head is a veil of white transparent material. She wears white gloves. Her veil and dress are sometimes decorated with flowers, ribbons and the like.
>
> The newlyweds, accompanied by friends and relatives, arrive at the Palace of Weddings in colorful wedding automobiles that have on their carriage a wedding emblem (two rings) and light blue flags on the radiator.
>
> At the entrance to the Palace of Weddings their friends meet them, open the doors of the car, and help the arrivals to get out of it. The groom gives his hand to the bride. Their friends open the door for them and the newlyweds go into the Palace. Before the registration, their friends invite them to the separate rooms for the groom and for the bride.
>
> In these rooms have already gathered all the invited relatives and friends. Many of them carry bouquets of flowers in their hands.
>
> At the appointed time an official of the Palace invites the bride and groom with their parents and guests into the room of nuptial celebrations: "Respected bride and groom, dear parents of the bride and groom, respected guests! I request you to go into the room of nuptial celebration!"
>
> Ceremonially is heard the First Piano Concerto of Tchaikovsky. The groom takes the bride by the arm. They go up a white marble staircase. Behind them, two by two, follow parents, friends and everyone else. The doors of the ritual room slowly and widely open, and all go into the room. The groom and bride stop opposite a large table, behind which stands in ceremonial clothing with an emblematic

ribbon across his or her shoulder, the leader of the ritual as well as a deputy [of the local Soviet] and a director of the Palace who are called upon to conclude the ceremony of marriage. The parents sit in seats especially reserved for them, two to the left of the groom and two to the right of the bride. All others seat themselves in chairs placed along the wall, forming a semi-circle in the hall.

The music quiets down and the ceremony of marriage begins. Addressing the groom and bride the leader announces that he together with the deputy of the local Soviet is empowered to register their marriage.

Before the act of celebration of the wedding, the leader reminds them that the Soviet family is a union of people warmly loving each other who have decided to go through life together and is the most important unit of our state.

Soviet law takes care of the family, helps to strengthen it. Having concluded a family tie, the newlyweds are taking on not only new civil rights but also new great civil responsibilities.

No one is forced to conclude a marriage, but having entered it the spouses are obligated to obey its laws, its high moral requirements.

The main moral principle of the Soviet family is the consciousness of the responsibility for the life and happiness of the person close to you.

In connection with this, the leader asks the groom and bride: "Is your decision to enter marriage mutual, free, and sincere? Are you prepared to create a friendly, strong family, to care for each other and take care of a worthy upbringing for your future children? I request the bride to answer, I request the groom to answer."

Having received a positive answer from the bride and groom, the leader announces that in the presence of a deputy of the local Soviet and witnesses (he names their names) by mutual consent today (he indicates the date) this wedding is being registered.

"I ask the bride and groom," says the leader, "to sign the marriage registration book."

The young people go to the table and sign (first the bride, then the groom) after which they return to their former place.

"I ask the respected witnesses to testify to the act of marriage with their signatures."

The witnesses go to the table (one from each side) and sign.

At the moment of signing of the marriage act in the room is heard melodious music (the *Adagio* from Glazounov's Ballet *Raymonda*, *Nocturne* of Chopin, Tchaikovsky's *Serenade for Strings*, and others).

After the signing of the act the music quiets down and the leader continues.

"As a sign of fidelity and mutual love I ask you to place wedding rings on each other's hands."

The director brings rings on a tray. The husband places the ring on the fourth finger of the right hand of his wife and she likewise places a ring on his right hand.

Then the deputy of the local or city Soviet hands the Certificate of Marriage to the newlyweds. He speaks some warm heart-felt words and shakes their hands. After this the leader turning to the newlyweds announces with pomp:

"In correspondence with the law concerning marriage and the family of the Russian Soviet Federated Socialist Republic, your marriage is registered. I declare you husband and wife."

All stand and applaud. In the room is heard the magnificent melody of *The Hymn to the Great City* [Leningrad] by Gliere. All those present listen to this hymn with emotion until its last final chords. After that when the music quiets down the leader warmly congratulates the young people.

"Dear newlyweds! Today is your happiest and most joyous day, the day of your wedding. May it always remain for you a symbol of love, friendship and mutual fidelity."

The leader expresses the wish that a thirst for knowledge and striving for high culture be born in and unite the new spouses. May their work be creative and bring people joy. Never must they forget their parents, but must respect them and be attentive to them.

Then the leader turns with congratulations to the parents.

"Dear parents! I congratulate you with the great event in your life. I wish you strong health, personal happiness. I wish that the happiness of your children will become for you a great joy. I invite you to be the first to congratulate your children with their marriage."

The parents approach the newlyweds and congratulate them. Then to the sounds of a wedding march the newlyweds and their parents and friends after them go around the circle of all the guests who have gathered in the room, receive their congratulations and gifts, and setting out for the exit, at the doors of the room take leave of the leader of the ritual. The gifts and flowers are given over for the moment to their friends (to the witnesses) so as not to embarrass themselves.

Behind them gradually, as they walk around the circle, all those present in the room follow after them and form again a procession which goes into the banquet room or leaves by the staircase to the exit.

Friends accompany the newlyweds and their parents to cars, help them to settle into them comfortably and then themselves get into the first car so as to arrive earlier at the place where the wedding banquet will be held and to meet the young people at the entrance. (Rudnev 1971: 136-38)

The actual ceremonies held in Palaces of Weddings often do not go so smoothly due to overcrowding. Their assembly-line character has been criticized, and theatrical directors even have been employed to improve the performance of those conducting the ceremony. A number of cities have eliminated the rooms adjoining the ceremony where a first glass of champagne was offered due to excessive drinking ("Waiting Line for the Wedding" 1976).

Such ceremonies mark only the entrance into first marriages. Divorced and, ordinarily, widowed persons must register in ZAGS offices rather than in Palaces of Weddings, although there also has been an elaboration of ritual in these offices in recent years. Following the ceremony, newly married couples often visit an historic site in their city—such as an eternal flame in honor of those killed in the war or Lenin's mausoleum in Moscow—before proceeding to a wedding banquet. Special coupons are given to them to go to the head of any lines. It is considered praiseworthy for the couple to do something beneficial to the country immediately upon marrying. In a town in the Ukraine, for example, it has become customary for a couple to plant a tree in a park to commemorate their wedding ("Let It Be Like This Everywhere" 1969).

Since there are no established traditions for the wedding dinner that follows, folk customs often are drawn on. In many areas of the country, wedding banquets tend to become drinking bouts, and those responsible for creating new Soviet ceremonies have argued recently that it is time to organize this part of the wedding ritual also. With the development of new ceremonies and increased wealth in the Soviet Union, wedding parties are becoming more and more public celebrations with displays of status, although they have quite some way to go before they reach the levels known in the United States. The lavishness of some weddings has been criticized in the press, especially the amount of money spent on liquor. The extravagance is in part attributed to the fact that the parents of contemporary brides and grooms are generally of the war and immediate post-war generations who, deprived of expensive wedding celebrations themselves, are now compensating for it through their children (Sergienko 1976). Catering services for weddings have begun opening around the country, beginning with one in Leningrad in 1975 (Fedorova 1975).

Generally, the number of people invited to weddings is not very great— usually no more than 20 to 30. The Kiev catering firm Radost averaged about 69 guests per wedding in 1976 (Wren 1977). In some areas of the country, however, weddings can be very large. Wedding ceremonies in Uzbekistan generally have 200 to 300 guests ("Under the Impact of a New Way of Life" 1975); weddings in the Caucasus may have 1,500 people (Benet 1976: 138). While much of this has to do with local custom, it is clear that wedding parties are becoming larger than they once were. This means more gifts for the couple, of course, and a number of articles have appeared in the Soviet press criticizing weddings that have been purposely large so as to acquire presents. Indeed, some weddings are held more or less only for this purpose, and thus constitute another form of fictitious marriage. For example, a couple who married to provide a "Komsomol wedding" to make the local secretary of the Young Communist League look as if he were doing his job well, then divided the gifts and parted company ("Comrades Have Lovely Soviet Wedding; But Irked Party Finds It Was a Fraud" 1958). Some years ago *Pravda* criticized a couple married in Kiev for having a second ceremony on a collective farm in Shpoliansk where the groom's father held an important position in the local bureaucracy. He invited officials dependent on him who did not know the couple but provided many expensive gifts, after which the couple left immediately for Kiev (Odinets and Riaboshtan 1968).

It thus may be argued that the introduction of new and more public wedding ceremonies in recent years in the USSR has been a move away from personal, private entrance into marriage toward a more public and, at times, mercenary conception of marrying.

3

TRENDS AND VARIATIONS
IN MARRIAGE RATES

     If love is assumed to be a universal human potential, then were mate-selection to be free of all calculations whatsoever, as Soviet ideologists anticipate will be the case under full communism, rates of entrance into marriage presumably would vary little over time or place; men and women would fall in love and marry without regard to considerations external to their relationships; and the frequency and timing of their marriages would be relatively unaffected by economic and political events or by seasons of the year, except insofar as such events and seasons affect the availability of potential spouses. The frequency and timing of Soviet weddings have been far from random, however, and it is of interest to examine the ways in which these characteristics of marriage have varied in the postwar USSR.

     The present chapter brings together the available vital statistics on year-to-year fluctuations in marriage rates prior to and after World War II; postwar marriage rates by age, sex, and region of the USSR; first marriages and remarriages; and seasonal variations in marriages.

YEAR-TO-YEAR FLUCTUATIONS IN RATES
PRIOR TO WORLD WAR II

     In Table 3.1 are presented the annual changes in marriage rates per 1,000 population for Russia and the USSR from 1861 to 1979. Data are lacking altogether for some years, and for others it has been necessary to extrapolate from small geographic areas to the entire country. In light of the difficulties of data collection and the crudeness of the rates, the absolute levels indicated in the table should be viewed with a degree of skepticism, but the year-to-year fluctuations are important and of interest. Table 3.1 is the closest approximation to a long-span historical time series on marriage rates in Russia and the USSR that can be obtained.

Many of the yearly fluctuations in crude marriage rates in the period prior to World War II are connected with political events, wars, and military service. Thus it seems likely that the high rates of marriage that prevailed in European Russia in the early 1860s were at least partly the result of the abolition of serfdom in 1861. Marriages that had previously been prevented between serfs were now made possible, and presumably a fair number of weddings in 1861-62 took place between men and women who had until then been forced to delay getting married. The decline in marriage rates subsequent to 1874 is connected to the introduction of universal military service at that time. Universal military service discouraged young men from entering marriage, and the percentage of married recruits in the Imperial Army fell from 38.4 percent in 1874 to 32 percent in 1878 (Rashin 1956: 171-72). The popularity of marriage before, during, and after wars in Russia followed much the same pattern to be found in other countries. Thus the Russo-Turkish War of 1877-78, the Russo-Japanese War of 1904-5, the Revolution of 1905, and particularly World War I were all followed by periods of high marriage rates due to the many marriages that had been delayed by these conflicts. The low marriage rates during World War I have been shown to have been the result not only of the mobilization of men for the army, but also of the abstention from marriage on the part of the rest of the population (Kohn 1932: 70).

Although the statistical data on the early years immediately after the 1917 Bolshevik Revolution are scanty, marriage rates evidently revived in 1918 and, at least in the cities, soared in 1919 to heights unrecorded elsewhere in the world. Although hostilities continued, the likelihood of potential husbands being away for long periods of time at the front was considerably less during the Revolution and Civil War than it had been during World War I, and the liberalization of marriage laws in 1918 eliminated previous restrictions on marriage. The marriage rates for 1919 for Moscow and Petrograd are far greater than can be explained on the basis of these two factors, however, and indeed are in a sense abnormal. Presumably many if not most of the marriages contracted in 1919 were fictitious. The wives of Red Army soldiers received an extra bread ration at the time as well as heating, apartments, and the like, and in such hard times there was a direct economic incentive to proclaim oneself officially married whether or not it was actually the case (Petrogradskoe Stolichnoe Statisticheskoe Biuro 1920: 13-14). The expected rise in marriage at the end of hostilities can be seen at the end of the Civil War in 1922.

After wars and military service, changes in the economic well-being of the Russian population account for much of the fluctuation in marriage rates. Czarist Russia was primarily an agricultural country, and the popularity of marriage varied with good and bad harvest years. Interestingly, however, the great famine of 1891-92 does not seem to have resulted in a sharp decline in the popularity of marriage. Periods of general economic crisis also were periods of low marriage

TABLE 3.1

Marriage Rates per 1,000 Population: Russia and USSR, 1861–1977, Available Years*

Year	Marriage rate	Year	Marriage rate
1861	11.6	1905	7.6
1862	10.9	1906	9.6
1863	9.4	1907	9.0
–	–	1908	8.0
1867	10.2	1909	8.0
1868	9.6	1910	8.4
1869	10.1	1911	8.0
1870	10.4	1912	7.8
1871	10.4	1913	8.3
1872	10.4	1914	6.8
1873	9.7	1915	3.4
1874	9.8	1916	3.1
1875	9.7	1917	4.6
1876	8.4	1918	(8.3)
1877	7.4	1919	(19.6)
1878	9.2	1920	8.9
1879	10.2	1921	11.2
1880	9.6	1922	12.7
1881	9.8	–	–
1882	9.5	1924	11.4
1883	9.6	1925	10.0
1884	8.9	1926	11.0
1885	8.6	1927	10.9
1886	8.5	1928	10.4
1887	9.0	1929	11.3
1888	9.8	1930	10.4
1889	8.8	–	–
1890	8.4	1934	(7.9)
1891	8.6	–	–
1892	8.9	1939	(8.3)
1893	8.9	1940	6.3
1894	9.5	–	–
1895	9.3	1946	12.4
1896	8.8	1947	10.8
1897	9.1	1948	11.0
1898	8.7	1949	11.4
1899	9.3	1950	11.6
1900	8.9	1951	11.6
1901	8.6	1952	10.4
1902	8.6	1953	10.9
1903	8.9	1954	11.2
1904	7.6	1955	11.5

1956	11.8	1966	8.9
1957	12.4	1967	9.0
1958	12.5	1968	8.9
1959	12.2	1969	9.4
1960	12.1	1970	9.7
1961	11.0	1971	10.0
1962	10.0	1972	9.4
1963	9.1	1973	10.1
1964	8.5	1974	10.3
1965	8.7		

*Data in parentheses refer to very small geographic areas and are included only for the sake of completeness. Data for 1861 to 1917 refer to 50 gubernii of European Russia. Data for 1918 and 1919 refer to Moscow and Petrograd only. Data for 1920 to 1922 refer to 18 gubernii of the RSFSR. Data for 1924 to 1927 refer to the European part of the USSR (European part of the RSFSR, Ukrainian SSR, and Byelorussian SSR). Data for 1928 to 1930 refer to the Ukrainian SSR. Data for 1934 refer to the Azerbaidzhan SSR only. Data for 1939 refer to the Uzbek SSR only. Data for 1940 to 1974 refer to the entire USSR within its present borders.

Sources: *1861–1911*: Rashin 1956:171. These figures have been used rather than the official ones of the Central Statistical Committee since they are based on more accurate estimates of midyear population. *1912*: Calculated on the basis of the number of marriages reported for 50 gubernii of European Russia in Tsentral'nyi Statisticheskii Komitet 1915: II = 2; and midyear population given in Rashin 1956:47. *1913*: Calculated on the basis of the number of marriages reported for 50 gubernii of European Russia in Narodnyi Kommissariat Zdravookhraneniia 1923:104; cited in Kohn 1932:49; and midyear population given in Rashin 1956:47. *1914*: Calculated on the basis of the number of marriages reported for 50 gubernii of European Russia in Narodnyi Kommissariat Zdravookhraneniia 1923: 104; cited in Kohn 1932:49; and midyear population for 1913 given in Rashin 1956:47; plus natural increase as given in Kohn 1932. *1915*: Calculated by projecting estimates given in Kohn 1932 of natural increase and number of marriages on the basis of 41 gubernii and 27 gubernii respectively. *1916*: Calculation of midyear population same as for 1915 but Kohn 1932, estimate based on 15 gubernii. Number of marriages based on average of two estimates given by Kohn 1932: 52. *1917*: calculation same as for 1916 but Kohn 1932 estimates based on six gubernii for both natural increase and number of marriages. *1918–19:* Calculated on basis of figures given in Statisticheskii spravochnik g. Moskvy i Moskovskoi gub. 1927 g. 1928:12; and Petrogradskoe Stolichnoe Statisticheskoe Biuro 1920:10. *1920–22*: Kuvshinnikov 1925:128. *1924–26*: Ts.S.U. 1928. *1927*: Calculated on the basis of figures given in Institut International de Statistique 1932:XXIII. *1928–30*: Institut International de Statistique 1932:XXIII. *1934*: Ts.S.U. Azerbaidzhanskoi SSR 1964:16. *1939*: Calculated on the basis of figures given in Kharchev 1964:168. *1946–49*: Ts.S.U. 1975b:97. *1940, 1950–73*: Ts.S.U. 1975a:150. *1974*: Vestnik statistiki 1975a:91. *1975*: Vestnik statistiki 1976:90. *1976*: Vestnik statistiki 1977:81. *1977*: Vestnik statistiki 1978:87.

rates. This is perhaps most visible in the low marriage rates of 1884-86 and 1901-2. Epidemics also affected the popularity of marriage (Kurkin 1902: 512; Khotsianov 1963: 88).

The various changes in legal statutes concerning marriage and divorce after 1917 seem to have had some but not a great deal of effect on year-to-year fluctuations in marriage rates. Thus the code of 1918 that freed marriage of the restrictions it had had under the czars and substituted civil registration for religious ceremonies did contribute to an increase in the marriage rate. The relatively high marriage rates prevailing throughout the 1920s in the Soviet Union were due in part to the great ease of marriage and divorce.

The 1926 family code was contradictory in its effects on marriage rates. On the one hand, by giving recognition to already existing liaisons as marriages, the 1926 code discouraged the registration of marriages and consequently the marriage rate; on the other hand, the establishment of the famous "postcard divorces" and the very casual means of entering marriage encouraged registration of marriages. No clear impact of the 1926 code is thus visible as a result; rather marriage rates simply continued to be high throughout the 1920s.

Data are missing for the 1930s, so it is not possible to state with any certainty the nature of the annual changes in marriage rates during that period. It seems clear, however, that the collectivization of agriculture must have caused a very severe drop in the number of marriages contracted in the early 1930s. Evidence from villages in the Moscow and Riazan regions shows a sharp decline in marriages in 1932-34 at the height of the collectivization, followed by an upswing during the latter half of the decade and the second Five-Year Plan. In one of the villages there also is a sharp drop at the climax of the purges in 1937 (Khotsianov 1963: 87, 96). The Soviet government's virtual blackout concerning all marriage and divorce statistics for the 1930s supports the suspicion that marriage rates must have been subject to extreme fluctuations during this part of Stalin's reign.

Even if one had the data, it would be difficult to determine whether the legislation of 1936 had much of an effect on marriage rates in view of the extremely high degree of social change in the 1930s and the threat of war. On the eve of World War II, marriage was the least favored that it had been since the Revolution throughout the USSR. During the war weddings became rare occurrences, to be followed by a marriage boom of huge proportions after the victory over Nazi Germany.

YEAR-TO-YEAR FLUCTUATIONS IN RATES SINCE WORLD WAR II

Crude marriage rates for the postwar USSR already have been presented in Table 3.1. More refined rates per 1,000 men aged 15 to 44 and per 1,000 women aged 15 to 44 appear in Table 3.2. In addition, rates per 1,000 men aged 15 to 69 and per 1,000 women aged 15 to 49 in the Ukrainian SSR from 1945 to

TABLE 3.2

Marriage Rates of Men and Women 15 to 44 Years of Age: Russia and USSR, 1897, 1926, 1940, 1950–77 (per 1,000 population)

Year	Men	Women	Male marriage rate as percent of female marriage rate
1897	42.2	39.7	106.3
1926	47.4	41.6	113.9
1940	26.9	25.5	105.5
1950	55.4	42.8	129.4
1951	55.3	43.3	127.7
1952	48.9	38.7	126.4
1953	50.7	40.7	124.6
1954	51.3	41.8	122.7
1955	52.3	43.2	121.1
1956	53.6	44.8	119.6
1957	56.5	47.8	118.2
1958	58.3	49.8	117.1
1959	57.7	49.9	115.6
1960	58.3	50.9	114.5
1961	53.5	47.2	113.3
1962	48.6	43.3	112.2
1963	43.8	39.5	110.9
1964	40.4	36.8	109.8
1965	40.8	37.5	108.8
1966	41.4	38.5	107.5
1967	41.3	38.8	106.4
1968	40.3	38.4	104.9
1969	42.0	40.5	103.7
1970	43.4	42.3	102.6
1971	44.5	43.7	101.8
1972	41.8	41.3	101.2
1973	44.7	44.3	100.9
1974	45.9	45.6	100.7
1975	47.7	47.4	100.6
1976	44.9	44.7	100.4
1977	47.5	47.4	100.2

Sources: *1897*: Average of numbers of marriages for three years (1896, 1897, 1898) used. Tsentral'nyi Statisticheskii Komitet 1896:88; 1897:88; 1898:88; 1905. *1926*: Calculated on the basis of Institut International de Statistique 1932:77; and 1926 census (i.e., not midyear population) as given in Eason 1973:52. *1940*: Number of marriages taken from Ts.S.U. 1975a:150. Base population is estimate as of 1.1.41 (i.e., not midyear population) as given in Eason 1973:53. *1950–77*: Calculated on the basis of data in Ts.S.U. 1975a:150; Vestnik statistiki 1975a:90; 1976:85; 1977:74; 1978:81. Baldwin 1973.

TABLE 3.3

Marriage Rates of Men 15 to 69 Years of Age and Women 15 to
49 Years of Age: Ukrainian SSR, 1945–70 and 1975
(per 1,000 population)

Year	Men	Women	Male marriage rate as a percent of female marriage rate
1945	18.4	16.2	113.6
1946	45.8	36.7	124.8
1947	41.7	32.2	129.5
1948	45.6	36.0	126.7
1949	44.0	36.8	119.6
1950	44.0	36.4	120.9
1951	42.8	36.9	116.0
1952	35.2	30.6	115.0
1953	37.9	31.9	118.8
1954	37.7	32.0	117.8
1955	36.8	33.6	109.5
1956	39.3	34.1	115.2
1957	42.8	38.0	112.6
1958	42.1	37.5	112.3
1959	42.2	37.4	112.8
1960	42.0	35.2	119.3
1961	41.9	36.4	115.1
1962	38.2	33.9	112.7
1963	36.3	32.3	112.4
1964	30.9	30.5	101.3
1965	31.1	29.9	104.0
1966	30.9	31.5	98.1
1967	32.0	33.1	96.7
1968	29.1	31.3	93.0
1969	31.8	36.4	87.4
1970	31.9	36.4	87.6
1975	34.2	41.0	83.4

Sources: Chuiko 1975:44; United Nations 1977:466; Baldwin 1975:26.

1975 appear in Table 3.3. Due to lack of information concerning the base population by region or other characteristics for intercensal years, it is not possible to present refined annual data for other areas of the country.

As in other countries that had been engaged in World War II, the year 1946 saw a huge number of marriages contracted in the USSR. In contrast to the experience of other countries, however, the rise in marriage rates was prolonged over several years. In the United States, for example, marriage rates fell back to normal by 1948–49 (see Carter and Glick 1976: 41–42), but in the Soviet Union rates did not begin to fall significantly until after 1951.

The main cause of this prolonged rise in the popularity of marriage was that the demobilization of the Soviet army occurred in a series of stages over a long span of time after the war, but there were a number of other reasons as well. As a result of the 1944 family legislation, those living in the many consensual unions that had grown up before and during the war now found it desirable to legalize their relationships so as to define the juridical status of children in light of the new discrimination against illegitimate offspring (Kharchev 1964: 168-69) and to avoid the tax against bachelors and spinsters. Many marriages had been delayed by the war and now were contracted. More important, the war had created a huge number of widowers and widows, as well as a fair number of divorces as a result of long separations during the war, and the pool of eligibles for new marriages was greatly enlarged. In addition, in the rush to return to a more normal life after World War II, there was evidently a tendency for young men to rush into marriage in their early years in greater proportions than formerly. (Data for the USSR as a whole are lacking to prove this point on a national level, but do exist for the Ukraine. See Chuiko 1975: 44-45.) These factors all led to an extended period of high marriage rates after the war.

The fall in marriage rates after 1951 is in part due to the fact that the cohort of men who married directly after the war was used up during 1945-51, and it was not possible to continue the high intensity of contraction of marriages. This was so in spite of the fact that there were a great many women in the USSR after the war who under ordinary circumstances would have married and presumably desired to do so. The war resulted in the deaths of so many men that huge numbers of women were unable to find partners of any sort. It has been estimated that some 24.9 percent of women in all marriageable ages in the Ukraine were unable to enter into marriage as a result of the death of their actual or potential partners during the war (Korchak-Chepurkovskii and Chuiko 1968: 76).

A second major peak in marriage rates in the postwar period is observable in 1957-61. The main cause of this second peak is to be found in the program of troop demobilization of the Soviet armed forces begun under Khrushchev in late 1955. Achieved again in several stages, this demobilization resulted in a cut of 1,840,000 men in the course of 1955-57 from the 1955 peak strength of the Soviet army of 5.7 million, with further reductions of 300,000 men in 1958-59 and an estimated 600,000 in 1960-61 (see Wolfe 1970: 164-66). Given the great shortage of marriageable men, this demobilization provided a spur to marriage rates over several years.

The rise in marriage rates as a result of this demobilization was not felt uniformly throughout the country, however, but seems to have had most impact on Central Asian marriage rates. Table 3.4 presents crude marriage rates averaged over four-year periods for the USSR as a whole and for the 15 Union republics. As can be seen from the table, the rise in marriage rates in 1958-61, the period of the demobilization, was much steeper for the republics of Central Asia (Uzbek SSR, Kazakh SSR, Kirgiz SSR, Tadzhik SSR, Turkmen SSR) and for predominantly Moslem Azerbaidzhan than it was for the other areas of the country.

Central Asia and Azerbaidzhan were less affected by World War II and consequently had and have more equal sex ratios than do other Union republics. Assuming proportional representation of the various nationalities among the demobilized troops, marriage rates in these areas should have been less affected by such demobilization of the armed forces than in other republics, but this was not the case. The explanation as to why marriage rates peaked higher in these areas most likely lies in the ethnic composition of the demobilized troops. The demobilized troops probably were drawn disproportionately from the Central Asian and Azerbaidzhan republics.

The low level of marriage rates in the early and mid-1960s is due in part to the demographic echo of the war. The relatively small cohort of the population born during World War II came of marriageable age in 1963, 1964, and 1965 and caused something a depression in marriage rates at that time. Some of the lesser frequency of marriage in the early and mid-1960s cannot be attributed simply to demographic factors. The easing of restrictions on divorce and the streamlining of divorce procedures in 1965 enlarged the pool of eligibles for marriage and contributed somewhat to a rise in marriage rates (crude divorce rates for the USSR since 1950 are presented in Table 3.5). Higher marriage rates since 1967 are mostly due to the larger cohorts of marriageable age in the late 1960s and early 1970s.

To what extent are the annual changes in postwar Soviet marriage rates explicable by changes in the economic well-being of the population? Table 3.6 compares the marriage rates per 1,000 men aged 15 to 44 with annual per capita real disposable income, the annual number of apartments built, and the gross yield in grain production from year to year in the USSR. Although there have been drops as well as rises in the postwar Soviet marriage rates, per capita real disposable income has consistently risen. Although marriage rates are known to fluctuate with business cycles and changes in income in other countries (see, for example, Easterlin 1968), the lack of fluctuation in the spending power of the Soviet population and continuous virtual absence of unemployment in the USSR make any explanation of the year-to-year changes in Soviet marriage rates by changes in income impossible.

The degree of yearly increase in per capita real disposable income has fluctuated during the postwar period, and it is perhaps arguable that perceived

TABLE 3.4

Crude Marriage Rates by Four-Year Periods: USSR and Union Republics, 1950–73 (per 1,000 population)

	1950–53	1954–57	1958–61	1962–65	1966–69	1970–73
USSR	11.1	11.7	12.0	9.1	9.1	9.8
RSFSR	11.8	12.2	12.1	9.1	9.2	10.3
Ukrainian SSR	10.8	11.3	11.4	9.1	9.5	9.9
Byelorussian SSR	9.7	11.5	11.1	8.7	8.4	9.3
Uzbek SSR	9.6	10.7	13.3	8.5	8.3	9.1
Kazakh SSR	11.1	12.5	13.7	10.1	8.8	9.4
Georgian SSR	8.7	9.4	10.3	9.0	8.2	7.8
Azerbaidzhan SSR	8.3	10.7	12.3	9.8	7.6	6.8
Lithuanian SSR	8.5	10.5	10.2	8.8	9.4	9.1
Moldavian SSR	10.3	10.5	9.8	7.1	8.1	10.1
Latvian SSR	9.2	10.8	11.0	9.2	9.9	9.8
Kirgiz SSR	11.1	11.9	13.5	9.0	8.4	9.1
Tadzhik SSR	9.4	9.4	12.1	10.1	9.0	9.0
Armenian SSR	13.9	12.0	11.7	8.4	7.5	7.7
Turkmen SSR	10.8	11.9	13.5	9.0	8.0	8.6
Estonian SSR	8.9	10.4	10.1	8.6	8.9	8.8

Source: Calculated on the basis of figures in Ts.S.U. 1975a:150–65.

TABLE 3.5

Divorce Rates per 1,000 Population: USSR, 1950-77

Year	Divorce rate	Year	Divorce rate
1950	0.4	1964	1.5
1951	0.4	1965	1.6
1952	0.5	1966	2.8
1953	0.5	1967	2.7
1954	0.6	1968	2.7
1955	0.6	1969	2.6
1956	0.7	1970	2.6
1957	0.9	1971	2.6
1958	1.1	1972	2.6
1959	1.1	1973	2.7
1960	1.3	1974	2.9
1961	1.3	1975	3.1
1962	1.3	1976	3.4
1963	1.3	1977	3.5

Sources: Ts.S.U. 1975a:150; Vestnik statistiki 1975a:91; 1976:90; 1977:81; 1978: 87.

relative future progress in one's economic position affects readiness to enter marriage more than actual economic position in the USSR. That this may be so to some extent is visible from a comparison of marriage rates with annual increase in per capita real disposable income in Table 3.6. Thus the drops in the marriage rate in 1964 and 1972 (these drops occur even when the rates are standardized for age) occurred in years in which there was somewhat less of an increase in real income than in other years. The match in changes in real disposable income and marriage rates is far from perfect, however.

In view of the nature of the Soviet economy, it is arguable that per capita real disposable income makes less difference in economic well-being than the actual supply of goods and services. Thus the popularity of marriage may depend more on the availability of housing than on income. Given the great difficulties with the housing shortage in the postwar period and the effect of housing in the Soviet Union on such matters as fertility (see Heer 1975), it seems reasonable to suppose that changes in the availability of housing do affect marriage behavior. It is possible to show a relationship between the availability of housing and differences in the prevalence of marriage by region for given points in time (see Chapter 4). It is very difficult, however, to demonstrate empirically the effect of yearly differences on the provision of housing on the popularity of marriage since Soviet construction of new apartments has maintained a fairly consistent rate of over 2 million a year (see Table 3.6), and there is no way of knowing how many newlyweds are allotted their own apartments from year to year. It seems clear that the availability of housing is an important factor in the decision to marry and must affect annual changes in marriage rates. As seen in Chapter 2, about one-sixth of broken engagements occur because of lack of housing, but there is no way of showing this empirically for the country as a whole.

Although migration from rural areas to towns and cities has been quite extensive in the postwar period, it was not until the early 1960s that more than half the Soviet population was to be found in urban areas. Good and bad harvests might explain year-to-year fluctuations in marriage rates in recent years just as they did in the nineteenth century. Gross yield grain production is presented in Table 3.6, and some effect of increases and decreases in grain production can be seen to accompany annual changes in marriage rates. For example, the low incidence of marriage in 1964 was preceded by a decrease in grain production in 1963, and the dip in the marriage rate in 1972 was accompanied by a poor harvest. The question remains as to what is to be really considered the cause here, since the provision of food to the population does not necessarily depend on a given year's harvest. For example, Soviet purchases of grain abroad have been considerable in recent years and, as indicated above, there has been an absolute increase in real disposable income every year.

In the absence of strong correlations between annual changes in marriage rates and the economic data available, it is only possible to make some ad hoc speculations as to the reasons for these changes. It is arguable that Soviet perception of the general situation in a given year has more to do with Soviet marriage rates than the actual economic well-being of the population. Marriage involves long-term investment in the future, and Soviet would-be newlyweds must assess their future economic prospects. As indicated above, year-to-year fluctuations in Soviet marital behavior do not seem to be related to the degree of increase in income. It would seem that Soviet couples are acting in accordance with their perception of the rate of progress rather than of there being any progress at all in their economic well-being. Formation of households in the United States, like other long-term investment decisions, is known to respond only sluggishly to the impact of ordinary short and mild business contractions and to be related more closely to longer business cycles (Easterlin 1968: 50-51), so it is clear that in the West as well the main factor is perception of long-run future opportunities. The difference seems to be that in the Soviet Union the question is not whether the future state of the economy can be expected to be better than at present or in the past as it is in the United States, but how rapidly improvement can be expected.

Insofar as marriage represents an investment in the future, it also is arguable that at points in postwar Soviet history when the future has seemed less than sure politically that the Soviet population has been less ready to marry. There was a drop in the popularity of marriage in 1952 during the period of political tightening and incipient purge prior to the death of Stalin. Dips in the

TABLE 3.6

Marriage Rates per 1,000 Men Aged 15 to 44 and Three Indicators of Economic Well-Being of the Postwar Soviet Population (per Capita Real Disposable Income, Total Apartments Built, and Gross Yield Grain Production)

Year	Marriages per 1,000 men aged 15 to 44	Per capita disposable income (rubles)	Annual percent increase in per capita real disposable income	Total number of apartments built (thousands)	Gross yield grain production (million tons)	Annual percent increase in grain production
1950	55.4	219.2	n.a.	1,073	81,200	15.7
1951	55.3	n.a.	n.a.	n.a.	78,700	-3.1
1952	48.9	n.a.	n.a.	n.a.	92,200	17.2
1953	50.7	n.a.	n.a.	1,245	82,500	-10.5
1954	51.3	n.a.	n.a.	n.a	85,568	3.7
1955	52.3	366.2	10.8*	1,512	103,687	21.2
1956	53.6	369.4	0.9	1,548	124,950	20.5
1957	56.5	411.1	11.3	2,060	102,639	-17.9
1958	58.3	423.5	3.0	2,382	134,721	31.3
1959	57.7	441.9	4.3	2,711	119,538	-11.3
1960	58.3	481.8	9.0	2,591	125,490	5.0
1961	53.5	506.2	5.1'	2,435	130,790	4.2
1962	48.6	549.4	8.5	2,383	140,183	7.2

Year					
1963	43.8	557.4	1.5	2,322	107,492	−23.3
1964	40.4	574.1	3.0	2,184	152,071	41.5
1965	40.8	637.9	11.1	2,227	121,141	−20.3
1966	41.4	694.4	8.9	2,291	171,184	41.3
1967	41.3	741.5	6.8	2,312	147,887	−13.6
1968	40.3	811.6	9.5	2,233	169,540	14.6
1969	42.0	841.2	3.6	2,231	162,402	−4.2
1970	43.4	885.8	5.3	2,266	186,795	15.0
1971	44.5	934.2	5.5	2,256	181,175	−3.0
1972	41.8	968.0	3.6	2,233	168,238	−7.1
1973	44.7	1,023.8	5.8	2,272	222,530	32.3

*Average annual.

n.a.: Not available.

Sources: Marriage rates: calculated on the basis of figures in Ts.S.U. 1975a:150; and Baldwin 1973. Per capita real disposable income: calculated on the basis of figures provided in personal communication by Sheldon T. Rabin, USSR Branch, Office of Economic Research, United States Central Intelligence Agency; Bronson and Severin 1966: 526; 1973:393. Data in the Bronson and Severin articles have been reworked so as to yield a series consistent with the Rabin data. Total number of apartments built: Ts.S.U. 1961:205; 1963k:107; 1965:609, 1966:611; 1974b:610. Gross yield grain production: Ts.S.U. 1973c:323; 1974b:392.

marriage rate also are observable in 1964 during the fall of Khrushchev and in 1972 during the internal political tightening concomitant with détente. In contrast, the liberal period under Khrushchev was a period of great popularity of marriage. Unfortunately, without further information such explanations of annual fluctuations in Soviet marriage rates must remain speculative.

POSTWAR MARRIAGE RATES BY AGE, SEX, AND REGION

The upheavals of the twentieth century have wreaked havoc with the age and sex distribution of the Soviet population. While surpluses of females have been a feature of Russian society since the nineteenth century, the loss of males during World War II was particularly severe. In the years immediately after the war, there were males available for less than three-fourths of all females in the prime marriageable ages. Although by the early 1960s sex ratios in the younger age groups had evened out, the sex ratios in the older age groups of the population continued to be very low. Indeed, as the cohorts that suffered most from the war grow older, the disproportions in the older age groups are growing worse. Estimates are that the sex ratio of the Soviet population will not even out before the end of this century (see Table 3.7).

As a result of these low sex ratios, the supply of men who can marry has been extremely low for long periods of Soviet history. The supply of marriageable men was particularly poor directly after World War II, but even today in the older age groups the supply of men who can marry is extremely limited. This situation has had drastic effects on women's chances of marrying. There do not exist any surveys that might indicate the extent to which the population was aware of the hopelessness of women's finding marriage partners after the war, but it seems clear that while individual women kept searching for a husband, there was a general awareness of the lonely position in which Soviet women found themselves. The figure of the woman unable to marry because of the war is a familiar one in Soviet fiction—perhaps the best known of such female characters is the nurse in Solzhenitsyn's *Cancer Ward* (Solzhenitsyn 1968)—and poetry:

> You tried to find him everywhere.
> He must exist,
> He is someplace.
> You asked:
> Where is he? Where?
> There was no answer.
> Your youth is gone.
> You paled and withered.
> You, whose beauty shone once,
> You do not know the verity

TABLE 3.7

Sex Ratios in the Marriageable Ages: Russia and USSR, 1897–1980, Selected Years (males per 100 females)

Age group	1897	1926	1939	1941	1950	1959	1970	1980
All marriageable ages	98.2	89.1	87.3	88.5	69.7	74.2	78.9	83.1
15–19	94.5	92.0	97.5	98.7	98.2	101.1	104.2	103.6
20–24	100.3	94.6	99.6	98.6	89.5	97.8	101.8	102.9
25–29	98.2	83.9	95.3	96.6	67.1	96.2	97.9	102.5
30–34	96.0	90.2	93.6	94.5	64.1	82.9	96.9	99.4
35–39	104.0	89.6	88.0	90.4	64.3	64.1	96.3	95.0
40–44	97.3	95.3	84.7	85.9	66.1	62.4	85.5	93.4
45–49	105.1	96.0	84.4	84.0	55.6	62.3	63.2	91.9
50–54	91.0	86.9	74.2	78.2	58.1	62.3	60.7	80.7
55–59	107.5	81.4	74.6	74.4	61.3	50.2	55.2	58.3
60–64	92.2	80.4	68.3	70.9	58.8	54.0	56.3	54.2
65–69	106.4	82.3	64.1	66.2	55.3	53.2	44.4	47.3
70 and over	93.0	74.5	54.0	57.6	46.0	46.8	43.1	40.7

Note: 1941 is estimate as of 1/1/41; 1950 is estimate as of 1/1/50; 1980 is estimate as of 1/1/80; all other years are as of census dates.
Sources: Tsentral'nyi Statisticheskii Komitet, 1905:46–48; Eason 1973: 52–53; Baldwin 1973: 23, 24, 26, 27, 16.

That a wife to no one
You long since are
A widow. . . .
You do not know
That he was killed
In War
Before you met him.
(Vladimir Semenov 1958, translated by Vera Dunham in Field 1968:
12-13)

As sex ratios have become more normal in the years since the war, the likelihood of a woman's finding a husband has increased and so have women's rates of entrance into marriage. Stated differently, the position of women on the Soviet marriage market has been improving over the past 30 years.

The opposite has been the case for men. The dearth of men after the war substantially raised the price of men on the Soviet marriage market. Faced with a wide choice of potential wives and himself in great demand, an eligible male after the war was in a very advantageous position. The attractions of marrying for him were considerably greater than those for women, and it was therefore more costly for a man not to marry than for a woman not to do so. That is to say, the cost of not participating in the marriage market was greater for men than it was for women since men could strike a better bargain than could women. While marriage rates for females have been affected primarily by changes in the availability of partners, marriage rates for men have been affected primarily by changes in the cost of not participating at all in the marriage market. Marriage rates of males typically have been higher than those of females, but whereas female rates have been increasing as the sex ratio evens out, male rates have been decreasing as the choice of partners for men has become more limited and the cost of not participating in the marriage market has decreased.

An alternative interpretation is that faced with the war's creation of so many widows and spinsters, Soviet men were under considerable social and moral pressure to marry, and that this pressure has since eased somewhat due to the comparative normalization of sex ratios. Soviet demographers have been chiefly concerned with female marriage behavior because of its importance to fertility and do not conceptualize marriage in market terms for ideological reasons, as has been seen. To the extent that they have remarked on this question of changes in male marriage rates, they tend to subscribe to this second interpretation of changing social pressure or to ignore the issue altogether (Chuiko 1975: 46; Perevedentsev 1974).

Changes in the participation of men and women in the marriage market are visible from Tables 3.2 and 3.3. Whereas the marriage rate of men aged 15 to 44 was 129.4 percent of the rate for women similarly aged in 1950 when the sex ratio was still far from evened out and the marriage market particularly favorable to men, by 1977 the rates for men and women had become equal. In the Ukraine women's rates actually were higher than those for men by the late 1960s.

Age-specific marriage rates by sex are presented in Table 3.8. As can be seen from the table, only in the very youngest age groups (under 20 years of age) are the marriage rates of women significantly higher than those of men (4.47 times the male rate on the average). In the 20-to-24-year age group male and female rates are most nearly equal, with women in this age group tending to marry somewhat more than men until 1969. Since 1969, due to a lowering of the age at marriage in recent years (see Chapter 5), the male rate has exceeded that for females in this age group. In the age groups 25 to 29 and older the male rates are consistently higher than those for females. At 25 to 29 years of age men are about 1.8 times more likely to marry than women; at 30 to 34 years of age they are about 1.4 times more likely to marry. In the age groups after that the male rate is often more than three times the female rate. Again, for the years directly after the war the difference between men and women in the probability of marrying is particularly striking. The differences between male and female rates for the older age groups have continued to be very great throughout the 1960s and 1970s due to the continuing low sex ratios among the cohorts most affected by World War II.

Vital statistics and data on the marital status of the Soviet population for available years are combined in Table 3.9 to yield more accurate marriage rates per 1,000 unmarried population by age and sex. In comparison to the rather depressed marriage rates immediately preceding World War II, male marriage rates soared in 1959 due to the extremely favorable postwar marriage market for men. By 1969-70, however, participation in the marriage market had become considerably less attractive to unattached men, and their participation was a fraction of what it had been in the late 1950s in virtually all age groups. The only age group in which male marriage rates increased was that aged 20 to 24 due to a slight lowering of the age at marriage. In contrast, although eligible women also were marrying more in the late 1950s than in the years immediately preceding World War II, the increase in their participation in the marriage market was a fraction of the increase in the participation of men. With the greater supply of men in the 1960s, marriage rates for eligible women went up or stayed approximately the same in all age groups except the very oldest from 1959 to 1969-70.

These differences in participation in the marriage market in the postwar period were characteristic of all the regions of the USSR, and in all 15 Union republics decreases in male marriage rates from 1958-59 to 1969-70 were greater than any decreases in female rates over the same period. In Table 3.10 are presented unstandardized and indirectly standardized (on the basis of the 1970 age distribution of the total USSR population) marriage rates for the unmarried population 16 years and older by Union republic. Since the 1950s saw extremely high numbers of marriages due to the demobilization of the Soviet army, the 1969-70 rates are almost all somewhat lower than those ten years previous. Again, the decrease is greatest for the Central Asian Moslem republics of the country (and for Armenia) due to the greater representation of the populations of these republics among the demobilized troops.

TABLE 3.8

Age-Specific Marriage Rates by Sex (All Marriages): USSR, 1940 and 1950–77 (per 1,000 marriages)

Year	15–19	20–24	25–29	30–34	35–39	40–44	45–49	50–54	55–59	60+	All ages 15+
					MEN						
1940	7.4	42.6	57.5	15.9	15.9	6.8	6.8	3.6	3.6	3.6	20.4
1950	12.5	79.0	94.8	47.0	34.0	24.6	24.6	9.3	9.3	9.3	40.3
1951											40.2
1952											35.5
1953											36.8
1954											37.3
1955											37.9
1956											38.7
1957											40.6
1958											41.5
1959	14.9	112.1	72.0	26.0	16.7	15.2	15.2	16.4	16.4	16.4	40.7
1960	17.1	110.2	71.4	22.1	22.1	12.9	12.9	17.4	17.4	17.4	40.9
1961	14.5	104.8	67.8	19.1	19.1	11.1	11.1	14.6	14.6	14.6	37.5
1962	n.a.	n.a.	n.a.	n.a.	n.a.	n.a.	n.a.	n.a.	n.a.	n.a.	34.1
1963	7.9	93.9	63.9	20.0	11.8	9.1	9.1	12.8	12.8	12.8	30.9
1964	7.7	89.4	62.8	19.7	11.5	9.1	9.1	13.0	13.0	13.0	28.6
1965	9.8	93.0	66.5	20.4	11.7	9.2	8.9	10.0	14.3	17.0	29.0
1966	10.5	92.3	72.9	24.8	13.0	10.0	10.0	12.1	12.1	14.4	29.6
1967	11.6	95.4	75.6	25.9	12.9	9.7	9.7	12.3	12.3	13.1	29.6
1968	13.0	105.0	71.6	24.3	12.0	8.8	8.5	10.6	10.6	10.6	28.9

Year											
1969	12.0	126.3	69.2	23.9	11.0	7.8	7.2	7.7	9.4	9.0	30.0
1970	11.1	135.5	65.8	23.6	10.9	7.5	6.8	7.3	8.7	8.6	30.9
1971	9.8	139.6	65.1	23.5	11.2	7.3	6.5	7.1	8.1	7.9	31.5
1972	8.7	125.6	62.9	21.8	11.0	6.9	5.9	7.0	7.0	7.0	29.0
1973	8.8	134.4	62.3	22.5	11.7	6.7	6.7	6.9	6.9	6.8	30.9
1974	9.3	134.4	61.5	22.7	12.2	7.3	6.1	6.8	6.8	6.8	31.4
1975	9.6	135.9	60.4	22.8	12.6	6.9	6.9	6.8	6.8	6.8	32.1
1976	10.0	125.0	52.8	21.5	12.0	7.0	7.0	7.0	7.0	6.9	30.0
1977	10.8	132.0	53.0	23.4	12.3	7.3	7.3	7.0	7.0	7.0	31.5

WOMEN

Year											
1940	32.1	57.1	27.6	9.4	9.4	4.2	4.2	1.1	1.1	1.1	18.0
1950	26.1	84.7	53.3	27.9	18.3	10.2	10.2	2.3	2.3	2.3	28.2
1951											28.3
1952											25.2
1953											26.4
1954											27.0
1955											27.7
1956											28.4
1957											30.0
1958											30.7
1959	57.7	111.2	40.8	19.5	13.8	7.9	7.9	7.9	8.7	3.9	30.2
1960	61.2	111.2	41.4	16.9	16.9	8.5	8.5	6.6	6.6	6.6	30.5
1961	54.3	108.0	40.8	14.8	14.8	7.3	7.3	5.4	5.4	5.4	28.0
1962	n.a.	n.a.	n.a.	n.a.	n.a.	n.a.	n.a.	n.a.	n.a.	n.a.	25.6
1963	37.9	100.5	40.3	16.3	9.8	6.8	6.8	4.9	4.9	4.9	23.4
1964	38.3	94.8	39.3	16.1	9.8	7.0	7.0	5.2	5.2	5.2	21.8
1965	46.1	95.5	39.3	16.4	10.1	7.6	6.7	6.2	9.3	4.6	22.2

TABLE 3.8 (Continued)

Year	15–19	20–24	25–29	30–34	35–39	40–44	45–49	50–54	55–59	60+	All ages 15+
1966	47.3	102.0	40.3	19.7	11.3	7.9	7.9	7.7	7.7	3.3	22.8
1967	47.5	111.2	38.0	19.4	11.1	7.6	7.6	8.3	8.3	2.8	22.9
1968	50.4	109.6	34.2	17.6	10.2	7.2	6.4	4.7	4.7	4.7	23.1
1969	53.0	121.2	31.9	16.4	9.2	6.4	5.6	3.6	3.6	3.6	23.6
1970	54.9	122.8	31.2	15.7	8.7	6.1	5.2	5.5	5.5	5.5	24.5
1971	57.0	121.6	32.6	15.2	9.0	5.9	5.1	3.1	3.1	3.1	25.1
1972	53.3	108.2	33.6	14.1	8.6	5.5	4.6	2.9	2.9	2.9	23.4
1973	57.4	112.9	41.6	14.4	8.9	5.3	5.3	4.9	4.9	4.9	24.9
1974	59.4	112.3	36.3	14.5	9.0	5.7	4.9	2.9	2.9	2.9	25.4
1975	59.4	113.7	36.3	14.8	9.1	5.4	5.4	5.0	5.0	1.8	26.1
1976	58.1	103.2	32.6	14.7	8.8	5.5	5.5	5.2	5.2	1.9	24.6
1977	62.6	107.8	33.1	16.3	9.0	5.7	5.7	5.3	1.9	1.9	26.7

n.a.: Not available.
Sources: Calculated on the basis of figures in Ts.S.U. 1975a:172. Vestnik statistiki 1963:93; 1965:96; 1976:88; 1977:78; 1978:84; United Nations 1968:544–45; 1969: 669; 1970:741; 1971:778; 1972:632; 1973:369; Baldwin 1973. Rates for 1940 calculated using estimate of age structure of population as of 1/1/41 (i.e., not midyear population) given in Eason 1973:53.

In every one of the 15 Union republics, however, the decrease in the participation of males in the marriage market was greater than any decrease in the participation of females. In other words, there does not seem to have been any regional variation in the extent to which changing market conditions of finding a spouse affected the participation of men and women in the marriage market. In all cases, women's participation was primarily affected by the increase in the supply of potential husbands, while men's participation was primarily affected by the decrease in the possibility to pick and choose among potential wives.

Over a longer time span age-specific marriage rates of men in the USSR have tended to vary more than have age-specific marriage rates for women. Comparison of age-specific rates of the marriageable population for the postwar period with those for 1926-27 in the Ukraine and Byelorussia shows relative consistency in the marriage rates for women in most age groups, while fluctuations for men are more severe (see Tables 3.11 and 3.12). Proportions of women in each age group entering marriage were not too different in 1969-70 than they had been in 1926-27, while proportions of men entering into marriage in 1969-70 in comparison to the 1920s fluctuated considerably by age group. In these republics as in the USSR as a whole (see also Table 3.13 on Latvia), considerable increases in the marriage rates of women in virtually all age groups are visible in 1969-70 in comparison with 1958-59, while the likelihood of men entering marriage in almost all age groups decreased over the same period.

Rates by age at marriage for the 15 Union republics are presented in Table 3.14. The patterns of age-specific marriage rates shown there contrast strongly for men and women and between republics. Few men marry before age 20 in all republics. Thereafter male rates rise, reaching a peak at ages 25 to 29 (exceptions are the Georgian and Azerbaidzhan SSRs with peaks at ages 35 to 39, and the Latvian SSR with a small edge in the age group 20 to 24). The rise is particularly steep in Central Asia and Armenia, with over four out of ten men marrying in the age group 25 to 29. The Baltic republics show the smallest peaks with only about 17 men in 100 marrying during this age period. Thereafter, the marriage rates for men show a fairly steady decline in the Baltic republics and in the Turkmen SSR, but elsewhere there are secondary peaks at ages 35 to 39 and 45 to 49. After the age of 50 the proportion of eligible men marrying decreases considerably, particularly in the Baltic republics; but even at this age in a number of the Central Asian republics and Moldavia, the RSFSR, and the Ukraine, the number of eligible men marrying approximates one in ten.

The pattern is quite different for women, with larger proportions marrying in the very early ages (under 20), earlier peaks, and steady declines to much reduced rates in the older ages. Considerably higher proportions of women in the age group 15 to 19 marry than do men, particularly in the Central Asian republics; more than one in ten in this age group marry in the Tadzhik SSR. The peak marriage age (20 to 24 years) is earlier for women than for men in all 15 republics. In general, these peaks for women are all considerably higher than the corresponding peaks for men except in the republics of the Caucasus. The peaks

TABLE 3.9

Marriage Rates per 1,000 Unmarried Population by Age and Sex: USSR, 1940, 1959, and 1969-70 (marriages per 1,000 unmarried population)

MEN

Age	1940	1959	1969–70	1959 as percent of 1940	1969–70 as percent of 1959	1969–70 as percent of 1940
15 and over	60.1	129.6	100.8	215.6	77.8	167.7
15–19	7.8	14.2	11.8	182.1	83.1	151.3
20–24	64.1	151.2	183.8	235.9	121.6	286.7
25–29	219.5	351.7	311.0	160.2	88.4	141.7
30–34	⎱ 173.1	342.0 / 350.3	208.5 ⎱ 128.5	⎱ 202.4	61.0 / 36.7	⎱ 74.2
35–39	⎰	376.4	164.2	⎰	43.6	⎰
40–44	⎱ 109.2	⎱ 402.1	141.4 ⎱ 143.1	⎱ 368.2	⎱ 35.6	⎱ 131.0
45–49	⎰	⎰	146.7 ⎰	⎰	⎰	⎰
50–54	⎱ 21.9	⎱ 162.8	158.5	⎱ 743.4	⎱ 56.1	⎱ 417.4
55–59			172.7 ⎱ 91.4			
60 and over	⎰	⎰	67.2 ⎰	⎰	⎰	⎰

84

WOMEN

Age						
15 and over	43.2	62.6	55.3	144.9	88.3	128.0
15–19	36.9	60.2	59.3	163.1	98.5	160.7
20–24	147.8	229.2	275.6	155.1	120.2	186.5
25–29	129.4	165.0	185.5	127.5	112.4	143.4
30–34	} 49.5	} 87.5	} 108.3	} 144.6	} 123.8 117.7	} 170.3
35–39		71.6	84.3		117.7	
40–44		52.6	56.5		107.4	
45–49	} 15.5	} 18.9	29.7 } 24.5	} 121.9	} 129.6	} 158.1
50–54			19.2			
55–59		9.6	5.8		60.4	
60 and over	1.9			} 505.3		} 305.3

Sources: Calculated on the basis of figures in Vestnik statistiki 1963:93; United Nations 1968:544–45; 1970:741; 1971:778; Ts.S.U. 1972:12–13, 263. Base population for 1940 estimated by applying USSR Central Statistical Administration estimate of the marital status of the entire Soviet population within the country's present borders as of 1939 (Ts.S.U. 1962a:73) to Eason estimate of age and sex distribution as of 1/1/41 (Eason 1973:53).

TABLE 3.10

Marriages per 1,000 Unmarried Population 16 Years and Older, Standardized and Unstandardized for Age:
USSR and Union Republics, 1958–59 and 1969–70

	Unstandardized			Standardized*		
	1958–59	1969–70	1969–70 as a Percent of 1958–59	1958	1969–70	1969–70 as a Percent of 1958–59
			MEN			
USSR	136.8	113.4	82.9	154.5	113.4	73.4
RSFSR	136.7	112.2	82.1	155.4	114.2	73.5
Ukrainian SSR	131.7	125.3	95.1	142.3	115.2	81.0
Byelorussian SSR	132.6	113.2	85.4	148.6	109.5	73.7
Uzbek SSR	183.5	122.1	66.5	207.2	131.8	63.6
Kazakh SSR	151.1	109.9	72.7	188.6	122.2	64.8
Georgian SSR	103.6	89.3	86.2	115.6	84.0	72.7
Azerbaidzhan SSR	145.8	87.1	59.7	180.5	92.7	51.4
Lithuanian SSR	93.8	100.8	107.5	98.5	93.5	94.9
Moldavian SSR	152.5	125.6	82.4	160.2	121.6	75.9
Latvian SSR	103.4	97.5	94.3	103.1	89.0	86.3
Kirgiz SSR	186.3	126.8	68.1	211.2	135.2	64.0
Tadzhik SSR	151.6	128.4	84.7	173.2	137.2	79.2
Armenian SSR	144.2	84.1	58.3	174.4	92.2	52.9
Turkmen SSR	167.4	111.3	66.5	189.6	127.7	67.4
Estonian SSR	90.6	81.5	90.0	90.4	74.7	82.6

WOMEN

USSR	64.4	58.8	91.3	61.8	58.8	95.1
RSFSR	61.5	56.1	91.2	58.8	55.6	94.6
Ukrainian SSR	58.4	56.9	97.4	56.7	56.6	99.8
Byelorussian SSR	59.0	55.8	94.6	57.9	55.5	95.9
Uzbek SSR	117.9	85.8	72.8	108.8	87.8	80.7
Kazakh SSR	94.1	74.4	79.1	88.0	72.8	82.7
Georgian SSR	60.0	55.9	93.2	59.5	54.8	92.1
Azerbaidzhan SSR	93.0	59.6	64.1	87.6	58.5	66.8
Lithuanian SSR	54.5	60.9	111.7	54.7	60.3	110.2
Moldavian SSR	74.7	66.4	88.9	71.2	65.5	92.0
Latvian SSR	50.4	52.8	104.8	50.6	53.3	100.9
Kirgiz SSR	103.6	76.3	73.6	96.1	77.2	80.3
Tadzhik SSR	105.7	97.1	91.9	91.4	94.9	103.8
Armenian SSR	93.7	63.7	68.0	88.8	63.3	71.3
Turkmen SSR	114.8	90.5	78.8	100.7	88.7	88.1
Estonian SSR	45.4	45.8	100.9	45.5	46.9	103.1

*Standardized on the basis of the age distribution of the total USSR population in 1970.
Sources: Calculated on the basis of figures in Ts.S.U. 1972:tables 3 and 6; 1975a:150–65; Baldwin 1973.

TABLE 3.11

Marriage Rates per 1,000 Unmarried Population by Age and Sex: Ukrainian SSR, 1926–27, 1958–59, and 1969–70

Age	1926–27	1958–59	1969–70	1958–59 as Percent of 1926–27	1969–70 as Percent of 1926–27	1969–70 as Percent of 1958–59
			MEN			
15 and over	110.2	124.1	112.6	112.6	102.2	90.7
15–19	30.7	15.6	12.4	50.8	40.4	79.5
20–24	222.0	141.5	202.0	63.7	91.0	142.8
25–29	373.5	408.8	333.7	109.5	89.3	81.6
30–34	361.8	328.7	225.7	90.9	62.4	68.7
35–39	320.6	347.9	192.0	108.5	59.9	55.2
40–49	186.1	332.7	169.3	178.8	91.0	50.9
50–59	75.2	245.3	206.2	326.2	274.2	84.1
60–69	20.3	220.3	160.3	1085.2	789.7	72.8
			WOMEN			
15 and over	85.2	56.8	54.2	66.7	63.6	95.4
15–19	72.3	61.7	69.7	85.3	96.4	113.0
20–24	303.9	214.0	289.9	70.4	95.4	135.5
25–29	194.1	139.5	176.7	71.9	91.0	126.7
30–34	100.2	67.2	98.5	67.1	98.3	146.6
35–39	46.6	13.7	48.8	29.4	104.7	356.2
40–49	21.2	15.1	23.2	71.2	109.4	153.6
50–59	6.7	12.5	13.6	186.6	203.0	108.8

Sources: Chuiko 1975:48; Institut International de Statistique 1932: 77; Ts.S.U. 1931:6; 1972:20–21, 263; 1975a:152.

for women are somewhat lower in the Baltic republics, as they are for men. They also are lower for women in Georgia and somewhat higher in Central Asia than elsewhere. In the Turkmen SSR as many as 65 of 100 eligible women marry at the peak ages 20 to 24. Age-specific marriage rates for women after age 25 decline steadily for all 15 republics to considerably reduced rates in the older ages, indeed to less than one in 100 for age 50 and over.

The above discussion of the changing rates of men's and women's entrance into marriage contradicts or at least provides an alternative to a common view on the consequences of extremely unequal sex ratios. With so many women available after the war, it often is believed that men found it unnecessary to marry since women's services were available outside of wedlock, and clearly this must have been the case for a large number of men. Solzhenitsyn describes the postwar situation in precisely such terms and indeed uses a market explanation for it:

> The young men she met all danced and went for walks with the same aim in mind: to warm themselves up a bit, have their fun and then clear out. They used to say among themselves, "I could get married, but it never takes me more than an evening or two to find a new 'friend,' so why should I bother?"
>
> Indeed, why marry when women were so easy to get? If a great load of tomatoes suddenly arrived in the market, you couldn't just triple the price of yours, they'd go rotten. How could you be inaccessible when everyone around you was ready to surrender? (Solzhenitsyn 1968: 184)

It is clear from the data presented, however, that men actually married more given the poor postwar sex ratios. To some extent the figures on male marriage rates represent entrance into very casual unions, multiple remarriages, bigamy, and the like. In the years after the war there were many reports of men repeatedly marrying or of having several wives (see Geiger 1968: 245-46). *Pravda* at one point even reported the case of a man who had so many wives he had to write all their names down in a notebook to remember them (Narinyani 1952).

Most marriages were not of this sort. While some men may take advantage of a population's low sex ratio and choose not to marry, even more men evidently take advantage of such a low sex ratio to get a more desirable wife than they could otherwise obtain. Very low sex ratios, in other words, can encourage men to marry.

Some Soviet commentators from within the context of their own society look around them, see that men are marrying at lower rates than in the recent past, and conclude that something is wrong. They see the new reluctance of men to marry as a social problem (Perevedentsev 1972; Kuznetsova 1975, 1979). What they do not seem to realize is that in historical context the postwar years were as abnormal in their consequences for men as they were for women, and that the decline in male marriage rates can be viewed as the expected adjustment to a changing market situation.

TABLE 3.12

Marriage Rates per 1,000 Unmarried Population by Age and Sex: Byelorussian SSR, 1926–27, 1958–59, and 1969–70

MEN

Age	1926–27	1958–59	1969–70	1958–59 as Percent of 1926–27	1969–70 as Percent of 1926–27	1969–70 as Percent of 1958–59
15 and over	73.4	129.8	100.4	176.8	136.8	77.3
15–19	12.0	8.1	7.6	67.5	63.3	93.8
20–24	114.5	145.3	183.6	126.9	160.3	126.4
25–29	269.4	418.3	322.1	155.3	119.6	77.0
30–34	272.9 }	382.9 } 402.8	226.0 } 208.5	} 147.6	} 76.4	59.0 } 51.8
35–39		463.1	171.0			36.9
40–44	153.2 }	467.9 } 405.1	156.8 } 159.3	} 264.4	} 104.0	33.5 } 39.3
45–49		359.8	163.9			45.6
50–59	60.3	210.1	205.9	348.4	341.5	98.0
60+	7.1	88.7	56.1	1249.3	790.1	63.2

WOMEN

Age						
15 and over	61.1	58.2	52.8	95.3	86.4	90.7
15–19	39.4	35.7	49.5	90.6	125.6	138.7
20–24	200.4	191.1	274.8	95.4	137.1	143.8
25–29	154.3	162.9	184.6	105.6	119.6	113.3
30–34		80.3	96.8			120.5
35–39		54.5	47.9			87.9
30–39 }	65.1	68.6	72.0	105.4	110.6	105.0
40–44		22.4	24.5			109.4
45–49		11.9	16.1			135.3
40–49 }	16.6	16.2	20.2	97.6	121.7	124.7
50–59		12.0	15.1	285.7	359.5	125.8
60+		6.5	2.7	1300.0	540.0	41.5

Sources: Shakhot'ko 1975:87; Institut International de Statistique 1932:77; Ts.S.U. 1931:5; 1972:24–25, 264; 1975a:153.

TABLE 3.13

Marriage Rates per 1,000 Unmarried Population by Age and Sex: Latvian SSR, 1958–60 and 1969–70

Age	1958–60	1969–70	1969–70 as Percent of 1958–60
		MEN	
15+	97.6	91.2	93.4
15–19	13.0	13.4	103.1
20–24	134.4	152.2	113.2
25–29	262.9	220.4	83.8
30–34	229.8	75.2	32.7
35–39	203.9	114.1	56.0
40–49	125.2	98.1	78.4
50+	39.3	33.3	84.7
		WOMEN	
15+	49.1	51.0	103.9
15–19	35.6	49.8	139.9
20–24	184.0	242.9	132.0
25–29	177.7	192.2	108.2
30–34	108.4	111.4	102.8
35–39	66.5	63.9	96.1
40–49	23.0	62.5	271.7
50+	3.5	3.7	105.7

Sources: Ts.S.U. Latviiskoi SSR 1966:20; 1972:27; Ts.S.U. 1972:52–53, 266.

TABLE 3.14

Marriage Rates per 1,000 Unmarried Population by Age and Sex: Union Republics, 1973

Union Republic	All ages 15 and over	15–19	20–24	25–29	30–34	35–39	40–44	45–49	50 and over
					MEN				
RSFSR	109.2	10.5	236.2	266.2	138.8	169.3	119.4	200.0	80.5
Ukrainian SSR	120.1	10.4	256.8	268.1	179.5	251.1	153.8	222.5	83.1
Byelorussian SSR	108.5	6.4	227.9	285.6	177.1	205.4	158.4	207.7	71.6
Uzbek SSR	126.5	9.9	309.5	404.3	289.3	282.1	170.8	191.2	52.7
Kazakh SSR	106.9	8.0	222.8	311.0	184.5	231.5	134.8	209.6	97.4
Georgian SSR	88.6	4.8	108.8	263.2	222.8	298.6	167.7	226.4	66.8
Azerbaidzhan SSR	83.8	3.5	119.5	299.3	253.3	314.3	201.3	257.6	79.5
Lithuanian SSR	88.2	9.5	166.4	183.0	154.6	123.1	111.0	92.1	35.7
Moldavian SSR	133.6	11.0	326.7	370.2	301.8	313.6	241.5	254.7	94.4
Latvian SSR	91.0	11.2	172.2	169.4	145.5	128.6	115.0	112.8	34.5
Kirgiz SSR	127.3	6.6	303.0	403.1	270.7	287.9	202.2	309.6	115.4
Tadzhik SSR	127.5	9.6	286.2	384.2	368.2	337.0	207.1	233.8	60.8
Armenian SSR	92.5	3.1	145.0	446.5	264.6	314.1	190.7	262.9	68.7
Turkmen ssr	108.1	13.0	248.7	383.8	218.2	188.9	106.5	132.9	33.2
Estonian SSR	75.7	11.0	153.6	161.0	105.9	83.3	63.7	67.9	20.4

TABLE 3.14 (Continued)

Union Republic	All ages 15 and over	15–19	20–24	25–29	30–34	35–39	40–44	45–49	50 and over
					WOMEN				
RSFSR	57.7	65.8	300.2	208.3	79.1	60.9	24.1	22.1	4.6
Ukrainian SSR	57.8	79.9	317.9	176.7	76.7	62.3	22.2	20.9	5.9
Byelorussian SSR	56.7	58.7	301.6	195.2	72.2	48.9	22.5	17.2	5.3
Uzbek SSR	93.0	95.5	519.1	348.5	124.9	87.1	36.6	26.1	4.6
Kazakh SSR	75.4	57.4	373.8	271.8	97.5	84.6	25.9	27.4	6.8
Georgian SSR	57.7	46.2	230.5	198.7	77.0	73.2	30.8	25.0	6.7
Azerbaidzhan SSR	60.1	56.3	280.4	209.5	68.6	60.2	26.1	20.8	4.6
Lithuanian SSR	55.1	43.6	236.3	155.2	94.8	61.5	32.7	24.2	4.5
Moldavian SSR	75.3	65.6	351.6	127.2	65.3	48.9	29.3	24.6	7.8
Latvian SSR	50.9	54.7	247.0	152.2	111.3	70.4	36.8	27.7	4.2
Kirgiz SSR	81.2	74.8	477.7	297.3	102.1	79.4	32.1	29.6	6.8
Tadzhik SSR	100.2	114.1	550.4	329.8	137.5	95.6	35.7	25.4	4.6
Armenian SSR	72.6	52.5	330.8	194.7	48.9	54.3	24.1	26.8	6.4
Turkmen SSR	90.0	60.1	646.5	398.9	122.3	78.4	30.7	21.7	4.3
Estonian SSR	43.7	48.5	231.1	150.6	79.9	50.4	24.1	16.9	2.7

Sources: Ts.S.U. 1975a:174–75; 1972:tables 3 and 6. Base population is as of 1970, the nearest available census year.

FIRST MARRIAGES AND REMARRIAGES

Most of the marriages that occur each year in the USSR are first marriages, but about 15 percent of the persons who wed have been married before. This is a lower proportion than in the 1920s when about one in five persons marrying had been previously married (see Table 3.15). Although postwar data prior to 1965 are lacking to make a fuller comparison, it appears that the easing of restrictions on divorce in 1965 did increase the proportion of all marriages that were remarriages. For several years in the late 1960s in particular, there was a bulge in remarriages due to weddings that had been delayed by the difficulties in legally divorcing. The proportion of remarriages in the Soviet Union at the present time and in the 1920s is smaller than in the contemporary United States (see Carter and Glick 1976: 82).

Somewhat more of all remarriages involve men than women. In view of the better market position of men, this is to be expected. Although figures in Table 3.15 refer to marriages rather than to persons who remarry since many remarry more than once, it seems clear that men's chances of remarrying are greater than women's. A study of divorce in Vilnius has found that men desire to remarry more than do women, although the complaint is made that men do not do so enough (Kuznetsova 1975).

Regional data on first marriages and remarriages are available for the Ukraine and Byelorussia for some recent years. The patterns just described for the USSR also are true of these two republics, although the number of remarriages are proportionately greater in the Ukraine and smaller in Byelorussia than in the Soviet Union as a whole due to relatively higher and lower divorce rates in those republics than the nationwide average. (See Table 3.16. In 1974 the crude divorce rate for the USSR was 2.9; for the Ukrainian SSR 3.2; for the Byelorussian SSR 2.5.)

Unfortunately it is not possible to determine accurately the likelihood of entrance into marriage in the USSR depending on previous marital status. Even if Soviet vital statistics differentiated marriages by previous marital status more than they do, census data do not provide the breakdown into never married, divorced, and widowed that would be necessary to compute the rates.*

It is possible to make some approximations to age-specific first-marriage rates. In Table 3.17 are first marriages per 1,000 population by age for available years since 1965. As can be seen in the table, women are more likely to enter into first marriage at younger ages, and there is a tendency for a larger proportion of women under the age of 20 to enter into first marriages in more recent years.

---

*A study of marriages in the Estonian SSR in 1972 does show what is to be found in other countries of the world, namely that there is a tendency for marriages to be homogamous in relation to previous marital status of the spouses with the never-married marrying the never-married, the divorced the divorced, and so on (Tavit 1975).

TABLE 3.15

Percent of Brides and Grooms Entering First Marriages and Remarriages: USSR, 1923-27 and 1965-77

Year	Grooms			Brides		
	First Marriages	Remarriages	Total	First Marriages	Remarriages	Total
1923	80.7	19.0	100.0a	81.3	18.7	100.0
1924	80.6	19.2	100.0b	82.4	17.5	100.0c
1925	79.5	20.5	100.0	81.4	18.6	100.0
1926	81.1	18.8	100.0c	83.5	16.3	100.0b
1927	79.3	20.5	100.0b	82.4	17.4	100.0b
1965	88.1	11.9	100.0	89.0	11.0	100.0
1966	84.3	15.7	100.0	85.5	14.5	100.0
1967	83.4	16.6	100.0	85.3	14.7	100.0
1968	83.5	16.5	100.0	85.3	14.7	100.0
1969	85.3	14.7	100.0	86.9	13.1	100.0
1970	85.6	14.4	100.0	87.3	12.7	100.0
1971	85.8	14.2	100.0	87.3	12.7	100.0
1972	85.6	14.4	100.0	86.8	13.2	100.0
1973	85.3	14.7	100.0	86.8	13.2	100.0
1974	85.0	15.0	100.0	86.7	13.3	100.0
1975	84.8	15.2	100.0	86.2	13.8	100.0
1976	84.3	15.7	100.0	85.4	14.6	100.0
1977	83.8	16.2	100.0	85.5	14.5	100.0

aIncludes 0.3 percent unknown.
bIncludes 0.2 percent unknown.
cIncludes 0.1 percent unknown.

Note: 1923 refers to RSFSR and Byelorussia only; 1924, 1925, 1926, and 1927 to the European USSR; 1965-74 to the USSR within present borders.

Sources: Institut International de Statistique 1932:77; Vestnik statistiki 1967:94; 1969:93; 1970:95; 1971a:95; 1971b:89; 1973:88; 1974:89; 1975a:172; 1975b:89; 1976:88; 1977:78; 1978:84; unpublished data, United Nations.

TABLE 3.16

Percent of Brides and Grooms Entering First Marriages and Remarriages: Ukrainian SSR, 1966–73, and Byelorussian SSR, 1969–70 (percent)

Year	Grooms			Brides		
	First Marriages	Remarriages	Total	First Marriages	Remarriages	Total
	Ukrainian SSR					
1966	82.1	17.9	100.0	85.0	15.0	100.0
1967	81.9	18.1	100.0	84.8	15.2	100.0
1968	81.6	18.4	100.0	84.5	15.5	100.0
1969	83.7	16.3	100.0	85.6	14.4	100.0
1970	82.6	17.4	100.0	85.2	14.8	100.0
1971	84.7	15.3	100.0	86.3	13.7	100.0
1972	83.8	16.2	100.0	86.7	13.3	100.0
1973	83.3	16.7	100.0	86.5	13.5	100.0
	Byelorussian SSR					
1969	88.0	12.0	100.0	91.1	8.9	100.0
1970	88.1	11.9	100.0	91.0	9.0	100.0

Source: Unpublished data, United Nations.

TABLE 3.17

Age-Specific First Marriage Rates by Sex: USSR, 1965–77
(per 1,000 population)

Year	15– 19	20– 24	25– 29	30– 34	35– 39	40– 44	45– 49	50– 54	55– 59	60+	All ages
						MEN					
1965	9.8	91.3	61.4	15.6	7.7	5.6	5.6	8.5	8.5	12.4	25.6
1966	10.5	89.9	65.3	17.8	7.5	5.2	5.2	7.9	7.9	9.5	25.0
1967	11.5	92.5	67.4	17.8	7.0	4.7	4.7	8.0	8.0	8.4	24.7
1968	12.9	102.3	62.7	16.6	6.2	3.9	3.9	6.4	6.4	6.4	24.1
1969	11.9	123.2	60.8	16.4	5.6	3.3	3.3	4.8	4.8	5.0	25.6
1970	11.0	131.0	57.3	16.0	5.6	3.0	3.0	4.2	4.2	4.5	26.5
1971	9.8	136.0	56.5	15.8	5.5	2.7	2.7	3.7	3.7	4.1	27.0
1972	8.6	122.1	54.6	14.3	5.3	2.4	2.4	3.1	3.1	3.3	24.9
1973	8.7	130.1	53.1	14.4	5.5	2.4	2.4	3.0	3.0	3.0	26.4
1974	9.3	130.5	52.0	13.9	5.6	4.6	2.6	1.7	1.7	1.7	26.7
1975	9.6	132.3	50.1	13.6	5.7	2.3	2.3	2.7	2.7	2.9	27.2
1976	10.0	121.7	43.4	12.6	5.1	2.3	2.3	2.9	2.9	3.0	25.3
1977	10.8	127.6	43.1	13.4	5.0	2.3	2.3	2.9	2.9	3.1	26.4

WOMEN

1965	45.9	109.1	33.5	12.3	7.3	5.1	5.1	5.9	5.9	3.9	19.8
1966	46.9	103.9	32.1	13.6	7.3	5.2	5.2	5.7	5.7	2.5	19.5
1967	47.2	94.7	29.1	12.9	7.0	4.8	4.8	6.2	6.2	2.1	19.6
1968	50.0	96.3	25.6	11.1	6.1	4.2	4.2	4.9	4.9	1.9	19.7
1969	53.6	115.6	23.8	9.8	5.3	3.6	3.6	3.9	3.9	1.3	20.5
1970	54.4	106.8	23.3	9.2	4.9	3.2	3.2	3.6	3.6	1.3	21.4
1971	56.5	115.4	24.3	8.3	4.7	3.0	3.0	3.1	3.1	1.2	21.9
1972	41.9	102.3	25.2	7.5	4.2	2.6	2.6	2.9	2.9	1.0	20.3
1973	56.9	106.7	26.5	7.3	4.0	2.6	2.6	3.0	3.0	0.9	21.6
1974	59.1	106.3	26.9	7.2	3.9	5.3	3.7	0.6	0.6	0.6	22.0
1975	60.7	107.1	26.4	7.4	3.8	2.3	2.3	2.8	2.8	1.0	22.5
1976	57.7	97.0	23.0	7.0	3.4	2.3	2.3	3.0	3.0	1.1	21.0
1977	62.2	101.3	23.5	7.9	3.4	2.3	2.3	3.0	3.0	1.1	22.2

Sources: Vestnik statistiki 1967:94; 1969:93; 1970:95; 1971b:89; 1973:88; 1974:89; 1975b:89; 1976:88; 1977:78; 1978:84; Ts.S.U. 1975a: 172; Baldwin 1973; unpublished data, United Nations.

Because of the recent trend to earlier marriages, male first-marriage rates at ages 20 to 24 have shifted from being lower than the comparable female rates to being greater than them since 1968. As is true of all marriages, after the age of 25 men are more likely to enter into first marriages than are women.

First marriages in 1969 to 1970 per 1,000 unmarried persons by age and sex are shown in Table 3.18 for the entire USSR, the Ukraine, and Byelorussia. Male first-marriage rates before age 20 are very low, but then rise to a peak at ages 25 to 29 that is higher than the corresponding peak for female first-marriage rates at ages 20 to 24. Thereafter the rates for men decline more rapidly than those for women.

SEASONAL VARIATIONS IN MARRIAGES

Monthly variations in marriage rates in czarist Russia were characterized by two principal features. First, as in all chiefly agricultural countries, there was a harvest pattern whereby most marriages were contracted during the winter and fall, relatively few during the spring, and almost none at all during the summer. Thus the months of December, January, and February generally accounted in the late nineteenth and early twentieth centuries for some 40 to 45 percent of all marriages contracted in European Russia in the course of a year. September, October, and November accounted for some 35 to 40 percent of all marriages. The spring months of March, April, and May saw only about 15 percent. During the remaining summer months of June, July, and August, when the most work in the fields was necessary, fewer than 10 percent of all weddings in the year took place. Marriages by month of occurrence in European Russia for the decade 1894-1904 are presented in Table 3.19.

Second, the prohibition of the Russian Orthodox church against marrying at certain times of the year greatly affected seasonal variations in marriage. The most important prohibition against marrying in the Orthodox church occurs during the Velikii Post (Great Fast) during the seven weeks preceding Easter, but there also are prohibitions against marriage during the Petrov Fast (May 27-June 28, o.s.), the Ouspenskii Fast (August 1-August 14, o.s.), the Christmas Fast (November 15-December 24, o.s.), and during the Christmas period itself. In addition there are separate days throughout the year on which it is forbidden to marry. As regards restrictions on the timing of marriage for members of other religions, the differences in dates between Catholic and Russian Orthodox Easter are not sufficiently great so as to have much effect on statistics on monthly variations in marriages (no data are available by week or by day). The main restriction on the timing of Jewish marriage is from the second day of Passover, which always occurs during the Orthodox Great Fast since the timing of Orthodox Easter depends on when Passover falls, for 49 days ending with Shavuot.

The important effect of religious restrictions on the timing of marriage can be seen in Table 3.19. The month of March typically was the time of the least

TABLE 3.18

First Marriages per 1,000 Unmarried (Never Married, Divorced, Widowed) Population: USSR, 1969–70, and Union Republics for which Data are Available on Age at First Marriage, 1969–70

Age	USSR 1969–70		Ukrainian SSR 1969–70		Byelorussian SSR 1969–70	
	Men	Women	men	Women	Men	Women
All ages 15+	86.1	48.2	93.7	46.3	88.8	48.0
15–19	11.7	58.8	12.3	68.4	7.6	49.3
20–24	179.1	262.8	196.9	274.7	180.9	266.4
25–29	263.3	138.4	286.9	128.6	292.4	150.7
30–34	142.2	64.2	135.1	55.9	160.7	67.7
35–39	84.3	32.2	79.3	26.2	85.1	33.5
40–44	60.8	14.2	61.0	12.5	n.a.	n.a.
45–49						
50–59	90.1	8.1	111.0	8.7	n.a.	n.a.
50+						
60+	36.5	1.9	26.7	1.4	n.a.	n.a.

n.a.: Not available.
Sources: Vestnik statistiki 1971a:95; 1971b:89; Ts.S.U. 1972:tables 2 and 6; unpublished data, United Nations.

TABLE 3.19

Marriages by Month of Occurrence: 50 Gubernii of European Russia, 1894–1904 (percent)

Month	1894	1895	1896	1897	1898	1899	1900	1901	1902	1903	1904
January	22.12	33.08	31.57	20.93	27.08	20.88	24.71	32.95	19.94	27.01	35.85
February	22.77	6.62	1.76	21.24	11.63	22.11	16.53	5.34	21.31	12.74	4.05
March	0.96	0.95	2.06	1.05	0.91	0.79	1.15	0.93	0.90	0.94	1.00
April	2.64	6.08	8.44	3.51	4.55	2.60	4.26	6.15	3.14	4.63	6.27
May	7.15	8.47	7.93	6.32	8.86	6.73	8.67	8.84	6.13	9.60	8.78
June	5.62	1.95	3.12	5.98	2.21	5.37	3.02	1.93	5.94	5.66	2.35
July	4.37	4.96	5.00	3.40	4.16	4.28	4.73	4.87	3.74	3.57	5.05
August	1.91	1.88	1.89	2.20	2.25	1.64	2.00	2.10	1.81	1.78	1.97
September	3.68	3.79	4.33	4.48	4.37	3.72	3.83	4.81	4.53	4.28	3.94
October	14.42	16.99	16.00	15.62	15.97	16.50	15.72	17.42	15.65	14.92	15.36
November	13.30	14.12	16.68	14.09	16.94	14.05	14.36	13.82	15.80	15.05	14.25
December	1.06	1.11	1.22	1.18	1.07	1.33	1.02	0.84	1.11	1.10	1.13
Total	100.00	100.00	100.00	100.00	100.00	100.00	100.00	100.00	100.00	100.00	100.00
N	848,383	842,631	809,847	857,371	825,602	898,202	873,018	862,408	877,909	919,082	801,312
Date of Orthodox Easter (o.s.)	April 17	April 2	March 24	April 13	April 5	April 18	April 9	April 1	April 14	April 6	March 28

Note: All months and dates are in the old-style (o.s.) calendar.

Sources: Tsentral'nyi Statisticheskii Komitet 1894:88; 1895:88; 1896:88; 1897:88; 1898:88; 1899:88; 1900:88; 1907:103; 1908:89; 1909:89; 1910b:94.

number of marriages due to the Great Fast prior to Easter. Effects on other months of the timing of Easter also can be seen from the table. December was the second least likely month of marriage due to the Christmas Fast. While the low number of marriages in August can be attributed to the demands of agricultural work, the low number of weddings then and during the other summer months also is attributable to the impact of religious holidays.

Since the Revolution, industrialization and urbanization have moved the population away from a harvest pattern in the timing of marriage. Data on the RSFSR for 1926 already show an increase in the proportion of marriages contracted during the spring and summer: some 32 percent of all marriages as compared with 25 percent or less in the prerevolutionary period. In the 1950s and early 1960s the harvest pattern had weakened considerably but was still visible. In data for the population as a whole (see Table 3.20), the spring and summer months accounted for about 40 percent of all marriages in 1950; by 1960 this had increased to over 45 percent and by 1977 marriages were distributed throughout the year sufficiently evenly that the spring and summer months accounted for nearly 50 percent of all marriages. Since 1968, in contrast to any harvest pattern, August consistently has been the most popular month for marriages. Almost twice as many marriages now occur in August than occur in May, the least popular month for weddings.

Some suggestions as to why the Soviet bride is now an August bride can be made. In view of the enforced one-month period of waiting between application for registration of a marriage and its actual registration (one month is the required time period set by law, but there is commonly a wait of up to three months, see Chapter 2), Soviet would-be newlyweds now have time to plan their wedding in advance whether they like it or not, and therefore may be more likely to have it coincide with vacations taken in August, which are more feasible now with greater affluence, and with a time of year when food is plentiful for wedding banquets. Students who decide to marry at the end of the academic year would as a result of this waiting period also not register their marriage until August. (Examinations may explain why May is so unpopular.) Many of those entering into fictitious marriages to retain residence permits in large cities such as Moscow and Leningrad are graduating students trying to avoid being sent elsewhere in the country at the end of their education. It seems likely that they exhaust all their remedies before entering into such marriages or, in other words, wait until the end of the academic year in June to file application for registration of a marriage, thereby swelling the ranks of those marrying in August.

To what extent is there still a religious pattern observable in the timing of marriages? Although only civil marriage has been officially recognized as valid in the Soviet period and religious marriage is discouraged, and although the data collected in official vital statistics are data on civil registration of marriages rather than on religious weddings, the Soviet population might well tend to retain religious traditions in a secular context and time civil entrance into marriage in accordance with religious rules. Some instances of this are known to the author

TABLE 3.20

Marriages by Month of Occurrence: USSR, 1950, 1955, 1960–77 (percent)

Month	1950	1955	1960	1961	1962
January	9.00	10.80	10.10	10.3	9.35
February	9.70	10.50	10.10	9.60	9.62
March	8.30	7.50	7.60	7.60	8.89
April	8.40	7.80	7.90	8.50	7.52
May	8.00	7.20	7.30	7.20	7.35
June	7.60	7.00	7.20	7.00	7.74
July	7.80	7.00	7.60	7.70	7.70
August	7.60	7.20	7.90	8.10	8.15
September	7.50	6.80	7.30	7.60	7.47
October	8.20	8.50	8.40	8.30	8.04
November	9.70	10.60	9.50	9.30	8.98
December	8.20	9.10	9.10	8.80	9.19
Total	100.0	100.00	100.0	100.0	100.0
N	2,080,817	2,259,534	2,591,509	2,404,041	2,221,526
Date of Orthodox Easter (O.S.)	March 27	April 4	April 4	March 27	April 16

Month	1963	1964	1965	1966	1967	1968
January	9.28	8.93	9.11	8.50	8.22	8.56
February	9.30	9.50	9.20	8.59	8.26	9.25
March	7.90	8.60	8.09	7.72	8.20	8.25
April	7.87	7.31	7.98	8.83	7.68	8.20
May	7.17	7.05	7.11	7.22	6.91	6.85
June	7.69	7.48	7.46	7.46	7.68	7.81
July	7.92	7.89	8.31	8.45	8.23	8.36
August	8.80	8.80	8.61	8.68	8.64	9.80
September	7.37	7.37	7.48	7.52	7.89	7.88
October	8.05	8.33	8.23	8.35	8.44	7.70
November	9.28	9.20	9.01	9.26	9.75	8.87
December	9.37	9.54	9.41	9.42	10.10	8.49
Total	100.00	100.00	100.00	100.00	100.00	100.00
N	2,051,432	1,939,780	2,008,673	2,087,599	2,131,888	2,120,900
Date of Orthodox Easter	April 1	April 20	April 12	March 28	April 17	April 8

TABLE 3.20 (Continued)

Month	1969	1970	1971	1972	1973	1974	1975	1976	1977
January	7.92	8.13	7.87	7.64	7.59	7.46	7.42	7.72	7.68
February	8.05	8.55	8.57	8.05	8.04	8.37	7.63	7.74	7.82
March	7.44	7.89	7.37	7.21	8.32	7.20	8.44	7.71	6.97
April	8.74	7.67	8.14	9.01	6.69	8.24	6.47	7.43	8.88
May	6.90	6.78	6.43	6.21	6.63	6.02	6.72	6.69	6.17
June	7.26	7.57	7.26	7.45	8.20	7.86	7.73	7.91	7.47
July	8.44	8.65	8.92	8.97	8.64	8.78	8.71	9.93	10.02
August	9.90	9.88	9.78	10.30	10.85	11.41	11.47	10.82	10.41
September	8.21	8.19	8.28	9.55	9.27	8.60	8.47	8.67	9.01
October	8.45	8.72	8.56	7.96	7.84	7.95	8.30	8.74	8.35
November	9.37	8.89	9.26	9.01	9.36	9.74	9.44	8.57	8.87
December	9.31	9.08	9.56	8.64	8.57	8.37	9.19	8.08	8.37
Total	100.00	100.00	100.00	100.00	100.00	100.00	100.00	100.00	100.00
N	2,250.600	2,365,259	2,459,900	2,333,470	2,516,267	2,606,700	2,722,800	2,596,300	2,775,900
Date of Orthodox Easter (o.s.)	March 31	April 13	April 5	April 27	April 16	April 1	April 20	April 18	March 28

Sources: Vestnik statistiki 1963:93; 1967:93; 1969:81; 1970:90; 1971a:88; 1971b:85; 1973:83; 1974:86; 1975b:78; 1976:85; 1977:74; 1978: 81; Ts.S.U. 1975a:150.

in which young Soviet couples, while not religious believers, still identified sufficiently with the church or synagogue so as to avoid registering their marriage
(they did not have a religious ceremony in addition) on religious holidays such as
Easter and Yom Kippur. Thus although the available statistics concern civil marriage, there is a question as to the lingering effects of religiosity.

In Table 3.21 is presented a seasonal index (unadjusted) of marriages for
years in which Russian Orthodox Easter has fallen on approximately the same
date in the old calendar. Were religious restrictions to have great impact on marriage rates, marriage could be expected to be unlikely pretty much throughout
March and April in all these years. As can be seen from the table, marriage during March and April (also in December) was extremely unlikely in 1894 and
1899, perhaps a little more likely in 1910. Less than a decade after the Revolution in 1926, however, although the effect of orthodoxy was still visible it was
considerably reduced. By the 1960s and 1970s very little of a religious pattern
can be observed for the USSR as a whole. Although marriages are somewhat less
likely in April than in other months, March does not seem to be affected, and in
any case all differences between months are now relatively small. Thus it does
not seem that Russian Orthodoxy exerts much of an influence today on the timing of marriage for the Soviet population generally.

It may be objected that the data for the 1950s, 1960s, and 1970s in Tables
3.20 and 3.21, as opposed to the earlier data, include many Central Asian Moslems and others of various faiths whose religions do not prohibit marriage at the
same times as the Russian Orthodox church. This objection would carry more
weight if it were possible to note some impact of Ramadhan, the Moslem month
of fasting during which marriages ordinarily do not take place, on marriage rates.
There does not seem to be any effect of Ramadhan whatsoever. In 1962 Ramadhan fell during the 30 days beginning February 5, in 1967 during the 30 days
beginning December 4, and in 1973 during the 30 days beginning September 29
(new calendar). For none of these years can there be observed any corresponding
change in the monthly distribution of marriage.

To the extent that it is possible to disaggregate the data, however, regional
variations in the continuing impact of religion are observable. Monthly statistics
on marriage are not available for most areas of the country but do exist for the
Ukraine and Byelorussia for selected years (Tables 3.22 and 3.23). Observation
of the data on the Ukraine shows that while a religious pattern is not nearly so
evident as before the Revolution, nonetheless Ukrainians are somewhat less likely
to register their civil marriages during the periods prohibited by the church. (The
date most relevant to present purposes is that of Easter, and this is the same for
both Ukrainian Uniates and Orthodox. As noted above, the date for Catholic
Easter tends to fall within the same month as that for the other sects.) Thus in
1963 Easter fell on April 1 (o.s.), affecting primarily marriages contracted during
March, and March is as a result the least represented month for marriages in the
Ukraine for that year. In contrast, in 1967 Easter fell on April 17 (o.s.), thereby
affecting April the most, and April was as a result that year the least popular

TABLE 3.21

Seasonal Index (Unadjusted) of Marriages: European Russia and USSR, Selected Years in Which Russian Orthodox Easter Occurred at Approximately the Same Time of Year, 1894–1973 (proportion of average monthly number of marriages)

Month	1894	1899	1910	1926	1962	1967	1973
January	2.65	2.52	2.81	1.71	1.12	0.99	0.91
February	2.73	2.65	2.56	3.22	1.15	0.99	0.97
March	0.12	0.09	0.14	0.91	1.07	0.98	1.00
April	0.32	0.26	0.33	0.38	0.90	0.92	0.80
May	0.86	0.82	0.87	0.74	0.88	0.83	0.80
June	0.67	0.64	0.66	0.79	0.93	0.92	0.98
July	0.52	0.51	0.47	0.59	0.92	0.99	1.04
August	0.23	0.21	0.26	0.44	0.98	1.04	1.30
September	0.44	0.46	0.50	0.48	0.90	0.95	1.11
October	1.73	1.99	1.74	0.75	0.97	1.01	0.94
November	1.59	1.69	1.52	1.49	1.08	1.17	1.12
December	0.13	0.16	0.14	0.50	1.10	1.21	1.03
Total	12.00	12.00	12.00	12.00	12.00	12.00	12.00
N	848,383	898,202	977,241	847,850	2,221,526	2,131,888	2,516,267
Date of Orthodox Easter (o.s.)	April 17	April 18	April 18	April 19	April 16	April 17	April 16

Note: 1894, 1899, 1910: 50 Gubernii of European Russia; 1926: RSFSR only; and 1962, 1967, 1973: USSR.

Sources: Tsentral'nyi Statisticheskii Komitet 1894:88; 1899:88; 1910a:88; Ts.S.U. RSFSR 1928:128–31; Vestnik statistiki 1963:93; 1969:81; 1974:86.

TABLE 3.22

Marriages by Month of Occurrence: Ukrainian SSR 1960 and 1963–71 (percent)

Month	1960	1963	1964	1965	1966	1967	1968	1969	1970	1971
January	10.10	8.64	8.90	9.70	8.60	7.80	8.40	8.60	8.00	7.91
February	10.90	9.50	0.40	11.20	9.00	8.60	9.90	9.00	9.10	8.89
March	6.80	6.84	8.16	7.40	6.60	7.20	7.20	6.30	6.60	5.53
April	7.50	7.67	6.17	7.00	8.60	6.20	7.30	8.30	6.60	6.97
May	8.20	7.71	7.88	7.90	8.30	7.40	7.60	7.80	7.90	7.30
June	7.30	7.61	7.89	7.50	7.20	7.70	7.90	7.00	7.50	6.83
July	7.80	7.71	7.88	7.90	8.70	8.00	8.50	8.50	8.70	8.83
August	8.00	8.62	9.23	8.60	8.60	8.40	10.20	10.50	10.80	10.17
September	7.60	7.65	7.46	7.40	7.60	8.00	8.20	8.30	8.60	8.51
October	8.50	7.95	8.35	8.20	8.50	8.80	8.00	8.30	9.30	9.09
November	10.10	10.71	10.17	9.60	10.20	11.40	10.20	10.40	9.90	10.66
December	7.20	9.39	7.82	7.60	8.10	10.50	6.60	7.00	7.00	9.32
Total	100.00	100.00*	100.00	100.00*	100.00	100.00	100.00	100.00	100.00	100.00*
N	458,934	409,374	366,450	407,514	422,083	453,136	421,024	462,305	465,786	507,963
Date of Ortho-dox Easter (o.s.)	April 4	April 1	April 20	April 12	March 28	April 17	April 8	March 31	April 13	April 5

*Figures do not add due to rounding.
Sources: Ts.S.U. Ukrainskoi SSR 1971:15; unpublished data, United Nations.

TABLE 3.23

Marriages by Month of Occurrence: Byelorussian SSR, 1960–63, 1968–73 (percent)

Month	1960	1961	1962	1963	1968	1969	1970	1971	1972	1973
January	11.70	11.10	10.50	10.40	8.73	8.82	8.40	8.89	8.50	8.18
February	10.40	9.40·	9.30	9.10	8.89	7.67	7.93	8.43	7.81	7.93
March	7.40	7.00	8.20	7.20	8.04	7.37	7.57	7.13	6.68	8.21
April	7.60	8.60	7.10	7.90	7.75	8.51	7.96	8.33	9.44	6.71
May	7.70	7.70	8.00	7.70	7.39	7.40	7.67	7.25	6.52	7.46
June	7.40	7.00	7.70	7.80	7.57	7.37	7.28	6.87	7.12	7.88
July	7.60	7.80	8.10	7.90	8.15	8.22	8.40	8.92	8.88	8.36
August	8.00	8.60	8.40	8.70	9.67	10.43	10.23	9.93	10.33	11.06
September	7.20	7.60	7.60	7.60	7.21	7.87	7.85	7.69	8.78	8.73
October	8.10	7.80	7.30	7.80	7.83	7.99	8.47	8.34	7.75	7.52
November	8.90	9.10	8.80	9.20	9.74	9.29	9.29	9.52	9.61	9.90
December	8.00	8.30	9.00	8.70	9.03	9.06	8.95	8.70	8.58	8.06
Total	100.00	100.00	100.00	100.00	100.00	100.00	100.00	100.00	100.00	100.00
N	90,252	83,774	79,419	73,697	74,014	79,334	83,658	85,503	82,964	87,615
Date of Ortho-dox Easter (o.s.)	April 4	March 27	April 16	April 1	April 8	March 31	April 13	April 5	April 27	April 16

Source: Unpublished data, United Nations.

month in which to marry in the Ukraine. In 1971 Easter again fell on April (o.s.) and again March was the least popular month. The same observation can be made for all the other available years (see Table 3.22). Soviet demographers have noted this phenomenon in the Transcarpathian region of the Ukraine. (See Kopchak and Kopchak 1977: 87-88.) Byelorussia, on the other hand, does not seem to have retained any particular religious pattern in the timing of marriages (see Table 3.23). Perhaps this is because of the generally weaker cultural development of Byelorussia and the traditionally greater significance of Easter in the Ukraine. Discussion of further regional variations will have to await availability of more data.

Although secularization has gone very far in the Soviet Union, there is evidence of at least some lingering effects of religious calendars on marriage. Propagation of atheism has on the whole been successful in changing the timing of marriage, but there is evidence that at least some members of Soviet society get around the secularization of their lives by adapting Soviet practices to their own religious and national ways of life.

4

MARITAL STATUS

Information on the marital status of the Soviet population in the postwar period is limited to that provided by the censuses of 1959 and 1970. Only information concerning the proportions currently married was collected in these censuses; no information on the proportions of the Soviet population divorced or widowed exists. Marital status by age was given in both censuses only by Union republic divided into urban and rural regions and for selected nationalities within Union republics as a whole. (In 1959 information on marital status also was published by oblast and for the autonomous republics, but only for the aggregated population aged 16 years and over, thereby making it nearly impossible to use due to the unknown effect of age and sex distributions.) The materials available are nonetheless of much interest since it is possible to correlate them with other information available from the censuses.

After examination of the number currently married in the USSR, the present chapter turns to a discussion of regional and nationality variations in marital status—information on variations in marital status by other characteristics is virtually nonexistent. Following this will be an examination of the correlates of these variations in marital status, in particular to the applicability of Becker's economic hypotheses regarding proportions married.

NUMBER MARRIED

As of the 1970 census there were 107,106,301 persons who claimed to be married in the USSR. As in past Soviet censuses, the number of people married was defined as the number of people factually in marriages rather than of those legally married. Since no check of legal documents was made at the time of the census, it was quite easy for women to say they were married when in fact they were not and for married men to claim they were bachelors. As a result there was a large discrepancy between the number of men and the number of women claiming to be married: fully 1,384,673 more women than men claimed to be married.

More women than men have claimed to be married in all censuses taken in Russia and the USSR with the possible exception of that for 1939 (see Table 4.1).* Although such excesses of women claiming to be married are to be found in the censuses of other countries, including those of the United States, the postwar Soviet figures are quite high, particularly the one for 1970.

There is no way to break down the census data so as to determine which women are claiming to be married for whom there are no corresponding husbands and why. The best that can be done is a distribution by geographic area. In Table 4.2 are presented the percentages, by Union republic and urban/rural location, of all women claiming to be married in 1959 and 1970 for whom there were no corresponding husbands. As can be seen from the table, there is no clear geographic pattern to the location of such women.

Soviet discussion of the phenomenon primarily attributes it to the differing views of men and women on their cohabitation outside of registered wedlock (for example, see Kuznetsova 1975). Since, as has been seen, men have been in great demand due to the low postwar sex ratios, their freedom to consider themselves unwed even when in registered marriages has been far greater than that of women. In view of the difficulties of divorce before the reforms of the late 1960s, some part of the discrepancy between men and women claiming to be married is probably due to men leaving their wives and creating second families without legally ending their first marriages.

In the Moslem areas of the country some of the discrepancy may be due to polygynous marriages not registered as such that are being tapped by the censuses. Similar data in the 1897 census have been shown to reflect polygyny in Central Asia (Tamimov 1970). In view of the criminal status of polygyny during the Soviet period, however, it seems doubtful that individuals in such relationships would want to admit them to government census takers. In this regard it is noticeable that the Moslem areas of the USSR are not more likely than others to be the location of such extra married women.

Presumably many Soviet women without husbands but with children prefer to identify themselves as married. Children tend to live with their mothers rather than with their fathers in the event of divorce and illegitimacy, and women in such instances are under pressure to lie concerning their marital status (for discussion of the social pressures involved, see Zhukhovitskii 1977).

---

*The exact numbers married as of the 1939 census are not known, and it was necessary to apply 1939 percentages married to an estimate of the age and sex distribution of the population as of 1941 in order to calculate the approximate number of men and women married as of 1941. The resulting apparent excess of men married may or may not reflect an excess of men married as of the 1939 census.

TABLE 4.1

Number Married by Sex and Urban/Rural: Russia and USSR, 1897, 1926, 1941 (estimate), 1959, 1970

Year	Men	Women	Difference (Women to Men)
1897			
Total	24,642,704	24,986,141	+ 343,437
1926			
Total	28,479,134	28,940,134	+ 461,000
Urban	5,624,316	5,144,772	− 479,544
Rural	22,854,818	23,795,362	+ 940,544
1941			
Total	39,838,530	39,634,760	− 203,770
Urban	—	—	—
Rural	—	—	—
1959			
Total	42,892,488	43,642,702	+ 750,214
Urban	21,439,903	21,909,932	+ 470,029
Rural	21,445,464	21,765,383	+ 319,899
1970			
Total	52,860,814	54,245,487	+1,384,673
Urban	31,174,047	31,808,807	+ 634,760
Rural	21,672,675	22,424,891	+ 752,216

Sources: Tsentral'nyi Statisticheskii Komitet 1905:78–79; Ts.S.U. 1931:2; 1972:12–13, 263. Estimate for 1941 calculated by applying Ts.S.U. estimate of marital status as of 1939 of Soviet population within present borders (Ts.S.U. 1962a:73) to Eason estimate of population by age and sex as of 1/1/41 (Eason 1973:53).

TABLE 4.2

Percentage of Women Claiming to be Married for Whom There Are No Corresponding Men Claiming to be Married: USSR and Union Republics by Urban/Rural, 1959 and 1970

Republic	1959			1970			1970 total as a percentage of 1959 total
	Total	Urban	Rural	Total	Urban	Rural	
Estonian SSR	6.4	8.0	4.2	1.3	2.0	0.0	20.3
Latvian SSR	5.2	7.4	2.2	1.4	1.7	0.8	26.9
Georgian SSR	5.1	4.5	5.5	6.1	5.4	6.8	119.6
Azerbaidzhan SSR	4.3	3.5	5.1	2.3	1.2	3.5	53.5
Turkmen SSR	4.3	4.6	4.0	2.1	0.4	3.9	48.8
Byelorussian SSR	3.5	5.8	2.4	2.3	1.5	3.0	65.7
Armenian SSR	3.2	2.2	4.2	4.3	5.3	2.4	134.4
Uzbek SSR	2.9	1.9	3.4	2.8	2.7	2.9	96.6
Tadshik SSR	2.8	1.5	3.5	2.2	1.9	2.4	78.6
Kirgiz SSR	2.7	1.0	3.6	2.0	2.0	2.0	74.1
Lithuanian SSR	2.7	4.6	1.5	1.7	1.6	1.9	63.0
Moldavian SSR	2.4	3.5	2.0	4.5	2.8	5.3	187.5
Ukrainian SSR	1.9	2.3	1.6	2.9	1.9	4.1	152.6
USSR	1.8	2.9	1.5	2.6	2.0	3.4	144.4
Kazakh SSR	1.0	0.2	1.7	1.9	0.6	3.3	190.0
RSFSR	1.0	1.5	0.4	2.2	1.9	2.7	220.0

Source: Ts.S.U. 1972: tables 3 and 6.

115

Particularly puzzling in the data in Table 4.2 is the rise in the percentage of women claiming to be married for whom there were no corresponding husbands from 1959 to 1970, most notably in the RSFSR, Ukraine, Kazakhstan, and Moldavia, while in other areas of the country this percentage fell, most notably in the Baltic republics. Possibly the explanation for this is to be found in different changes in the norms in these various republics concerning the propriety of unmarried cohabitation. It seems likely that in the Baltic republics, which continue to be closer in their cultural developments to Scandinavia and the West and historically have had large proportions single (see below), women are now more willing than formerly to live in consensual unions without claiming to be married for appearance's sake and/or admit they are unmarried generally. In less westernized areas of the Soviet Union with historically small proportions single, it was no longer possible by 1970 to explain spinsterhood on the basis of the war since the sex ratio had evened out for most age groups; spinsterhood now could be explained only by reference to the personal qualities of the woman herself. As a result, more women in 1970 than in 1959 in these areas may have preferred to claim they had husbands when in fact they did not.

MARITAL STATUS: LONG-TERM TREND

The changing age and sex distribution of the USSR has had enormous consequences for the proportion married at any given time. While the percentage married of men over 15 years of age ostensibly rose steadily from 64.4 percent in 1897 to 69.9 percent in 1970, standardization of the census data on marital status considerably changes the picture (Table 4.3). The age distribution of the population in 1970 was more conducive to a large proportion married than the age distribution in former years, and standardization on the basis of the 1970 age distribution increases the percentage of men married in all previous census years. Standardization of the age distribution, moreover, shows that there was considerable fluctuation up and down over time in the proportion married among men rather than a unilinear increase. Had the age distribution of the population been the same in all censuses, the proportion married among men would have increased from 1897 to 1926, then declined by 1939, again increased by 1959, and again declined, though to a lesser extent, by 1970. These fluctuations coincide with what already has been seen regarding historical changes in marriage rates whereby the popularity of marriage was greater in the 1920s and 1950s than in other periods of Soviet history.

The unstandardized proportion married of women 15 years of age and older in Russia and the USSR declined steadily from 64.1 percent in 1897 to 51.7 percent in 1959, then rose somewhat to 56.6 percent in 1970 but did not recoup prewar levels. Standardization on the basis of the 1970 age distribution decreases the percentage of women married in all previous census years. Had the age distribution in 1959 been the same as in 1970, less than half the population of women aged 15 and over would have been married (see Table 4.3). The gap between the percentage of men married and the percentage of women married grew steadily to 1959; only recently has it closed somewhat.

The rise in the proportion married from 1897 to 1926 among men is to be explained in part by a certain lowering of the age at marriage around the latter date. From 1926 to 1959, however, the proportions married among the youngest age groups decreased, and the increase in the overall proportion of males married from 1926 to 1959 thus was due primarily to increases in the percentages married in all but the youngest age groups (Table 4.4). As has been seen, the low sex ratios existing among most of the older age groups after World War II created a market situation more favorable to male entrance into marriage or, alternatively, to heavy sociodemographic pressure on men to marry. The resulting proportions of men currently married as of 1959 thus were extremely high, reaching fully 96.3 percent of all men aged 45 to 49 that year or nearly all of that generation of men most directly affected by the war (Table 4.4). Since 1959 the normalization of the sex ratio has made participation in the marriage market somewhat less attractive to men, and there has been a decrease in the percentage married in all age groups except the very oldest ones, which are experiencing even lower sex ratios as the war generation grows older (one other exception is the age group 20 to 24, as the age at marriage has declined slightly).

The proportion currently married among women declined for all age groups between 1926 and 1959 (Table 4.4). The low supply of men after the war made women's chances for marriage very slim. Since 1959, however, there has been an increase in the proportion married among women in all but the very youngest (16 to 17 years) age groups. Of interest is the fact that the difference in the proportion married among women in 1926 and in 1970 is not very great in most age groups, whereas the percentages of men married by age group have changed rather greatly over this longer span of time. As with marriage rates, it would seem that the proportion of women married is fairly steady but the proportion of men married rather volatile; the distribution of marital status among women over age 25 in the Soviet population does not look very different today from what it did in 1926.

Since the postwar censuses did not collect data on marital status beyond presently married or unmarried, it is not possible to determine with any accuracy whether the percentage ever married among the Soviet population has increased or decreased as a result of the shift to a self-selection system of courtship. Examination of the percentages married, widowed, and divorced, standardized by age for 1897 and 1926, does show a slight increase during that period in the proportions of men and women, aged 15 years and over, who had ever been married, similar to the slight increase in countries of the West over the same period (Goode 1963: 48).

All things considered, marriage is an extremely popular institution in the USSR. In spite of a certain decline in the popularity of marriage in the United States in recent years, the United States remains a country with a very high

TABLE 4.3

Percent by Marital Status, for Persons 15 Years Old and Over, by Sex, Standardized by Age and Unstandardized: Russia and USSR, 1897, 1926, 1939, 1959, 1970

Year	Total	Married	Never Married	Widowed	Divorced	Total	Unknown
			MEN				
Standardized for age[a]							
1897	100.0	67.0	27.4	5.4	0.1	32.9	0.1
1926	100.0	70.5	23.9	4.8	0.5	29.2	0.3
1939	100.0	68.2	—	—	—	31.8	—
1959	100.0	70.5	—	—	—	29.5	—
1970	100.0	69.9	—	—	—	30.1	—
Unstandardized							
1897	100.0[b]	64.4	30.1	5.4	0.1	35.6	0.1
1926	100.0	65.5	29.7	4.0	0.5	34.2	0.3
1939	100.0	66.4	—	—	—	33.6	—
1959	100.0	68.4	—	—	—	3.16	—
1970	100.0	69.9	—	—	—	30.1	—

WOMEN

Standardized for age[a]							
1897	100.0	63.3	16.6	19.9	0.1	36.6	0.1
1926	100.0	58.7	15.6	24.5	0.9	41.0	0.3
1939	100.0	55.5	—	—	—	44.5	—
1959	100.0	49.0	—	—	—	51.0	—
1970	100.0	56.6	—	—	—	43.4	—
Unstandardized							
1897	100.0[b]	64.1	22.4	13.4	0.1	35.9	0.1
1926	100.0	59.3	22.9	16.4	1.1	40.4	0.3
1939	100.0	58.5	—	—	—	41.5	—
1959	100.0	51.7	—	—	—	48.3	—
1970	100.0	56.6	—	—	—	43.4	—

[a]Standardized on the basis of the age distribution of the entire USSR population in 1970.

[b]Total adds up to over 100 due to rounding.

Sources: Tsentral'nyi Statisticheskii komitet 1905:78–79; Ts.S.U. 1931:2; 1962a:73; 1972:263; and distribution by single years of age and sex for 1970 given in Baldwin 1973.

119

TABLE 4.4

Marital Status by Age and Sex: USSR, 1926, 1939, 1959, 1970
(per 1,000 married population)

MEN

Age	1926	1939	1959	1970	Change					
					1926 to 1939	1926 to 1959	1939 to 1959	1926 to 1970	1939 to 1970	1959 to 1970
16 and over	683	690	695	722	7	12	5	39	32	27
16–17	8	4	5	4	– 4	– 3	1	– 4	0	– 1
18–19	122	53	41	39	–69	–81	–12	–83	–14	– 2
20–24	474	336	274	289	–138	–200	–62	–185	–47	15
25–29	808	738	800	772	–70	– 8	62	–36	34	–28
30–34	909	891	922	887	–12	13	31	–22	– 4	–35
35–39	939	929	953	933	–10	14	24	– 6	4	–20
40–44	944	940	962	946	– 4	18	22	2	6	–16
45–49	937	935	963	952	– 2	26	28	15	17	–11
50–54	914	921	956	952	7	42	35	38	31	– 4
55–59	885	900	943	948	15	58	43	63	48	5
60–69	791	823	908	920	32	117	85	129	97	12
70 and over	552	611	739	778	59	187	128	226	167	39

WOMEN

16 and over	616	605	522	580	-11	-94	-83	-36	-25	58
16-17	54	40	29	26	-14	-25	-11	-28	-14	-3
18-19	289	250	171	186	-39	-118	-79	-103	-64	15
20-24	686	614	501	559	-72	-185	-113	-127	-55	58
25-29	850	787	759	827	-63	-91	-28	-23	40	68
30-34	852	818	776	853	-34	-76	-42	1	35	77
35-39	818	800	725	839	-18	-93	-75	21	39	114
40-44	763	759	623	790	-4	-140	-136	27	31	167
45-49	702	688	549	719	-14	-153	-139	17	31	170
50-54	614	593	485	603	-21	-129	-108	-11	10	118
55-59	550	497	433	501	-53	-117	-64	-49	4	68
60-69	408	363	361	371	-45	-47	-2	-37	8	10
70 and over	202	168	169	196	-34	-33	1	-6	28	27

Sources: Ts.S.U. 1931:2; 1962a:73; 1972:263,

proportion currently married. While the proportion of women married in the USSR cannot be what it is in the United States due to the shortage of men, the proportion of men married in the Soviet Union exceeds that in the United States. Had the United States had the same age distribution in 1970 as that of the USSR, the percentage of U.S. men 15 years of age and older who were married would have been 67.8 percent as opposed to 69.9 percent of Soviet men (calculated on the basis of U.S. Bureau of the Census 1972: table 1. Unstandardized U.S. rate: 67.7 percent).

REGIONAL AND NATIONALITY VARIATIONS IN MARITAL STATUS

Historically, marriage patterns in the USSR have been of three sorts. In Hajnal's terms the Baltic areas traditionally have had a European pattern of marriage similar to that of Western Europe of relatively late age at first marriage and a high proportion remaining single at older ages. The central Slavic areas historically had an East European pattern whereby the proportion of women ever married at ages 20 to 24 was over 60 percent and fewer than 5 percent remained single at ages 45 to 49. The Central Asian areas historically have had a marriage pattern characteristic of many populations of Asia and Africa in which the proportion ever married among women 20 to 24 often was above 80 percent and very, very few people remained single throughout life (Hajnal 1953; 1965; Sklar 1970; Chojnacka 1976; Coale et al. 1979).

To a large extent traces of these regional differences in marriage patterns are still observable in the USSR today. In Table 4.5 are presented age-standardized proportions married of men and women 16 years and older by republic in 1959 and 1970. As can be seen from the table, the Baltic republics tend to have fewer adults currently married than elsewhere in the USSR, while the Central Asian republics are uniformly above the average for the USSR as a whole. The Slavic republics fall in between with the Transcaucasus somewhat between them and the Baltic areas. Moldavia is exceptionally high for the Western areas of the Soviet Union. Those areas with high proportions of adults married tend to have relatively larger proportions of those in the youngest age groups married, as well as low proportions single at ages 40 to 44 (Table 4.6). Thus there still is a tendency for the Baltic republics to maintain a European pattern in Hajnal's terminology, while the RSFSR, Ukraine, and Byelorussia follow more of an East European pattern, and the Central Asian republics more of a non-European pattern.

Be this as it may, there has been considerable movement over time from the various starting points to a unified Soviet marriage pattern in much the same manner as there has been movement from different starting points to some form of a conjugal family system throughout the world (Goode 1963). The various republics are becoming more alike in their marriage patterns. This has been shown to be so for female nuptiality since the nineteenth century (Coale et al.

TABLE 4.5

Married per 1,000 Population Aged 16 and Older, Standardized by Age: USSR and Union Republics, 1959 and 1970*

	Males		Females	
	1959	1970	1959	1970
USSR	730	722	502	580
BALTIC REPUBLICS				
Estonian SSR	639	651	489	546
Latvian SSR	660	667	502	561
Lithuanian SSR	666	683	527	592
WESTERN REPUBLICS				
RSFSR	729	721	482	565
Ukrainian SSR	726	729	504	583
Byelorussian SSR	726	726	501	581
Moldavian SSR	762	749	581	628
TRANSCAUSASIAN REPUBLICS				
Georgian SSR	707	698	553	620
Armenian SSR	742	722	575	641
Azerbaidzhan SSR	739	706	557	598
CENTRAL ASIAN REPUBLICS				
Uzbek SSR	752	735	599	650
Kazakh SSR	750	732	552	611
Kirgiz SSR	768	745	586	626
Tadzhik SSR	755	735	594	654
Turkmen SSR	744	723	586	640

*Standardized on the basis of the age distribution of the total population of the USSR in 1970.

Sources: Ts.S.U. 1972:table 6; Baldwin 1973.

TABLE 4.6

Percent of Single Males and Females in Selected Age Groups: Union Republics, 1970

Age group	Five Republics with the lowest third of all standardized proportions married over age 16	Five Republics with the middle third of all standardized proportions married over age 16	Five Republics with the highest third of all standardized proportions married over age 16
		MEN	
	(Less than 710)	720 to 730)	(More than 730)
16–17	98.9–99.8	99.2–99.8	99.2–99.5
18–19	96.0–97.5	92.7–97.8	95.0–95.9
20–24	73.9–82.4	64.6–78.8	68.1–71.0
40–44	4.2–12.6	3.4– 6.8	2.9– 5.1
		WOMEN	
	(Less than 590)	(590 to 627)	(More than 627)
16–17	97.2–99.1	93.2–99.2	92.8–97.8
18–19	81.3–88.5	70.6–89.4	59.6–80.7
20–24	43.1–51.1	32.7–52.0	23.6–44.8
40–44	21.2–23.9	17.0–21.0	14.6–17.7

Source: Ts.S.U. 1972:table 6.

1979) and has been clearly the case for both male and female nuptiality in the period since World War II. Thus the standard deviation of age-standardized proportions married in 1959 of men was 39.4, but by 1970 it had dropped to 28.5; the corresponding drop for women was from 41.4 to 34.2.

In general, marriage is more prevalent among the Soviet rural population than among the urban population (Table 4.7). Exceptions to this rule for men are the three Baltic republics, and in 1970 Kirgizia. Exceptions for women in 1959 were the RSFSR and the Ukraine, in 1970 the Ukraine alone. For both urban and rural populations there are the same regional differences to be found: the northern Baltic republics have small proportions married, the Central Asian republics have higher proportions married, and the Slavic and Transcaucasian regions fall somewhere in between as regards both urban and rural areas. Moldavia again is an exception to the rule with very high proportions married in both cities and countryside. There has been convergence between rural and urban patterns and convergence between the patterns of different republics for both males and females.

Variations among the nationalities in marriage patterns are similar to the regional variations just noted, as might be expected given the tendency for the members of most nationalities to be concentrated within their home territories. In Table 4.8 are presented age-standardized proportions married for the population 16 years and over for the 15 major Soviet nationalities. Marriage is most prevalent among Central Asians and Moldavians and least prevalent among the Baltic nationalities, with Slavs and Caucasians coming somewhere in between. The proportions of Russian men married tend to be almost precisely the mean of the proportion of males married of the various nationalities. The proportions of Russian women married are somewhat lower than the average.

Over time the various nationalities are converging in their marriage patterns. The range of the different nationalities as a percent of the proportion married for Russians has grown smaller since 1959 for both men and women, and the standard deviation of the variations in the nationalities' marital status has decreased for both men and women since 1959. On the one hand, the Central Asians with their historically very low proportions single have over time decreased their proportions married, while, on the other hand, the Baltic peoples with their historically high proportions single have over time increased their proportions married. Russians and other Slavs have changed their marriage patterns comparatively little. (These observations are based on male marriage rates. Female marriage rates have all gone up due to the improvement in sex ratios.)

CORRELATES OF MARITAL STATUS

What determines these differences in proportions married between the regions and nationalities of the USSR? While the full set of determinants of a marriage pattern is obscure and eventually leads to discussions of cultural history

TABLE 4.7

Married per 1,000 Population Aged 16 and Older, Standardized by Age: Urban and Rural Populations, USSR and Union Republics, 1959 and 1970*

	Men 1959			Women 1959		
	Urban	Rural	Urban as a Percent of Rural	Urban	Rural	Urban as a Percent of Rural
USSR	722	740	97.6	497	505	98.4
BALTIC REPUBLICS						
Estonian SSR	655	611	107.2	479	494	97.0
Latvian SSR	668	646	103.4	492	510	96.5
Lithuanian SSR	675	643	105.0	497	537	92.6
WESTERN REPUBLICS						
RSFSR	722	739	97.7	484	478	101.3
Ukrainian SSR	728	740	98.4	518	491	105.5
Byelorussian SSR	723	728	99.3	496	500	99.2
Moldavian SSR	733	771	95.1	550	591	93.1
TRANSCAUCASIAN REPUBLICS						
Georgian SSR	696	716	97.2	514	583	88.2
Armenian SSR	722	765	94.4	554	596	93.0
Azerbaidzhan SSR	710	769	92.3	516	597	86.4
CENTRAL ASIAN REPUBLICS						
Uzbek SSR	722	770	93.8	526	653	80.6
Kazakh SSR	733	764	95.9	526	575	91.5
Kirgiz SSR	745	780	95.5	535	617	86.7
Tadzhik SSR	734	766	95.8	523	637	82.1
Turkmen SSR	729	760	95.9	532	636	83.6

	Men 1970			Women 1970		
USSR	717	732	98.0	569	599	95.0
BALTIC REPUBLICS						
Estonian SSR	669	612	109.3	539	558	96.8
Latvian SSR	670	659	101.7	547	583	93.8
Lithuanian SSR	687	676	101.6	565	614	92.0
WESTERN REPUBLICS						
RSFSR	717	727	98.6	559	580	96.4
Ukrainian SSR	723	736	98.2	587	583	100.7
Byelorussian SSR	726	724	100.3	542	592	91.6
Moldavian SSR	733	758	96.7	606	639	94.8
TRANSCAUCASIAN REPUBLICS						
Georgian SSR	685	712	96.2	580	662	87.6
Armenian SSR	708	752	94.1	625	672	93.0
Azerbaidzhan SSR	683	741	92.2	567	640	88.6
CENTRAL ASIAN REPUBLICS						
Uzbek SSR	710	756	93.9	590	698	84.5
Kazakh SSR	724	743	97.4	590	636	92.8
Kirgiz SSR	732	725	101.0	582	665	87.5
Tadzhik SSR	718	749	95.9	593	702	84.5
Turkmen SSR	707	744	95.0	598	688	86.9

*Standardized on the basis of the age distribution of the total population of the USSR in 1970.
Sources: Ts.S.U. 1972:table 6; Baldwin 1973.

TABLE 4.8

Married per 1,000 Population Aged 16 and Older, Standardized for Age:
Major Nationalities, USSR, 1959 and 1970*

Nationality	1959	Percent of figure for Russians	Nationality	1970	Percent of figure for Russians
			MEN		
Kirgiz	799	109.0	Moldavians	761	105.7
Uzbeks	775	105./	Kirgiz	759	105.4
Moldavians	772	105.3	Uzbeks	753	104.6
Tadzhiks	771	105.2	Tadzhiks	747	103.8
Kazakhs	768	104.8	Turkmen	743	103.2
Turkmen	767	104.6	Ukrainians	736	102.2
Azeri	753	102.7	Byelorussians	729	101.3
Armenians	738	100.7	Kazakhs	729	101.3
Ukrainians	734	100.1	Russians	720	100.0
Russians	733	100.0	Azeri	715	99.3
Byelorussians	733	100.0	Armenians	714	99.2
Georgians	706	96.3	Georgians	698	96.9
Lithuanians	656	89.5	Lithuanians	689	95.7
Latvians	640	87.3	Latvians	660	91.7
Estonians	623	85.0	Estonians	638	88.6

WOMEN

Kirgiz	660	135.5	Tadzhiks	698	123.1
Uzbeks	651	133.7	Uzbeks	691	121.9
Tadzhiks	650	133.5	Turkmen	678	119.6
Turkmen	630	129.4	Kirgiz	668	117.5
Kazakhs	623	127.9	Kazakhs	638	112.5
Moldavians	580	119.1	Moldavians	631	111.3
Azeri	580	119.1	Georgians	628	110.8
Armenians	564	115.8	Armenians	628	110.8
Georgians	558	114.6	Azeri	614	108.3
Lithuanians	528	108.4	Lithuanians	594	104.8
Ukrainians	506	103.9	Ukrainians	588	103.7
Byelorussians	501	102.9	Byelorussians	584	103.0
Russians	487	100.0	Russians	567	100.0
Latvians	486	99.8	Latvians	549	96.8
Estonians	478	98.2	Estonians	532	93.8

*Standardized for age on the basis of the age distribution of the total USSR population in 1970.
Sources: Ts.S.u. 1973a:383; Baldwin 1973.

and the like, what is of interest in the present context is the extent to which these differences in proportions married are explicable by reference to economic considerations in marriage and to a market model. Analysis of 1960 census data for the United States has shown that regional differences in proportions married in the United States can be explained in part using Becker's economic interpretation of mate-selection. In particular, Becker's hypothesis regarding the greater economic gain to marrying where the relative wage differentials of men and women are greater—and husbands and wives therefore more likely to specialize either in market or in household production—has been confirmed for proportions of U.S. females married (Freiden 1974; Santos 1975; for the basic argument behind Becker's theory, see Chapter 1).

In light of the Soviet ideological denial of a market structure to mate-selection in the Soviet Union, it is of interest to know whether the same sort of reasoning can explain the regional and nationality differences in proportions married in the USSR. While the data problems in the Soviet case are such that it is not possible simply to replicate Freiden's U.S. study for the USSR, sufficient data do exist to answer the question in general terms. The main problem with the Soviet data is its aggregation; in examining differences in proportions married by regions the number of cases is limited to the 15 Union republics. In examining differences in proportions of nationalities married, the number of cases is considerably greater; since the proportions married for some of the 44 ethnic groups whose marriage behavior was reported in the 1970 census were given for several areas of the USSR, the total number of cases comes to 103. Data by nationality are available, however, on only five relevant explanatory variables.

Below follows discussion of a series of variables relevant to predictions regarding proportions married by region on the basis of an economic market model. Because of the limitations of the data it was thought best not to attempt more than simple zero-order correlations with the data on proportions married by region. Several of the propositions are subsequently tested using the more extensive data on nationalities with which partial correlations were then also computed.

Sex-Ratios

Becker (1973: 836-41) and Freiden (1974: S34-S37) present a formal economic analysis of the effect of sex ratios on the proportion of women and men married, but the basic hypothesis can be stated in fairly simple terms. Increases in the supply of men reduce the price women must pay in marrying in the sense that women can appropriate more in the division of output (market and nonmarket income) between mates under such circumstances, and a larger proportion of women thereby are induced to marry. It therefore is predicted that the proportion of women married with be positively related to the ratio of men to women. The argument concerning the effect of increases in the supply of women on the proportion of men married is similar: it is predicted that the proportion of men married will be positively related to the ratio of women to men.

In most societies the importance of marriage for females is greater than for males because of the enforcement of rules of legitimacy, the economic dependence of women, and so on. The expectation thus can be added to Becker's and Freiden's hypothesis that the demand by females for husbands is more elastic in relation to the supply of men than is the demand by males for wives in relation to the supply of women—that is, one would expect higher correlations between the proportions of women married and sex ratios than between the proportions of men married and sex ratios.

To test these hypotheses for the postwar USSR the sex ratio (number of males per 100 females) in each five-year age group from 15 to 59 and in the age groups 60 to 69 and 70+ was correlated with the age-standardized proportion married by sex for both 1959 and 1970 for urban and rural populations (data on sex ratios taken from Ts. S.U. 1972: table 3). Since men tend to marry women somewhat younger than themselves, this definition of sex ratio is not totally satisfactory, but since the data are not available by single years of age there would be equivalent problems with using adjacent five-year age groups. Similar analysis of the effect of sex ratios on proportions of females married in the United States has shown that redefining the sex ratio to take account of this problem of differences in ages makes little difference in the results obtained (Freiden 1974: S-42).

In Table 4.9 are presented the correlation coefficients between the age-standardized proportions married and the various sex ratios. Most of the correlations are positive as predicted, and the correlations for women are considerably stronger than those for men as predicted. With a few exceptions in the younger age groups, all the negative correlation coefficients are extremely small. The overall observation, in other words, is that the higher the number of males relative to females, the more women are likely to be married; the higher the number of females relative to males, the more men are likely to be married, with the latter correlation weaker than the former.

To the extent that there is any support for the idea that men are less likely to marry when there are a great number of women present because they can more easily obtain the services of women outside of marriage, it is in the younger age groups. There is some evidence, in other words, that large supplies of women may induce young men to postpone marriage for a while, but that eventually the proportion of them marrying will be greater than where there are few women. This observation is consonant with evidence on a postwar rise in the age at marriage in the Soviet Union (see Chapter 5).

The evidence on sex ratios thus tends to support an economic interpretation of Soviet mate-selection.

TABLE 4.9

Correlation Coefficients between Standardized Proportions Married and Sex Ratios by Age Group and Residence: USSR, 1959 and 1970

Age Group	MEN			WOMEN		
	Total	Urban	Rural	Total	Urban	Rural
			1959			
15–19	0.454	0.399	-0.189	0.615	0.410	0.088
20–24	-0.039	0.128	-0.499	-0.244	0.046	-0.699
25–29	0.430	0.359	0.278	0.204	0.203	0.146
30–34	0.763	0.633	0.655	0.873	0.566	0.891
35–39	0.395	0.162	0.429	0.721	0.467	0.768
40–44	0.047	-0.305	0.247	0.491	-0.028	0.752
45–49	0.405	0.073	0.444	0.832	0.559	0.884
50–54	-0.064	-0.186	-0.106	0.504	0.346	0.536
55–59	-0.305	0.189	-0.247	0.304	0.694	0.298
60–69	0.466	0.486	0.201	0.876	0.582	0.815
70+	0.606	0.566	0.422	0.899	0.792	0.883

1970

15-19	-0.776	-0.508	-0.693	-0.701	0.106	-0.909
20-24	-0.682	-0.352	-0.786	-0.754	-0.080	-0.870
25-29	-0.075	0.352	-0.575	0.004	0.031	-0.111
30-34	0.029	0.212	-0.271	0.214	0.169	0.173
35-39	0.103	0.136	0.042	0.339	0.480	0.321
40-44	0.313	0.010	0.468	0.734	0.515	0.865
45-49	0.316	0.061	0.447	0.816	0.604	0.859
50-54	-0.136	-0.110	0.110	0.220	-0.118	0.553
55-59	-0.040	-0.082	0.000	0.312	0.128	0.408
60-69	-0.038	-0.075	-0.040	0.562	0.601	0.512
70+	0.442	0.245	0.465	0.893	0.776	0.948

Relative Education of Males and Females

Where wage rates of husbands and wives are highly unequal (usually wage rates of husbands exceed those of wives), one spouse (usually the husband) will specialize in market production while the other concentrates time in the home. The economic gains from marriage, and therefore the proportion of males and females married, are hypothesized to be positively related to the relative wage differential (Becker 1973: 815-22; Freiden 1974: S-38). In Becker's terms a negative correlation between proportions married and relative wage differentials would imply mutual caring or love between mates rather than self-seeking utility (see Chapter 1). Examination of these hypotheses empirically is thus probably the nearest thing to a direct test of Soviet claims that love is the only motive in marrying in the USSR and that economic considerations play virtually no part in mate-selection.

Soviet data on the relative wage rates of males and females are insufficient for this purpose, but it seems reasonable to substitute relative education of males and females for relative wage rates, since in bureaucratized Soviet society a reasonably close correlation exists between educational level and income. While rates of return to formal education have been shown to be lower in the Soviet Union than in the West, it is clear that the higher the Soviet citizen's education, the higher the citizen's earnings (for discussion of sex differentials in income, see Chapman 1977; Swafford 1978; Ofer and Vinokur 1979). The male/female education differential was operationalized as the proportion of women ten years of age or older with some secondary education or more as a percentage of the proportion of males ten years of age or older with some secondary education or more (data from Ts. S.U. 1973d). Note that operationalization in this manner means that the higher this indicator the smaller is the gap between men's and women's education.

The figures on relative education differentials were correlated with the age-standardized proportions married by region for urban and rural populations. The hypothesis is that the greater the percentage of men's education women's education is, the smaller the proportions of men and women who are married. In view of the greater cultural stress placed on marriage for females, one would expect that the correlations would be higher for men than for women— that is, men can be expected to be more responsive to variations in the economic gain to marrying than women.

The male-female education differential turns out to have the predicted effect on proportions married. The correlations for the urban population are -.569 for men and -.477 for women in 1959, and -.091 for men and -.168 for women in 1970. For the rural population the correlations are -.905 for men and -.589 for women in 1959, and -.642 for men and -.288 for women in 1970. All correlations are thus in the predicted direction, with those for men stronger as predicted in all cases but one. The decrease in the strength of the relationship between 1959 and 1970 is due in part to a decline in the difference in men's and women's education during this period. Whereas in 1959 the standard deviation of female education as a percent of male education was 5.27 and 11.53 for the urban and rural populations respectively, by 1970 it had decreased to 3.78 and 7.01 respectively.

The evidence on the importance of the relative differences in education between men and women, which here are being taken to be indicative of corresponding relative wage differentials, supports an economic interpretation of Soviet mate-selection. In the USSR as well as in the United States, it seems, "caring" in Becker's sense does not prevail. As will be seen with the data by nationality below, relative wage differentials (that is, relative education differentials) are highly correlated with proportions married even when other factors are controlled.

Employment of Women

The more women are independently employed in the labor force outside the home, the less advantageous marriage is to them and to their potential husband. This is due to the lesser extent to which women need male earnings for survival and to their greater potential loss of income were they to specialize in household production (and resulting lesser likelihood that they will so specialize in household production). It therefore can be predicted that the larger the percentage of females employed in the labor force outside the home, the lower will be the age-standardized proportions of both men and women married.

Reported employment of women in rural areas is problematic in Soviet statistics because of problems with the definition of employment in the agricultural labor force given the system of workdays. This variable therefore was limited to correlations with urban proportions married and was operationalized as the proportion of all urban females employed in nonagricultural activities (data from Ts. S.U. 1973b). The hypothesis is that the larger the proportion of urban females employed in a region, the lower the age-standardized proportion married of men and women.

The correlations support the hypothesis. Correlation coefficients between the proportion of urban females employed and age-standardized proportions of women married are -.837 for 1959 and -.679 for 1970; correlation coefficients with age-standardized proportions of men married are -.623 for 1959 and -.244 for 1970. The decrease in the strength of these correlations in the intervening decade is due most likely to the fact that the proportion of urban women employed increased substantially from a mean of 53.97 percent of all urban females in 1959 to a mean of 77.61 percent of all urban females in 1970. As of 1970, in other words, men were faced with potential partners who were more or less all likely to be employed, and the correlation with this factor of necessity decreased.

It does not appear that the extensive employment of women in the USSR has been compatible with being married. Soviet society evidently has not been able to increase women's economic independence and avoid a decrease in the popularity of marriage at the same time. The evidence of women's employment also lends support to an economic interpretation of Soviet mate-selection.

Kolkhozniki as a Percentage of Rural Population

Historically in the central areas of Russia, land was distributed according to a labor principle. Landowners, until the abolition of serfdom, had been interested in obtaining as much labor as possible from their serfs and therefore had linked the allotment of land to serfs to the number of working members in a serf's family (Blum 1972: 513). Until the end of the last century the obshchina or village commune periodically would redistribute the land held by its members, with the labor contribution of a given family the basis of allotment of strips of land. This labor principle of land distribution was a major cause of early and common marriage in central Russia since the husband's family, through a son's marriage, gained laborers and therefore more land. Given the male principle of land allotment it was only through marriage that a woman could make sure of her economic existence (Chojnacka 1976). A side effect of this situation was that loyalty was principally to family rather than to land.

In the Baltic areas this system of land allotment did not exist. Instead, private ownership of land and a primogeniture inheritance system as in much of Western Europe prevailed, which discouraged early or common marriage. In contrast, in Central Asia land was divided equally among sons, thereby encouraging early and frequent marriage (Matley 1967: 278-79).

In the Soviet period with collectivization of agriculture, the pattern peculiar to Central Russia has in a sense been extended to all areas of the Soviet Union. To the extent that there still is land allotment, such allotment primarily concerns the private plots that are guaranteed to members of collective farms by the Soviet Constitution. These are distributed by the general meeting of the collective farm on much the same principles of labor distribution as pertained before the Revolution. Thus the "Model Charter of the Collective Farms" approved by the Third All-Union Congress of Collective Farmers in November 1969, which forms the basis for collective-farm legislation throughout the country, states that:

> The personal plot of the collective farmer's family (collective farm household) is granted by decision of the general meeting of collective farm members, and its size is established with consideration for the number of members of the collective farmer's family (collective farm household) and their labor participation in the collective farm's communal sector. (translated in Matthews 1974: 396)

In some areas of the country newlyweds are specifically encouraged to engage in private farming, are given livestock as a wedding present by the collective farm, and so on (Ulianova 1979).

Although private plots also are made available to workers in state farms and to workers and employees in other institutions, they are not a matter of right as they are for collective-farm households, nor do they play nearly as large a role in the income of state farmers and others as they do in the income of kolkhozniki. In areas where collective farms are prevalent in agriculture, the proportion married thus can be expected to be greater due to the system of allotment of private plots.

This variable was operationalized as the proportion of kolkhozniki in the rural population (data from Ts. S.U. 1973b) and tested against the age-standardized proportions of men and women married in rural areas. The hypothesis is that the greater the percentage of collective farmers in the rural population, the larger the age-standardized proportions of men and women married.

The correlations bear out the hypothesis. The correlation coefficients between kolkhozniki as a percentage of the rural population and proportions married are +.363 for men and +.412 for women in 1959, and +.304 for men and +.348 for women in 1970. It thus seems likely that there continues to be a link between marriage and the economic incentive of gaining more land in the USSR similar to that pertaining in the nineteenth century.

Income Level

Becker (1973: 821-22) predicts that with increases in monetary income there is greater incentive to marry, and this coincides with observed inverse correlations between economic income levels and divorce rates (Goode 1956; 1962). Since the cost of marrying is relatively constant, increases in income also increase the gain from marriage—marriage becomes cheaper to enter into and therefore more attractive. It therefore can be hypothesized that the higher the income level of a region, the greater will be the proportion married.

Statistics on absolute levels of real disposable income are not available for the different regions of the USSR, so it is not possible to test this hypothesis directly. A number of indicators of general material well-being and economic development by region do exist, however, and it therefore is possible to make substitutions for data on levels of real disposable income. In particular the produced national income per capita, educational level, and degree of urbanization of the population by region give a fair approximation to differences in the income levels of the Soviet population. These three indicators were operationalized and correlated with the age-standardized proportions married of men and women in rural and urban areas. Educational level was operationalized as the proportion of the population over ten years of age with some secondary education or more (data from Ts. S.U. 1973d). The degree of urbanization was operationalized as the percentage urban of the total population of a republic, using census definitions of urban (data from Katz et al. 1975: 448). Produced national income per capita was taken from available figures for 1960 and 1970 (data from Katz et al. 1975: 452).

The hypotheses are that the higher the educational level of a region's population, the higher the produced national income per capita, and the more urbanized the area, the larger the age-standardized proportions of men and women married will be.

These hypotheses are not corroborated by the data. The correlation coefficients between produced national income per capita and proportions married are -.676 and -.664 for urban men and women respectively in 1959, and -.481 and -.655 in 1970 (corresponding coefficients for the rural population are -.723, -.652, -.818, and -.877). Those between educational level and proportions married are -.369 and -.137 for urban men and women respectively in 1959, and -.157 and -.402 in 1970 (corresponding coefficients for the rural population are +.446, +.465, +.302, and +.549). The coefficients between degree of urbanization and proportions married are -.551 and -.472 for urban men and women respectively in 1959, and -.592 and -.403 in 1970. As can be seen, only the correlations with educational level for the rural population are in the predicted direction.

The same lack of corroboration of Becker's hypothesis regarding the relation between income level and proportions married has been noted for the United States (Freiden 1974). Analysis of the data for ethnic groups below shows, however, that the negative correlations obtained can be explained by the variation in relative wage differentials (relative education differentials). The wealthier, more developed areas of the Soviet Union are precisely the areas in which differences in the relative wages and education of men and women tend to be small and in which women are more likely to be employed outside the home. As will be seen it is primarily the effect of relative wage differentials that is determining the negative correlations found here.

It may be noted that a fourth indicator of material well-being, the provision of housing, is also negatively correlated with proportions married. Heer (1975) in a study of fertility has shown that housing construction in a given area reflects less the needs of the Soviet population than the number of workers in the labor force. This is because much construction of new housing is done by industrial ministries rather than by local urban governments (Di Maio 1974), and cities in which women are extensively employed in the labor force tend to have more housing available. These in turn are areas that as a result can be expected to have lower proportions married.

In spite of the negative correlations between income levels and proportions married, the above discussion shows considerable support for the idea that differences in proportions married among regions of the USSR can be explained in economic market terms. Further support comes from analysis of the data on differences in the marital status of nationalities. Data regarding marriage on 44 ethnic groups were provided by the 1970 census, and since many of them were presented in more than one republic the total number of cases equals 103. Data by nationality concerning the above variables are limited, however, to the percent urban, educational level, relative education differential of men and women, and sex ratio. These variables were operationalized as for the correlations on regional differences, but because a breakdown of the nationalities by sex and age was not given in the 1970 census, the sex ratio of a given ethnic group in 1970 was taken as the proportion of males to 100 females of all ages in the ethnic group.

Since with the larger number of cases it is possible to do a set of partial correlations, data on an additional variable, traditional religion, were collected. There are major differences in the religious traditions of the various nationalities regarding the conception of marriage and traditional patterns of entrance into marriage that might well affect the observed proportions married for which it was felt it would be good to control. In particular, among the Eastern Orthodox and Catholics celibacy is an approved state, whereas for the Moslems there is no corresponding tradition (Sklar 1970: 146-52). The kin control of mate-selection among Moslem peoples (see Chapter 2) historically has encouraged early and frequent marriage. Insofar as sex roles affect entrance into marriage, the stress Moslem peoples place on virginity in the female at marriage encourages marrying girls off as soon after puberty as possible (Goode 1963: 104-5). Since the main division in the Soviet Union is between Christians and non-Christians, nationalities were assigned a value of one and non-Christian nationalities a value of zero in order to create a dummy variable that would measure traditional religion. (This procedure follows that used by Mazur in 1967. In view of the great similarities between Jews in Soviet Russia and the Christian population, Jews were added to the Christian group for purposes of measurement of this variable.)

In Table 4.10 are presented the age-standardized proportions married for 40 ethnic groups within their home territories in the USSR, along with information on their geographic region of location, traditional religion, and linguistic group. The regional variation noted above whereby the northern areas of the Soviet Union generally have lower proportions married than the southern regions and the western areas smaller proportions married than the eastern regions is observable for the ethnic groups that inhabit these areas. Table 4.10 also shows a clear tendency for Moslem groups to have higher proportions married than other ethnic groups. Thus 13 out of 22 non-Christian groups within their own territory are above the USSR average in proportions of males married, whereas only eight out of 18 Christian groups were similarly above the countrywide average. The difference is even more pronounced for women, with only six out of 18 Christian ethnic groups above the USSR average, while 17 out of 22 non-Christian ethnic groups are above it.

Since the proportions married in Table 4.10 are for the ethnic groups within their particular territory, comparison of the figures given there with those given for 1970 in Table 4.8 for the 15 major nationalities as a whole shows the difference in marriage behavior of a nationality within its principle area of settlement and outside it. There is something of a tendency for the marital behavior of an ethnic group when outside its own area of settlement to approach the marital patterns of the area to which it has migrated. In terms of marital status

TABLE 4.10

Married per 1,000 Population Aged 16 and Older, Standardized for Age and Selected Characteristics of Nationalities: Nationalities within Their Home Territories, USSR, 1970[a]

Geographic region	Ethnic group	Traditional religion	Men		Women	
			Below USSR average	Above USSR average	Below USSR average	Above USSR average
Siberia	Yakut (T)	Orthodox	592		506	
	Buryat (M)	Buddhist	675		513	
	Tuvan (T)	Buddhist	682			629
Baltic	Estonian (F)	Protestant	637		533	
	Latvian (B)	Protestant	660		549	
	Lithuanian (B)	Catholic	689			594
Caucasus	Ossetian (I)	Orthodox	651		537	
	Abkhaz (C)	Moslem	672		554	
	Balkar (T)	Moslem	683		561	

Group	Religion				
Ingush (C)	Moslem	686			586
Kalmyk (M)	Buddhist	696			581
Georgian (C)	Orthodox	698			629
Azeri (T)	Moslem	710			607
Armenian (C)	Orthodox[b]	719			642
Avar (C)	Moslem		726		587
Chechen (C)	Moslem		732		628
Lezgin (C)	Moslem		739		626
Dargin (C)	Moslem		741		603
Kabardin (C)	Moslem		744		611
Kumyk (T)	Moslem		746		607
Kurd (I)	Moslem		805		728
Western USSR					
Karelian (F)	Orthodox	704		522	
Russian (S)	Orthodox	719		565	
Byelorussian (S)	Orthodox		726	577	
Ukrainian (S)	Orthodox		736		584
Moldavian (R)	Orthodox		761		632
Gagauz (T)	Orthodox		789		696

TABLE 4.10 (Continued)

Geographic region	Ethnic group	Traditional religion	Men Below USSR average	Men Above USSR average	Women Below SSR average	Women Above USSR average
Central Asia	Karakalpak (T)	Moslem	716			704
	Kazakh (T)	Moslem		729		636
	Turkmen (T)	Moslem		742		676
	Tadzhik (I)	Moslem		747		698
	Uzbek (T)	Moslem		754		692
	Kirgiz (T)	Moslem		761		664
East European Russia	Komi (F)	Orthodox	691		520	
	Tatar (T)	Moslem	717		552	
	Chuvash (T)	Orthodox		728	501	
	Mari (F)	Orthodox		730	470	
	Mordvin (F)	Orthodox		735	539	
	Bashkir (T)	Moslem		743	560	
	Udmurt (F)	Orthodox		744	489	

Note: Capital letters in parentheses refer to ethnolinguistic groups: S, Slavic; C, Caucasus; T, Turkic; M, Mongolian; F, Finnic; B, Baltic; I, Iranian; R, Romance.

aStandardized on the basis of the age distribution of the total USSR population in 1970.

bArmenian Apostolic church, close to Orthodox.

Sources: Ts.S.U. 1973a:table 35; Baldwin 1973.

standardized for age, whereas 73.6 percent of Ukrainian male adults in the Ukraine are married, in regions of more common marriage, such as Moldavia and Kirgizia, they tend to marry more: 76.1 percent of Ukrainian men in Moldavia and 74.9 percent of Ukrainian men in Kirgizia are married. In areas where marriage is less common they tend to marry less: 71.4 percent of Ukrainian men in Estonia and 71.9 percent of Ukrainian men in Latvia are married. The behavior of Jews in those republics for which data are available shows the same tendencies. Thus the age-standardized proportions married of Jewish men in the Ukraine and Byelorussia are 69.5 percent and 70.0 percent respectively, but 72.0 percent in Moldavia where marriage is generally more common and only 67.5 percent in Latvia where marriage is relatively less common. (The corresponding figures for Jewish women are: Ukrainian SSR, 58.1 percent; Byelorussian SSR, 57.0 percent; Moldavian SSR, 63.3 percent; and Latvian SSR, 58.3 percent.)

Zero-order correlations based on the data for ethnic groups are presented in Table 4.11. As can be seen they are generally all in the predicted direction. Since intercorrelation of the variables is considerable, however, it is perhaps of more interest to look at some of the partial correlations relating to proportions married (see Table 4.12).

When other variables are controlled for, religion remains significantly related to the proportion married of women, although the relationship is reduced. In contrast, for men there seems to be nothing about religion per se that affects the proportion married; rather, religion tends to be very strongly associated with such factors as the male/female education differential. In light of the many restrictions placed on Moslem women that do not apply to Moslem men—religious law does not allow them to intermarry, for example (see Chapter 7)—this difference between the effect of religion on proportions married of males and females is perhaps understandable.

The same reduced but still significant relationship between the proportions of women married and the sex ratio when other variables are controlled demonstrates the continuing importance of this demographic factor for women's marital behavior in the USSR. Sex ratios also are positively and significantly correlated for men even when religion, urbanization, and education are controlled, but less strongly than for women, as predicted.

Controlling for other variables, in particular for the male/female education differential, essentially obliterates the relationships between the two indicators of material well-being—percent urban and educational level—and differences in marital status for both men and women. As already argued, in other words, the lack of the expected relation between income level and proportions married is explained to a great extent by the smaller education and wage differences between men and women in the more developed regions and nationalities.

Although for women the relationship between the male/female education differential and age-standardized proportions married is highly reduced when traditional religion and sex ratios are taken into account, and essentially removed when the other variables are added in the partials, the correlation between the

TABLE 4.11

Zero-Order Correlations between Variables Relating to Proportions Married: Soviet Nationalities, 1970 (N=103)

Name of variable	Proportion males married	Proportion females married	Traditional religion	Sex ratio	Percent urban	Educational level	Female educational level as percent of male level
Proportion of males married x_1	1.000	.590**	-.235*	.145	-.326**	-.283*	-.482**
Proportion of females married x_2		1.000	-.394**	.332**	-.300**	-.230*	-.388**
Traditional religion x_3			1.000	-.112	.520**	.480**	.566**
Sex ratio x_4				1.000	.013	.250*	-.193*
Percent urban x_5					1.000	.866**	.666**
Educational level x_6						1.000	.653**
Female educational level as a percent of male level x_7							1.000

*Significant at .05 level.
**Significant at .001 level.

TABLE 4.12

Selected Partial Correlations Relating to Proportions Married: Soviet Nationalities, 1970

Variable and order of correlation	Males	Variable and order of correlation	Females
Proportion Married and Traditional Religion			
r_{13}	-.235*	r_{23}	-.394**
$r_{13.7}$	.052	$r_{23.7}$	-..230*
$r_{13.4567}$	.057	$r_{23.4567}$	-.216*
Proportion Married and Sex Ratio			
r_{14}	.145	r_{24}	.332**
$r_{14.6}$	.232*	$r_{24.6}$	.414**
$r_{14.36}$	.209*	$r_{24.36}$	.356**
$r_{14.356}$	.168*	$r_{24.356}$	.331**
$r_{14.3567}$	.023	$r_{24.3567}$	.279*
Proportion Married and Percent Urban			
r_{15}	-.326**	r_{25}	-.300**
$r_{15.7}$	-.008	$r_{25.7}$	-.061
$r_{15.3467}$	-.064	$r_{25.3467}$	-.002
Proportion Married and Educational Level			
r_{16}	-.283*	r_{26}	-.230*
$r_{16.4}$	-.334**	$r_{26.4}$	-.343**
$r_{16.34}$	-.261*	$r_{26.34}$	-.181*
$r_{16.3457}$	.056	$r_{26.3457}$	-.056
Proportion Married and Female Educational Level as Percent of Male Level			
r_{17}	-.482*	r_{27}	-.388**
$r_{17.3}$	-.435**	$r_{27.3}$	-.218*
$r_{17.34}$	-.424**	$r_{27.34}$	-.179*
$r_{17.345}$	-.349**	$r_{27.345}$	-.112
$r_{17.3456}$	-.345**	$r_{27.3456}$	-.084

*Significant at .05 level.
**Significant at .001 level.

proportion of males currently married and the male/female education differential remains highly significant for men even when all other variables are controlled. That is, while women tend to be most affected in their marriage patterns by sex ratios and traditional religion, whether men are likely to be married or not greatly depends on the relative difference between their education and consequent wage power and the education and consequent wage power of their potential wives.

As already noted, the potential gain to marriage and therefore the proportion of women married have been found to be related to sex-specific relative education and relative wages in the United States (Freiden 1974: S-47-S-48). It would seem that for Soviet women this factor is overshadowed by sex ratios and traditional religion, but that Becker's observations regarding the economic gains to marriage where specialization is likely hold for the Soviet Union as well. Where women are likely to specialize in household production the attractiveness of marriage is considerably increased to both men and women, but particularly to men. In view of the huge time losses involved in housework in the USSR, this last finding seems quite reasonable. Given the poor development of Soviet service industries, the gain to males of marriage to a woman who is likely to specialize in household matters is very great. (For discussion of the time budgets of men and women, see Sacks 1976.)

This last finding also negates very strongly any idea that the marital status of the Soviet population is not based on economic considerations in addition to emotional attachment. The fact that men are clearly more likely to enter into marriage under conditions of specialization in household tasks supports Becker's discussion of the economics of marital decisions, not Engels's on the elimination of calculation in marriage under socialism. The finding is consistent with some other things that are known. Thus Mazur found that in 1959 the presence of elderly persons in the home increased the likelihood of fertility on the part of young people. His interpretation was that readily available child care in the presence of elderly household members with low education increased the feasibility of Soviet couples having children (Mazur 1973: 110). Under Soviet conditions of great difficulty in arranging for household services, it would seem that the utilization of family members—of elderly persons in the case of child care and of wives likely to specialize in household matters in the case of housekeeping more generally—is a major factor in the decision to expand a household, whether by adding new members through birth or through marriage.

Although it is generally recognized that enormous problems of budgeting time still exist for Soviet women in balancing the demands of family and full-time employment, the work role of women is nonetheless believed to have become so much a part of women's identity in the USSR that it is supposed to not affect women's marriageability. Such does not seem to be the case. Men are clearly more likely in the USSR to marry where women are likely to specialize in household production. To the extent that women's full-time employment has become accepted in the USSR it would seem to be something that men make their peace with rather than something actively preferred. Thus the Soviet case does not seem to give much hope for the idea that women can be employed on an equal basis with men and marriage still remain as universal an institution as where they are not so employed.

In general the data presented in this chapter show substantial empirical support for an economic interpretation of the Soviet marriage market. Sex ratios, gains to specialization, and land allotment all influence marital behavior as expected according to a market interpretation. All this is not to say that love plays no part in the determination of eventual proportions marrying, but that it is merely one item in a more general calculation that can best be described in market terms.

5

AGE AT MARRIAGE

In explaining the marital status of the Soviet population, it was noted that historically there have been three main patterns of nuptiality among the peoples of the USSR: a European pattern in the Baltics, an East European pattern in the Slavic areas, and a non-European pattern in Central Asia. A relatively late age at entrance into marriage for both men and women characterized the Baltics, and a relatively early age at marriage was standard in the central Slavic areas. In Central Asia—and much of the Caucasus—a very early age at marriage for women with a somewhat later age at marriage for men was typical. If Soviet mate-selection were in fact free of economic considerations, presumably the age at marriage now would be early—at least this would be the expectation in view of Soviet anti-Malthusianism and hatred of the necessity of people being forced to wait to marry until they can afford it (Iurkevich 1970a: 21).

Soviet legislation has tended to make the legal age at marriage uniform for the entire country, although significant regional differences still exist. A minimum age of 18 for both men and women was recommended in the "Basic Principles of Legislation of the USSR and Union Republics on Marriage and the Family" in 1968, along with a permissible lowering of age at marriage by two years with approval of the local Soviet in exceptional cases, such as where the bride is pregnant. The RSFSR has had such an equal minimum age at marriage of 18 for both men and women since 1926 and most of the other republics have followed suit, but the Ukraine and Uzbekistan have a minimum age of 17 for women. The lowering of up to two years was enacted into law in the RSFSR but not in the other republics. Uzbekistan has no code provision for age lowering; among the other republics, six allow only up to one year for women only, and the remaining seven allow it up to one year for both men and women (Juviler 1977).

The present chapter brings together most of the empirical evidence available to examine the long-range trend in average age at marriage, current regional variations in age at marriage, and the correspondence between the ages of brides and grooms.

AGE AT MARRIAGE: LONG-TERM TREND

In Table 5.1 are presented mean ages at marriage in Russia and the USSR for selected years from 1867 to 1977. Mean age at first marriage is available only since 1965, and age at marriage for the USSR as well as for imperial Russia is generally reported only in five-year age groups. The interval used for calculating average age at marriage was 15 to 69 since although it is true that the minimum age at marriage is generally 17 or 18 throughout the USSR, marriages do occur before that and such an interval is necessary for historical comparisons. Very few marriages occur after the age of 69.

For the country as a whole the average age at marriage was relatively low in the nineteenth century, began to rise after the Revolution, and continued to do so more or less uniformly until the late 1960s, since when it has been falling back to almost the levels of the 1920s. As can be seen from Table 5.1, grooms married at an average age of a little over 25 and brides at an average age of about 22 quite consistently throughout the late nineteenth and early twentieth centuries. The rise in average age at marriage after the Revolution was somewhat abated as of 1926, presumably due to the great ease of marriage and divorce enacted in the laws of that year. By the end of the decade of the 1930s, however, the average age at marriage had increased substantially and continued to do so until 1965 when it reached a peak of 31.1 years for all grooms and 28.5 years for all brides.

Some of the very late age at marriage observable as of 1965 is due to the fact that many people who had previously been unable to remarry found themselves able to do so that year due to the easing of divorce laws. The mean age at marriage for first marriage only also reached a peak that year: 29.7 years for grooms and 27.6 years for brides. While some first marriages were with the newly divorced, this late age at first marriage cannot be explained entirely in such terms, and the rise in age at marriage to 1965 must be accepted as a true rise. Since 1965 the age at marriage has been dropping steadily for both men and women for first marriages as well as for all marriages. As of 1977 the mean age at first marriage for grooms was 25.2 and for brides 23.2 years. This is higher than has been the case for the United States in recent years but not very different from the age at marriage prevailing in Russia in the nineteenth century or in the USSR of the late 1920s.

Since the mean age at marriage is so dependent on the age and marital structure of the population, the median age at marriage was computed for the same years (Table 5.2). The median age at marriage also has the advantage of not being affected by the problem of five-year intervals. The median ages at marriage are as expected somewhat lower than the average ages at marriage, showing

TABLE 5.1

Mean Age at Marriage: USSR, 1867–1977, Selected Years

Year	All marriages			First marriages only		
	Grooms	Brides	Difference	Grooms	Brides	Difference
1867–71	25.5	22.2	3.3			
1872–76	25.4	22.1	3.3			
1877–81	25.4	21.7	3.7			
1890–94	25.6	22.0	3.6			
1895–98	25.3	21.9	3.4			
1910	25.3	22.1	3.2			
1923	27.9	24.4	3.5			
1924	27.7	24.2	3.5			
1925	27.8	24.4	3.4			
1926	25.4	22.8	2.6			
1927	25.5	23.0	2.5			
1940	28.8	25.0	3.8			
1950	29.5	27.1	2.4			
1959	29.5	26.9	2.6			
1960	29.5	27.4	2.1			

Year						
1961	29.3	27.3	2.0			
1962	n.a.	n.a.	n.a.			
1963	29.9	27.9	2.0			
1964	30.7	28.4	2.3			
1965	31.1	28.5	2.6	29.7	27.6	2.1
1966	30.9	28.2	2.7	29.3	27.0	2.3
1967	30.7	27.9	2.8	29.0	26.6	2.4
1968	29.6	27.1	2.5	27.1	25.6	1.5
1969	28.5	26.0	2.5	26.7	24.5	2.2
1970	27.9	25.5	2.4	26.1	24.1	2.0
1971	27.6	25.2	2.4	25.8	23.8	2.0
1972	27.5	25.2	2.3	25.6	23.6	2.0
1973	27.3	24.9	2.4	25.4	23.4	2.0
1974	26.3	24.9	1.4	25.1	23.1	2.0
1975	27.2	24.9	2.3	25.2	23.2	2.0
1976	27.4	25.1	2.3	25.3	23.3	2.0
1977	27.3	25.0	2.3	25.2	23.2	2.0

Note: 1867 to 1910 refers to 50 gubernii of European Russia; 1923 refers to 50 gubernii of European Russia; 1923 refers to RSFSR and Byelorussia only; 1924–27 refers to European USSR only; 1940–77 refers to the total USSR within present borders.

n.a.: Not available.

Sources: Rashin 1956:173–74; Institut International de Statistique 1932:90; Vestnik statistiki 1963:93; 1965:96; 1967:94; 1969:93; 1970:95; 1971a:95; 1971b:89; 1973:88; 1975b:89; 1976:88; 1977:78; 1978:84; Ts.S.U. 1975a:172; United Nations 1968:544–45; 1969:669; 1970:741; 1971: 778; 1972:632; 1973:369; unpublished data.

TABLE 5.2

Median Age at Marriage: USSR, 1867–1977, Selected Years

Year	All marriages			First marriages		
	Grooms	Brides	Difference	Grooms	Brides	Difference
1867–71	23.0	20.2	2.8			
1872–76	23.0	20.2	2.8			
1877–81	23.2	20.1	3.1			
1890–94	23.8	20.4	3.4			
1895–98	23.7	20.5	3.2			
1910	23.7	20.5	3.2			
1923	23.9	22.3	1.6			
1924	23.8	22.1	1.7			
1925	23.7	22.0	1.7			
1926	23.4	21.9	1.5			
1927	23.5	22.1	1.4			
1940	27.1	23.2	3.9			
1950	26.5	24.5	2.0			
1959	25.0	23.6	1.4			
1960	24.9	23.6	1.3			

Year						
1961	24.9	23.7	1.2			
1962	n.a.	n.a.	n.a.			
1963	26.1	24.2	1.9			
1964	26.8	24.6	2.2			
1965	27.1	24.7	2.4	26.5	24.0	2.5
1966	27.4	24.7	2.7	26.7	23.7	3.0
1967	27.3	24.2	3.1	26.4	23.3	3.1
1968	26.5	23.5	3.0	25.3	22.6	2.7
1969	24.9	22.9	2.0	24.1	22.2	1.9
1970	24.3	22.6	1.7	23.7	22.1	1.6
1971	24.0	22.5	1.5	23.5	22.0	1.5
1972	24.0	22.5	1.5	23.5	21.9	1.6
1973	24.0	22.5	1.5	23.4	21.9	1.5
1974	24.0	22.4	1.6	23.4	21.8	1.6
1975	24.0	22.4	1.6	23.4	21.8	1.6
1976	24.0	22.5	1.5	23.4	21.8	1.6
1977	24.0	22.4	1.6	23.4	21.8	1.6

Note: 1867 to 1910 refers to 50 gubernii of European Russia; 1923 refers to RSFSR and Byelorussia only; 1924 to 1927 refers to European USSR only; and 1940 to 1977 refers to the total USSR within present borders.

n.a.: Not available.

Sources: See Table 5.1.

asymmetry in the distribution of ages, but the observations made in regard to average ages at marriage essentially also apply to the median ages.

The median age remained fairly constantly about 23.5 for grooms and somewhat over 20 for brides throughout the nineteenth century. After the Revolution the medians for both brides and grooms rose, then fell slightly as of 1926. A rise in the median age at marriage is then visible up to the late 1960s, followed by a decline since then. At the present time half of all Soviet grooms marrying for the first time marry by the age of 23.4 years, and half of all brides marrying for the first time by the age of 21.8 years.

What have been the causes of these fluctuations in age at marriage? Presumably a large part of the explanation for the rise in age at marriage from the Revolution to the late 1960s is to be found in the very rapid urbanization of the population, industrialization, and the increase in years of schooling. The destruction of landholding patterns, particularly among the Slavic populations who contribute so heavily to the picture for the country as a whole, also dealt a blow to early marriage: young people in the countryside found themselves more independent of their parents' desires to obtain further workers by marriage. The tremendous upheavals of the Civil War, the Five-Year Plans, collectivization, purges, and World War II presumably convinced few people the world was stable enough not to have to postpone marriage. Although the Soviet Union is the chief example of women's participation in the industrial labor force and the independence of women in allocation of their income, it is not the case that these factors, even when combined with ideological support of a self-selection courtship system, have brought about a lowering of age at marriage as in the West (see Goode 1963: 43-45).

The recent decline in age at marriage has caused concern among those Soviet demographers deploring increases in divorce rates (for example, see Atarov 1972), but has been encouraged by those concerned with fertility (see Perevedentsev 1971b). The reasons for the decline are thought to be various. In part it is due to a lowering of the draft age; in part it would seem that the general improvement in the standard of living and housing has made it possible for young people to be financially independent earlier than in prior decades. Another major factor is the greater ease of divorce in recent years. This hypothesis is supported by the observation that it is precisely since the changes in divorce laws as of 1965 that the age at marriage has been falling. Two additional factors Soviet demographers have pointed to are the greater availability of contraception, which means that marriage need not be postponed for purposes of limitation of family size, and the observed lowering of the age of puberty (Vishnevskii 1975a; Chuiko 1975: 64). It should be noted, however, that the average age at marriage in most of the USSR traditionally has followed the East European nuptiality pattern described by Hajnal. This pattern is the one to which all the populations of the world are gradually converging (Coale et al. 1979), and not all these factors necessarily must be at work to produce the pattern. In terms of the USSR as a whole, the age at marriage has now more or less returned to that prevailing in the 1920s.

REGIONAL VARIATIONS IN AGE AT MARRIAGE

As already noted, there has been a significant convergence of marriage patterns among the regions and nationalities of the Soviet Union from different starting points (see Chapter 4). As regards age at marriage, those areas and peoples with historically very low ages at marriage have seen them raised, while those regions and nationalities that traditionally married very late have tended to marry earlier.

These trends are visible for the recent period in the changing proportions married at young ages as reported by the last three censuses. In Table 5.3 are presented the changing proportions married at ages 18 and 19 since 1939 in the 15 Union republics. As can be seen, the proportion of women married at these ages has been increasing in the Baltic republics, decreasing in Central Asia and Moslem Azerbaidzhan (also Moldavia), and shows a pattern of decrease and return in the Slavic areas and Georgia and Armenia. Although the patterns for men at these young ages are less consistent, it is interesting to note the lowering of their age at marriage to 1959 in Central Asia, followed since by somewhat later marriage. Presumably the decline in age at marriage for Moslem men is due to the lessened importance of the necessity of being able to afford the kalym or bride-price (Tamimov 1970: 306). Grooms in the Baltics, as expected, have been growing younger.

Despite this convergence of patterns, there still are remnants of regional differences observable in ages at marriage. In Table 5.4 are presented the mean and median ages at marriage of brides and grooms in the 15 Union republics as of 1973. Unfortunately data by region are not available for first marriages separately. The highest mean and median ages at marriage are still to be found in the Baltic republics for both men and women and in the republics of the Caucasus particularly for men. As will be seen, a large spread in the ages of brides and grooms traditionally has been characteristic of the Caucasus. The lowest mean and median ages of brides are still to be found in Central Asia. While there is now considerable similarity between regions in age at marriage, the differences that characterized the czarist empire are still visible as of the 1970s. (For more detailed discussion of the reasons for the various marriage patterns, see Chapter 4.)

Very few registration statistics are available concerning urban and rural differences in age at marriage in the USSR for the postwar period. Lithuania has published some data, and data on the Ukraine were collected in the study by Chuiko (1975; see the data and calculations in Table 5.5). In both Lithuania and the Ukraine age at marriage, particularly for men, is now somewhat lower in

TABLE 5.3

Proportion Married at Age 18 to 19: USSR and Union Republics, 1939, 1959, 1970
(per 1,000 population)

Region	1939	1959	1970
	MEN		
USSR	53	41	39
RSFSR	63	38	40
Ukrainian SSR	41	36	35
Byelorussian SSR	37	23	22
Uzbek SSR	32	88	50
Kazakh SSR	44	58	43
Georgian SSR	45	35	40
Azerbaidzhan SSR	32	50	25
Lithuanian SSR	7	20	29
Moldavian SSR	128	66	49
Latvian SSR	7	28	37
Kirgiz SSR	43	76	41
Tadzhik SSR	36	83	45
Armenian SSR	35	33	27
Turkmen SSR	95	111	73
Estonian SSR	8	24	33
	WOMEN		
USSR	250	171	186
RSFSR	222	143	159
Ukrainian SSR	200	148	187
Byelorussian SSR	183	101	126
Uzbek SSR	585	406	343
Kazakh SSR	435	278	211
Georgian SSR	398	175	236
Azerbaidzhan SSR	620	326	269
Lithuanian SSR	47	93	106
Moldavian SSR	241	223	193
Latvian SSR	62	97	129
Kirgiz SSR	495	397	294
Tadzhik SSR	644	438	404
Armenian SSR	711	253	268
Turkmen SSR	597	443	336
Estonian SSR	63	93	115

Sources: Ts.S.U. 1962a:73; 1962b:21; 1962c:43; 1962d:21; 1962e:19; 1962f:29; 1963a:19; 1963b:31; 1963c:27; 1963d:27; 1963e:25; 1963f:29; 1963g:98; 1963h:25; 1963i:27; 1963j:44; 1972:table 6.

TABLE 5.4

Mean Age and Median Age at Marriage: Union Republics, 1973

	Mean Age			Median Age		
	Men	Women	Difference (Men to Women)	Men	Women	Difference (Men to women)
RSFSR	27.0	25.0	2.0	25.8	22.5	3.3
Ukrainian SSR	27.8	25.5	2.3	24.0	22.5	1.5
Byelorussian SSR	27.2	25.2	2.0	24.0	22.6	1.4
Uzbek SSR	26.6	23.0	3.6	24.0	21.4	2.6
Kazakh SSR	27.1	24.7	2.4	24.0	22.5	1.5
Georgian SSR	30.4	26.6	3.8	27.8	23.6	4.2
Azerbaidzhan SSR	29.1	24.4	4.7	26.8	22.3	4.5
Lithuanian SSR	28.3	26.3	2.0	24.8	23.5	1.3
Moldavian SSR	26.7	24.4	2.3	23.6	22.2	1.4
Latvian SSR	29.1	27.2	1.9	25.2	23.9	1.3
Kirgiz SSR	27.3	24.1	3.2	24.1	22.0	2.1
Tadshik SSR	27.0	22.6	4.4	24.4	20.8	3.6
Armenian SSR	28.2	24.1	4.1	25.9	22.3	3.6
Turkmen SSR	26.3	23.6	2.7	24.0	22.3	1.7
Estonian SSR	27.7	26.0	1.7	24.5	23.4	1.1

Source: Ts.S.U. 1975a:174–75.

TABLE 5.5

Mean Age and Median Age at Marriage by Urban/Rural: Lithuanian SSR and Ukrainian SSR, Years for which Data are Available

	Mean Age				Median Age			
	Urban		Rural		Urban		Rural	
	Men	Women	Men	Women	Men	Women	Men	Women
Lithuanian SSR – All Marriages								
1965	28.3	26.0	29.8	26.9	26.3	23.9	26.8	21.6
1967	28.5	26.2	29.6	26.9	26.5	24.0	26.9	24.3
1968	28.4	26.2	29.3	26.9	26.1	23.9	26.5	24.2
1969	28.0	25.4	29.3	26.9	25.6	23.7	26.2	23.9
1970	28.2	26.1	28.7	26.4	25.4	.23.7	25.5	23.6
1971	27.8	25.9	28.7	26.6	24.9	23.6	25.1	23.5
1972	28.1	26.1	29.0	26.8	24.9	23.6	25.1	23.5
Ukrainian SSR – First Marriages Only								
1946–54	28.2	25.4	26.4	23.7	26.1	24.1	25.1	23.3
1955–64	27.8	25.8	26.9	25.0	25.0	23.8	24.7	22.6
1965–69	26.7	24.6	29.8	27.3	24.0	21.2	24.5	21.5
1970	25.0	23.1	26.6	24.5	23.4	21.4	23.7	21.2
1971	24.7	22.9	24.0	24.0	23.1	21.3	23.3	21.0

Sources: Ts.S.U. Litovskoi SSR 1969:22; 1971:25; 1972:98; 1973:23; Chuiko 1975:61, 63.

urban areas than in rural areas; the traditionally lower age at marriage in rural areas has been reversed. Although private plots still affect marriage patterns (Chapter 4), the economic organization of agriculture has lost much of its significance for marriage. The general lowering of age at marriage in recent years is visible in both town and country.

CORRESPONDENCE BETWEEN THE AGES OF BRIDES AND GROOMS

Marriages between persons of greatly differing ages are suspect from the standpoint of Soviet ideology since they supposedly often represent cases of marriage for economic gain or for other reasons than love. Historically in Russia loveless unions between old and young were a commonly recognized type of marriage and are reflected in the literature and art of the nineteenth century. Perhaps the most famous example is a painting by Vasilii Pukirev entitled *Unequal Marriage* (*Neravnyi brak*, Tretiakov Gallery, Moscow). Painted in 1862, Pukirev's painting shows a wrinkled, elderly high official at the altar with his pale young bride and as such is a critique against such marriages. It was painted specifically to change attitudes of the time and is said to have prevented several old generals from marrying poverty-stricken young girls (Repin 1887: 228-29; cited in Valkenier 1975: 106). It often is referred to in discussions of marriage today (for example, see Chachin 1971).

Such marriages are claimed to have become less frequent over time in view of the greater equality of women and the growth of women's economic independence and cultural level. An immediate result of the removal of economic considerations in marriage is supposed to be an equalization in the ages of brides and grooms (Kharchev 1964: 185-89). Such an equalization in marriage ages has been generally observed throughout the world (Goode 1963: 40), and it is unclear how much of such an equalization is due to the specifics of the Soviet economic and political structure as such. Where there is a large gap in the ages of a would-be bride and groom, ZAGS registration officials often extend the obligatory waiting period as a matter of policy (Kulaeva 1974).

Examination of the differences between mean ages at marriage of grooms and brides and between median ages in Tables 5.1 and 5.2 does show a considerable decrease from the nineteenth century to the present in the age differences of husbands and wives. Indeed there has been something of a decrease in this respect for first marriages even since 1965. While the difference between mean ages at marriage in the nineteenth century was somewhat over three years, by 1977 it was about half of that.

Certainly the extremes in gaps in the ages of husbands and wives have been eliminated over time. While in Leningrad in 1920 7.5 percent of all grooms were at least 13 years older than their brides, by 1960 such unions had decreased to only 2 percent of all marriages (Kharchev 1964: 190). Similar observations have been made for areas such as Central Asia where vast differences in ages were traditionally very common (Tamimov 1970: 306). Studies in Armenia have shown that while marriages in which the husband was 11 to 13 years older than his wife were not infrequent among generations born prior to 1935, among those born since that date the gap in marriage ages rarely exceeds five to six years (Ter-Sarkisiants 1972: 111-13).

As in the case of mean age at marriage and marital status, the differences between the regions of the USSR have lessened as regards age differences between husbands and wives but are still visible. The largest differences between men and women in mean age at marriage and median age at marriage are still to be found in Central Asia, where Moslem cultural traditions have supported large gaps in the ages of spouses, and in the Caucasus (see Table 5.3). The largest age gaps between husbands and wives exist among the Chechens of the Caucasus (Benet 1976: 118).

Direct information concerning the ages of brides in relation to the ages of grooms is available only by five-year age groups. As a result it is not possible with any accuracy to do more than indicate the percentages of marriages in which the husband is older, equal in age to, or younger than the wife (equal in age in this case means within the same five-year age group). In Table 5.6 are presented ages of brides by ages of grooms for the Ukrainian SSR for selected years. In 1926 two out of three Ukrainian men under 20 years of age married women their own age, and one out of three married an older woman. Those aged 20 to 24 married primarily women their own age, while those 25 and above mostly married women younger than themselves. Immediately after World War II, a very large proportion of young men, including even those aged 25 to 29, married women older than themselves. Only with the normalization of the sex ratio did the share of men marrying older women return to rest primarily on the shoulders of the youngest age group. As can be seen from Table 5.6, however, the effect of poor sex ratios after the war has had a lingering effect on the proportion of marriages for virtually all ages in which the groom is younger than the bride. While the data for 1971 for the Ukraine are more similar to those for 1926 than to those for the 1950s, there nonetheless has been an increase for almost all age groups of the proportion of men marrying women older than themselves. The proportion marrying within their own age group also increased, while there was a corresponding decrease in the number of marriages in which men are older than their wives.

In Table 5.7 are presented the ages of brides by ages of grooms for the entire Soviet Union for those postwar years for which data are available. As can be seen from the figures, the percentage of marriages in which bride and groom are equal in age has increased over this period, while the proportions of marriages where the bride is younger than the groom and in which she is older have decreased. A consistently large proportion of marriages where the bride is over the age of 25 involve younger grooms; about a third of all brides over the age of 25 marry men younger than themselves. This is a considerably larger proportion than in the United States.

TABLE 5.6

Proportion of Grooms Married to Brides Younger, Equal, and Older in Age than Themselves by Age of Groom: Ukrainian SSR, 1926, 1951, 1959, 1971

	Percent married to brides who are											
	Younger than groom				Equal in age				Older than groom			
Age of groom	1926	1951	1959	1971	1926	1951	1959	1971	1926	1951	1959	1971
Less than 20	–	–	–	–	60.6	20.6	48.7	64.9	39.4	79.4	51.3	35.1
20–24	36.0	8.8	26.7	36.9	50.0	27.7	63.4	58.1	14.0	63.5	9.9	5.0
25–29	75.5	16.2	70.7	73.4	18.7	62.8	20.3	16.6	5.8	21.0	9.0	10.0
30–34	80.6	59.9	59.6	57.1	13.3	33.2	29.1	31.0	6.1	6.9	11.3	11.9
35–39	82.6	67.7	61.7	63.4	12.6	23.9	29.8	21.1	4.8	8.7	8.5	15.5
40–44	84.6	64.3	67.3	53.0	10.8	27.5	22.4	29.7	4.6	8.2	10.3	17.3
45–49	84.4	60.5	66.5	55.8	11.6	36.9	25.3	30.9	4.0	2.6	8.2	13.3
50–54	84.8	–	66.4	60.8	11.5	–	24.6	26.3	3.7	–	9.0	12.9
55–59	88.3	55.8	60.5	62.6	9.3	43.8	31.9	30.8	2.4	0.4	7.6	6.6
60 plus	82.8	–	51.7	57.3	17.2	–	48.3	42.7	–	–	–	8.4
Total	45.7	40.5	42.5	46.0	39.6	44.4	46.1	45.6	14.7	15.1	11.4	8.4

Source: Chuiko 1975:67.

TABLE 5.7

Age of Bride by Age of Groom: USSR, 1966–77

	Brides Younger than Grooms (as percent of all brides)					
Age of bride	1966	1967	1968	1969	1970	1971
Under 20	84.7	83.2	82.2	85.1	86.6	88.3
20–24	53.2	51.1	42.1	32.7	27.7	25.6
25–29	23.9	28.0	32.1	36.1	38.0	38.1
30–34	41.3	28.8	27.6	26.6	28.2	30.5
35–39	29.8	30.6	31.3	32.5	33.1	33.2
40–44	42.0	38.5	35.9	34.4	34.0	34.4
45–49	63.2	59.1	55.7	52.6	49.9	46.6
50 and over	–	–	–	–	–	–
All ages	53.1	47.0	46.3	44.5	43.1	43.0
	1972	1973	1974	1975	1976	1977
Under 20	88.6	89.3	88.8	88.6	87.3	87.1
20–24	26.1	26.1	26.9	27.1	26.8	26.3
25–29	34.7	31.1	29.0	27.8	26.2	27.2
30–34	33.8	38.3	42.5	44.7	47.0	40.5
35–39	32.4	31.9	31.5	33.2	31.9	38.6
40–44	35.2	36.7	38.3	39.7	39.8	38.8
45–49	43.7	40.9	37.2	37.5	37.0	38.2
50 and over	–	–	–	–	–	–
All ages	43.4	44.0	44.4	44.4	43.9	43.9

Brides Equal in Age to Grooms (as percent of all brides)

	1966	1967	1968	1969	1970	1971
Under 20	15.3	16.8	17.8	14.9	13.4	11.7
20–24	41.9	43.5	52.2	62.6	68.3	71.1
25–29	56.3	55.3	49.9	42.9	36.2	32.3
30–34	30.4	31.8	35.2	40.0	41.9	43.8
35–39	33.7	33.6	30.7	28.6	27.5	27.1
40–44	24.6	27.8	30.0	32.4	33.4	33.2
45–49	18.7	19.4	20.6	21.3	22.6	25.2
50 and over	96.7	96.0	95.1	95.0	94.2	93.5
All ages	34.2	41.2	42.4	45.6	47.8	48.6

	1972	1973	1974	1975	1976	1977
Under 20	11.4	10.7	11.2	11.4	12.7	12.9
20–24	70.9	71.0	70.2	70.1	70.4	70.7
25–29	33.8	36.4	40.9	43.8	45.4	45.1
30–34	42.0	38.0	32.4	27.6	25.3	26.5
35–39	29.2	32.7	36.5	38.1	39.4	37.5
40–44	32.3	31.2	28.0	27.0	26.9	28.4
45–49	27.7	31.3	32.3	33.6	34.1	33.0
50 and over	92.3	91.2	89.9	89.1	88.5	88.0
All ages	48.1	47.5	47.2	47.4	47.9	47.8

TABLE 5.7 (Continued)

	Brides Older than Grooms (as percent of all brides)					
Age of bride	1966	1967	1968	1969	1970	1971
Under 20	—	—	—	—	—	—
20–24	4.9	5.4	5.7	4.7	4.0	3.3
25–29	19.8	16.7	18.0	21.0	25.8	29.6
30–34	28.3	39.4	37.2	33.4	29.9	25.7
35–39	36.5	35.8	38.0	38.9	39.4	39.7
40–44	33.4	33.7	34.1	33.2	32.6	32.4
45–49	18.1	21.5	23.7	26.1	27.5	28.2
50 and over	3.3	4.0	4.8	5.0	5.7	6.4
All ages	12.7	11.8	11.3	9.9	9.1	8.4
	1972	1973	1974	1975·	1976	1977
Under 20	—	—	—	—	—	—
20–24	3.0	2.9	2.9	2.8	2.8	3.0
25–29	31.5	32.5	30.1	28.4	28.4	27.7
30–34	24.2	23.7	25.1	27.7	27.7	33.0
35–39	38.4	35.4	32.0	28.7	28.7	23.9
40–44	32.5	32.1	33.7	33.3	33.3	32.8
45–49	28.6	27.8	30.5	28.9	28.9	27.8
50 and over	7.6	8.8	10.0	10.9	11.5	12.0
All ages	8.5	8.5	8.4	8.2	8.2	8.3

Grooms Younger than Brides (as percent of all grooms)

Age of groom	1966	1967	1968	1969	1970	1971
Under 20	33.1	33.2	33.0	36.4	36.6	35.1
20–24	17.3	12.4	8.7	6.0	5.3	5.1
25–29	9.5	9.8	10.9	11.0	11.0	9.7
30–34	15.5	13.6	12.7	11.3	11.1	11.8
35–39	15.0	16.3	17.6	17.5	16.8	15.8
40–44	10.6	11.9	13.3	14.3	15.4	16.8
45–49	10.3	12.6	11.6	11.1	12.0	11.8
50 and over	–	–	–	–	–	–
All ages	12.7	11.8	11.3	9.9	9.1	8.4

Age of groom	1972	1973	1974	1975	1976	1977
Under 20	33.0	32.6	31.0	29.8	28.2	28.0
20–24	5.7	6.2	6.4	6.4	6.2	6.3
25–29	8.0	6.6	5.8	5.5	5.9	6.3
30–34	13.0	14.3	16.0	15.6	14.7	12.2
35–39	14.8	13.6	13.3	13.1	14.5	15.7
40–44	17.9	18.5	19.6	18.8	18.8	17.5
45–49	12.9	13.3	14.4	15.4	17.1	12.8
50 and over	–	–	–	–	–	–
All ages	8.5	8.5	8.4	8.2	8.2	8.3

TABLE 5.7 (Continued)

Age of groom	Grooms Equal in Age to Brides (as percent of all grooms)					
	1966	1967	1968	1969	1970	1971
Under 20	66.9	66.8	67.0	63.6	63.4	64.9
20–24	46.3	50.5	54.0	59.2	60.6	60.4
25–29	31.9	28.4	24.4	20.2	17.5	16.4
30–34	24.8	24.8	26.4	28.3	28.7	29.2
35–39	31.9	31.0	27.6	25.2	23.0	22.5
40–44	29.7	30.7	31.5	31.8	31.0	29.5
45–49	22.3	23.2	25.0	26.2	27.1	29.2
50 and over	74.3	75.8	74.9	74.3	74.4	74.0
All ages	34.2	41.2	42.4	45.6	47.8	48.6

	1972	1973	1974	1975	1976	1977
Under 20	67.0	67.4	69.0	70.2	71.8	72.0
20–24	59.3	57.8	56.7	56.6	56.2	55.9
25–29	18.2	20.8	24.0	26.1	27.6	27.7
30–34	28.2	25.3	21.3	18.6	17.8	18.9
35–39	23.5	25.9	28.0	29.0	30.3	29.0
40–44	28.0	26.5	23.3	22.1	22.1	22.9
45–49	30.3	31.9	32.1	31.7	31.4	29.9
50 and over	74.5	74.1	74.8	74.5	75.8	76.0
All ages	48.1	47.5	47.2	47.4	47.9	47.8

Grooms Older than Brides (as percent of all grooms)

Age of groom	1966	1967	1968	1969	1970	1971
Under 20	—	—	—	—	—	—
20–24	36.1	37.1	37.3	34.8	34.1	34.5
25–29	58.6	61.8	64.7	68.8	71.5	73.9
30–34	59.7	61.6	60.9	60.4	60.2	59.0
35–39	53.1	52.7	54.8	57.3	60.2	61.7
40–44	59.7	57.4	55.2	53.9	53.6	53.7
45–49	67.4	64.2	63.4	62.7	60.9	59.0
50 and over	25.7	24.2	25.1	25.7	25.6	26.0
All ages	53.1	47.0	46.3	44.5	43.1	43.0

Age of groom	1972	1973	1974	1975	1976	1977
Under 20	—	—	—	—	—	—
20–24	35.2	36.0	36.9	37.0	37.6	37.8
25–29	73.8	72.6	70.2	68.4	66.5	66.0
30–34	58.8	60.4	62.7	65.8	67.5	68.9
35–39	61.7	60.5	58.7	57.9	55.2	55.3
40–44	54.1	55.0	57.1	59.1	59.1	59.6
45–49	56.8	54.8	53.5	52.9	51.5	51.3
50 and over	25.5	25.9	25.2	25.5	24.2	24.0
All ages	43.4	44.0	44.4	44.4	43.9	43.9

Sources: Vestnik statistiki 1967:94; 1970:96; 1971a:95; 1971b:89; 1973:88; 1974:89; 1975b:89; 1976:89; 1977:78; 1978:84; United Nations 1968:593.

167

TABLE 5.8

Age Homogamy of Couples Marrying: Union Republics and Years for which Information Is Available (percent)

	Bride and groom equal in age	Bride is younger than groom	Bride is older than groom	Total	N
Estonian SSR					
1959–68	41.6	42.3	16.1	100.0	10,000
1959–69	42.0	42.1	15.9	100.0	10,000
1968	40.9	44.2	14.9	100.0	11,858
1969	45.4	40.9	13.7	100.0	12,247
1970	46.8	40.4	12.8	100.0	12,373
Armenian SSR					
1959	36.6	54.4	9.0	100.0	21,775
1966	29.6	63.7	6.7	100.0	18,673
Ukrainian SSR					
1968	39.4	49.4	11.2	100.0	420,455
1969	42.3	47.8	9.9	100.0	461,551
1970	45.0	45.9	9.1	100.0	464,820
1971	46.2	45.5	8.3	100.0	507,039
Byelorussian SSR					
1969	46.3	43.1	10.6	100.0	79,270
1970	48.9	41.3	9.8	100.0	83,576
1971	50.1	40.6	9.3	100.0	85,405
1972	50.3	40.6	9.1	100.0	82,872
1973	49.5	41.5	9.0	100.0	87,615

Sources: Vardanian and Karavaeva 1968:56; Ts.S.U. ESSR 1969:22; 1970:24; 1971:36–37; unpublished data, United Nations.

Evidently what happened was that with the poor sex ratios after the war, men found they could marry women with various attractive traits who were older than they. In all likelihood many of the marriages between younger men and older women directly after the war involved financial gain or gain in status for men that would not have been available to them had sex ratios been more normal. Perhaps also in the aftermath of the war older women represented succor and nurturance. The pattern thus established has lingered on, and there continue to be a sizable proportion of marriages of this sort among the older ages, even when the sex ratio is now relatively equal. Demographic considerations aside, the prevalence of marriages between younger men and older women perhaps is evidence that to some extent the criteria used in mate-selection in the USSR have been affected by the greater participation of women in the economy and by the ideological underplaying of characteristics of women connected with youth, such as beauty. (The growth of the Soviet cosmetics industry in recent years may be reemphasizing youth as a desirable trait in a wife, however. Articles on cosmetics bear titles such as "Women Have Become Younger!" Velikanova 1971.)

The decline in the proportion of marriages between older women and younger men is observable in each of the separate regions of the USSR for which data are available. In Table 5.8 the proportions of marriages by the relative ages of brides and grooms are presented for Estonia, Armenia, the Ukraine, and Byelorussia. Not only is the decline in age-heterogamous marriages visible in all areas, but regional differences consistent with what is known concerning cultural traditions and the participation of women in the labor force also can be seen. Thus Estonia with larger proportions of women working has a larger proportion of marriages between older women and younger men; Armenia, with less female employment and cultural traditions that grooms be much older than their brides, has a smaller proportion of such marriages.

The overall tendency, as in many other countries of the world, is nonetheless toward greater and greater age homogamy in the Soviet population. The frequency of marriage of young men to older women indicated above implies some effect on age differences in marriage of Soviet ideology and practice concerning women, but the Soviet Union is still far from approaching a normal curve in the distribution of ages of brides and grooms.

6

INTERMARRIAGE BETWEEN
OCCUPATIONAL AND
EDUCATIONAL GROUPS

Soviet denial of a market structure to mate-selection in the USSR has been most vociferous in regard to marriages within and between social strata. Soviet society is claimed to be "open to social mobility and the possibility of establishing the most diverse ties, including marriage" (Kuznetsova 1973). As was seen in Chapter 1, to some extent marriage across class lines is seen as a way of equalizing the remaining inequalities in the Soviet Union. If marriages were concluded without regard to considerations other than love, presumably Cupid's wings would fly across any and all divisions of the society however defined, and there would be more or less random mating in regard to socioeconomic status.

Market theories of marriage in contrast predict that those of similar socioeconomic status will tend to marry each other, and that the majority of marriages will be homogamous in regard to occupational level and education as potential mates find their approximate level on the market in competition with others. Becker's economic analysis of mate-selection specifies this general hypothesis further by predicting that like will marry like in assortative mating primarily where the traits involved are not close substitutes in household production (Becker 1973; 1974).

Where marriages are not homogamous in socioeconomic status, it is thought that some sort of trade-off must occur. In particular it is predicted that females will tend to marry up, that hypergamy is more prevalent than hypogamy (Parkin 1971: 55; Glenn et al. 1974: 684). Underlying this last point is the assumption that couples derive their status principally from the occupation of the husband (Merton 1941; Davis 1941). Since women's status in this view depends on that of the men they marry, women are motivated to be upwardly mobile through marriage, and since men do not lose in status from marrying beneath them, they are willing to do so in return for desired personal characteristics (Elder 1969). This assumption has been challenged by Soviet sociologists on the grounds that the equalization of women's position in Soviet society and the extensive participation of women in the labor force outside the home have created conditions in which the status of a Soviet conjugal pair derives as much from the occupation of the wife as from that of the husband (Aimre and Titma 1971: 252-53). In this regard it is of note that empirical studies of status homogamy in the United States have tended to focus on social origins of females rather than on their current occupational standing (for example, see Rubin 1968; Glenn et al. 1974).

The present chapter examines the available data on patterns of marriage between class and occupational groups in the Soviet Union, then turns to homogamy in education and income, followed by a brief note on geographic propinquity in the USSR.

MARRIAGE BETWEEN SOCIAL CLASSES AND BETWEEN OCCUPATIONAL GROUPS

In official Soviet conceptions since the late 1930s a threefold structural division is claimed to exist in Soviet society consisting of the working class, collective-farm peasantry, and intelligentsia. The first two are nonantagonistic classes associated with different forms of socialist property—the working class with state property "belonging to the whole people," the peasantry with the "cooperative" property of particular collective farms. While these first two are defined in terms of their relationship to the ownership of the means of production, the intelligentsia is distinguished by its employment in "mental labor." In the last two decades those engaged in mental labor generally have been divided into intelligentsia proper (specialists with higher education) and ordinary white-collar employees. Obviously these are extremely broad categories whose significance in actual social life can be challenged (farmers working on state farms are considered part of the working class, not of the collective-farm peasantry, for example), and Soviet sociologists in recent years have been moving toward more sophisticated ways of viewing their country's social structure (Yanowitch and Fisher 1973; Dobson 1977; and others). They remain, however, the categories in which official statistics are reported, with the word "employees" generally used to refer to all white-collar workers of whatever level.

The 1970 census collected information on the numbers of families mixed according to social class as thus officially defined by Soviet ideology—that is, on the numbers of families whose members belong to more than one of the three official structural divisions of Soviet society: the collective farmers, workers, and employees. While such figures are not the same thing as the numbers of marriages between such official classes, they nonetheless establish what the maximum number of such marriages can possibly be. In Table 6.1 are presented the number of mixed families per 1,000 families in the USSR and the Union republics in urban and rural areas.

TABLE 6.1

Proportion of Families Mixed in Social Class (Collective-Farm Peasantry, Workers, Employees): USSR and Union Republics by Urban/Rural, 1970
(per 1,000 families)

	Total	Urban	Rural
USSR	296	320	262
Tadzhik SSR	345	340	349
Uzbek SSR	317	337	303
Armenian SSR	308	310	304
Estonian SSR	305	329	260
RSFSR	300	326	256
Georgian SSR	297	282	312
Ukrainian SSR	296	309	281
Turkmen SSR	293	309	276
Latvian SSR	289	331	221
Kazakh SSR	285	324	240
Azerbaidzhan SSR	280	279	280
Byelorussian SSR	275	329	235
Kirgiz SSR	272	312	244
Moldavian SSR	240	307	208
Lithuanian SSR	229	286	176

Source: Ts.S.U. 1974a:252–71.

Only 29.6 percent of all families in the USSR in 1970 had members from more than one class or, in other words, at the very least in about 70.4 percent of all conjugal pairs both husband and wife belonged to the same broad social group. In all likelihood most of the mixed families enumerated result from differences in class status between parents and children; the figures in the table must be highly affected by intergenerational mobility. Some two-thirds of families mixed in social class so defined in Nizhnyi Tagil in 1956-58 were found to be mixed because of differences in the class positions of parents and children rather than in the class positions of husbands and wives (Krupianskaia et al. 1974: 161). If one takes this observation concerning mixed families in Nizhnyi Tagil as representative of the entire country, then in an estimated 90 percent of all couples in the USSR husband and wife both belong to the collective-farm peasantry or both belong to the workers or both belong to the employees.

As can be seen from Table 6.1, there is relatively little variation between republics or, for that matter, between urban and rural areas concerning the proportions of all families mixed in class. Some tendency does seem to exist for urban areas to be more mixed than rural ones. This is as expected given that classes in rural areas tend to be more isolated from each other; workers on state farms or in rural enterprises are not likely to come in contact with collective farmers on kolkhozes.

To what extent do the three main classes differ in their tendencies to choose spouses from other social groups? Census data are available only on the number of people of a given social class living in families where there are only members of that class. Using this information and the total base population of a given class, the proportion of members of a social class who live only with people of their own broad category was computed. Since social classes may differ as to the extent to which their members are likely to live in families to begin with, and the proportion of each class living in families of all kinds is un-known, the total population of each social class was indirectly standardized on the basis of the tendency of the 1970 Soviet population as a whole to live in families. In other words, the total population of each social class was multiplied by .8996 (the proportion of the entire Soviet population living in families in 1970) to yield the expected number of the given social class living in families of all sorts, had the tendency of the social class to do so been the same as that of the Soviet population as a whole. Thus the proportions of manual workers living in families who live in all-worker families in 1970 for the USSR as a whole was 635 per 1,000 standard population: that is, if the tendency for workers to live in families is assumed to be the same as for the USSR population as a whole, 63.5 percent of workers who were living in families were living ex-clusively with other workers. The proportions so computed are presented for the 15 Union republics for urban and rural areas in Table 6.2.

These figures are not the same as the actual percentages of class homoga-mous marriages; rather they indicate the extent to which members of a given social class have contact with other classes in their immediate families. However, they do give a rough indication of the location and relative levels of such mixed marriages. Judging by the data in the table, marriages between classes seem to be more frequent among employees than among workers, and more frequent among workers than among collective farmers. In urban areas collective farmers seem more likely to be in such mixed marriages than do either employees or workers; in contrast, in rural areas they seem to marry their own almost exclusively. There would not appear to be very marked differences between republics nor any particular pattern to where geographically members of the three broad classes are more or less likely to intermarry, with the possible exception that in the most advanced areas urban collective farmers are almost all in mixed families.

These differences concerning the propensity to intermarry on the part of employees, workers, and collective farmers that are indicated by data on family composition can be taken only as a very rough depiction of actual Soviet mar-riage patterns. As already mentioned, the bulk of mixed families are mixed between parents and children rather than between spouses. The figures in Table 6.2 do correspond in very general terms to what is known more directly

TABLE 6.2

Proportion of Employees, Workers, and Collective Farmers Living in Families Homogeneous in Social Class: USSR and Union Republics by Urban/Rural, 1970

(Number of members of given social class living in homogeneous families per 1,000 standardized population of that class living in families*)

Union Republics	Total			Urban			Rural		
	Employees	Workers	Collective Farmers	Employees	Workers	Collective Farmers	Employees	Workers	Collective Farmers
USSR	470	635	707	505	617	211	383	682	740
RSFSR	472	640	684	494	608	118	379	705	728
Ukrainian SSR	480	600	690	514	628	288	310	532	724
Byelorussian SSR	475	631	714	509	590	102	372	675	746
Uzbek SSR	397	639	764	507	635	402	240	643	780
Kazakh SSR	447	710	719	485	632	158	383	790	761
Georgian SSR	538	632	714	612	654	294	314	601	733
Azerbaidzhan SSR	508	683	774	582	689	379	327	671	794
Lithuanian SSR	501	679	763	529	639	66	377	741	795
Moldavian SSR	513	602	786	558	610	333	399	592	811
Latvian SSR	477	609	684	493	583	149	396	670	723
Kirgiz SSR	449	690	804	512	664	229	363	713	832
Tadzhik SSR	365	580	728	479	651	288	193	470	746
Armenian SSR	489	680	709	541	669	222	281	702	745
Turkmen SSR	443	633	792	536	670	331	204	573	806
Estonian SSR	475	586	574	487	576	87	421	610	613

*Standardized on the basis of the proportion of the total USSR population living in families in 1970.
Sources: Ts.S.U. 1973b: table 2; 1974a: table 29.

TABLE 6.3

Homogeneity of Class Origin in Marriages, 1900–45: Former Soviet
Citizens Interviewed after World War II
(percent of respondents whose spouse is of the same class origin)

| | Respondent's social class origin | | |
Date of Marriage	Nonmanual	Manual	All Classes
1900–20	82 (77)	72 (98)	76 (175)
1921–30	74 (121)	76 (168)	75 (289)
1931–45	79 (158)	81 (156)	80 (314)
Totals	77 (356)	77 (422)	77 (778)

*Total number of respondents on the basis of which the percentage is computed.
Source: Inkeles and Bauer 1959: 196.

about marriages between classes in the USSR, however, and as such they point
up two characteristics of such marriages: the extent to which opportunity for
contact with other classes affects the rates of marriages between them, and a
certain frequency of marriage across the manual/nonmanual line when social
classes are so broadly defined. These patterns are discussed below on the basis
of data directly concerning marriage rather than family composition.

From evidence directly concerning marriage, it would seem that over the
long run, in terms of the class origin of spouses, there has not been much change
in the relative homogeneity of Soviet marriages. The Harvard Project data show
if anything an increase in homogamy in terms of social class origins through
World War II (Table 6.3). Data on the social origins of grooms and brides in
Kiev in 1970 do not permit an exact statement concerning the extent to which
newlyweds there tend to be of similar origins, but if anything there is a slight
tendency for grooms as a group to move up the social ladder through marriage.
On the average they were slightly more likely than brides (not necessarily their
own) to come from families of kolkhozniki and workers rather than from families of employees (Table 6.4).

Whatever the case regarding social origins of brides and grooms, the majority of marriages are homogamous in terms of the current class status of newlyweds themselves. In Table 6.5 are presented the social class membership of Kiev
grooms by that of their brides in 1970, and in Table 6.6 the ratio of actual to
expected numbers of couples by social class. As can be seen, most marriages
occur within the confines of one or another of the broad official structural divisions. Brides who are workers are particularly likely to marry only grooms who
are workers. Class homogeneous marriages are about half again more likely to
occur than if mate-selection were random with regard to social class. Newlyweds

TABLE 6.4

Social Class Origins of Brides and Grooms: Kiev, 1970
(percent)

	Grooms	Brides
From families of workers	41.1	38.3
From families of white-collar employees	36.7	41.9
From families of collective farmers	14.3	12.2
From socially mixed families	6.1	6:0
Unknown	1.8	1.6
Total	100.0	100.0
	N = 1,000	N = 1,000

Source: Chuiko 1975:93.

similarly have been found to choose their mates overwhelmingly within the confines of their broad class in a study of the Moskvaretskii region of Moscow: 90 percent of the brides of engineers and equivalent personnel there in 1965 were employees—that is, they also were engaged in nonmanual work (Sysenko 1971). Evidence from Nizhnyi Tagil and Orel shows that the proportion of marriages that cross broad class lines has decreased considerably since World War II (Filippov and Chetyrkin 1970; Spiridonov and Gilinskii 1977: 184-85).

A second frequent combination, however, is that of marriages of male manual workers to female white-collar employees. Fully 42.4 percent of all employee brides in Kiev in 1970 were marrying workers. Evidently this combination is quite common and the most prevalent of all heterogeneous ones. Thus in over 80 percent of all interclass marriages in Nizhnyi Tagil in 1956-58 the husband was a worker and the wife an employee (see Table 6.7). About the same figure applies to interclass marriages in the Kalmyk ASSR (Van'kaev 1976: 225). To a great extent the frequency of such marriages is to be explained simply by the greater concentration of women in white-collar jobs of one sort or another. As can be seen from the ratios of actual to expected numbers of couples, this combination is not as frequent as it would be were marriages contracted randomly without regard to social class. Much of the apparent crossing of the manual/nonmanual line in such marriages therefore must be discounted as the result of the sex distribution of occupations and consequent lessened opportunity to marry within one's social class for male workers, rather than of freedom of mate-selection from class boundaries.

Weddings in Kiev in 1970 between male workers and female employees were nonetheless more frequent than vice versa even when comparing ratios of

TABLE 6.5

Social Class of Bride by Social Class of Groom: Couples Marrying in Kiev, 1970 (percent)

Grooms	Brides							
	Employed		Students, persons changing work	Total	Employed		Students, persons changing work	Total
	Workers	White-collar employees			Workers	White-collar employees		
Employed								
Workers	72.3	42.4	25.4	49.7	53.9	34.6	11.5	100.0
White-collar employees	16.7	36.9	30.8	28.1	22.1	53.4	24.5	100.0
Students, those serving in the Soviet army, and persons changing work	11.0	20.7	43.8	22.2	18.0	37.8	44.2	100.0
Total	100.0	100.0	100.0	100.0	37.0	40.9	22.1	100.0
				N = 1000				N = 1000

Source: Chuiko 1975:93.

TABLE 6.6

Ratio of Actual Number of Couples by Social Class to Expected
Number if Couples Married at Random: Brides and Grooms
in Kiev, 1970

	Brides		
	Employed		Students, persons changing work
Grooms	Workers	White-collar employees	
Employed			
Workers	1.45	0.85	0.51
White-collar employees	0.59	1.31	1.10
Students, those serving in the Soviet army, and persons changing work	0.50	0.93	1.97

Source: Calculated on the basis of Chuiko 1975:93. (See Table 6.5.)

TABLE 6.7

Combinations of Social Classes among Couples Heterogeneous in
Class: Nizhnyi Tagil, 1956–58
(percent of all heterogeneous couples)

Social combinations		Natives of Nizhnyi Tagil	Migrants to Nizhnyi Tagil
Husband	Wife		
Worker	white-collar employee	80.8	52.2
White-collar employee	worker	2.1	6.5
Worker	intelligentsia	8.5	6.5
Intelligentsia	worker	4.3	13.1
Intelligentsia	employee	4.3	21.7
	Total	100.0	100.0
		(47)	(46)

Note: Included among workers are pensioners who formerly were workers and house-
wives who formerly were workers or are the wives of workers. Included among intelligentsia
also are students in higher and specialized secondary educational institutions.
Source: Krupianskaia et al. 1974: 160–62.

actual to expected numbers of marriages. The implication is that when marriages do cross the manual/nonmanual line, they tend to be hypogamous. As will be shortly discussed, however, most of these marriages are of couples who are only superficially intermarrying and are basically homogamous or hypergamous marriages in regard to most relevant characteristics.

Data from various studies that provide information on marriages already in existence for some time and that divide social classes into finer occupational groups show generally the patterns already outlined. Tables 6.8 and 6.9 show the extent of status homogamy within various occupational groups respectively among parents of a sample of graduating secondary-school students in 1966 and among parents of a sample of students in the third year of higher education in 1969 in the Estonian SSR.

The isolation of rural areas clearly supports class boundaries in marital choice: three-quarters of fathers in agriculture were married to mothers in agriculture, and two-thirds of mothers in agriculture were married to fathers in agriculture in both samples. While the percentage of members of the agricultural intelligentsia (Table 6.9) who were married to spouses in the same occupational group was not as great as among agricultural personnel generally, comparison of the ratio of actual to expected numbers of marriages shows an extremely high propensity to homogamy in this group. Evidently the combination of geographic isolation and social divisions produces a situation in which the rural intelligentsia is particularly likely to marry its own in spite of the odds against doing so.

The social homogeneity of husbands and wives in rural areas has been documented for other parts of the Soviet Union. There seem to be few cases in which the wife of a sovkhoz director, kolkhoz chairman, agronomist, or other member of the rural intelligentsia is employed as a simple worker or kolkhoz member (Wädekin 1971: 518-19). As studies in Krasnodar territory, Kalinin oblast, and the Tatar ASSR have shown, however, the spouses of sizable minorities of the upper strata in rural areas work at some sort of manual labor. Common laborers virtually all marry their own (see Table 6.10).

In a rare complete enumeration of all the families of a village, the writer Soloukhin, in describing his native village of Olepino in central Russia as of 1959, shows the extent to which marriages in the countryside take place between members of the same strata. The wives of the top three kolkhoz officials in his village of some 34 households were all white-collar workers: the wife of the kolkhoz chairman was a teacher, the wife of the leader of the field brigade was a saleswoman in the village shop, and the wife of the agronomist was the kolkhoz accountant. In the middle stratum combinations were accountant and teacher, tractor driver and head of the local medpunkt (medical unit with perhaps two nurses), tractor driver and housewife, storekeeper and bookkeeper, and former kolkhoz chairman and teacher. The remaining marriages were primarily between common kolkhozniki with a few mixed with members of the middle stratum (Soloukhin 1960; as discussed in Wädekin 1971: 519).

TABLE 6.8

Extent of Status Homogamy among Parents of a Sample of Graduating Secondary-School Students: Estonian SSR, 1966*

Occupation of father	Occupation of mother					
	0	1	2	3	4	5
0 parental occupation not stated	107[a] 29.8%[b] 40.2%[c]	76 21.2% 12.9%	19 5.3 18.6%	28 7.8 12.6%	37 10.3 11.2%	0 0.0 0.0%
1 agricultural personnel	34 6.8% 12.8	383 76.9 65.1	9 1.8 8.8	9 1.8 4.1	14 2.8 4.2	0 0.0 0.0
2 workers in enterprises with up to 50 workers	12 11.4% 4.5	18 17.1 3.1	24 22.9 23.5	16 15.2 7.2	17 16.2 5.2	1 0.9 5.0
3 workers in trade and public catering	8 7.9% 3.0	3 3.0 0.5	5 5.0 4.9	38 37.6 17.1	9 8.9 2.7	1 1.0 5.0
4 workers in enterprises with more than 50 workers	46 8.8% 17.3	49 9.4 8.3	25 4.8 24.5	57 11.0 25.7	200 38.5 60.6	3 0.6 15.0
5 technical intelligentsia (engineers)	5 5.6% 1.9	4 4.5 0.7	5 5.6 4.9	12 13.5 5.4	13 14.6 3.9	6 6.7 30.0
6 office employees in offices and institutions	29 8.8% 10.9	31 9.4 5.3	10 3.0 9.8	42 12.8 18.9	24 7.3 7.3	3 0.9 15.0

Occupation of mother → / Occupation of father ↓	6	7	8	9	10	11	Total
0 parental occupation not stated	51 / 14.2 / 12.9%	21 / 5.8 / 16.3%	12 / 3.3 / 11.0%	4 / 1.1 / 28.6%	0 / 0.0 / 0.0%	4 / 1.1 / 6.6%	359 / 100.0%
1 agricultural personnel	19 / 3.8 / 4.8	9 / 1.8 / 7.0	6 / 1.2 / 5.5	0 / 0.0 / 0.0	0 / 0.0 / 0.0	15 / 3.0 / 24.6	498 / 100.0%
2 workers in enterprises with up to 50 workers	7 / 6.7 / 1.8	1 / 0.9 / 0.8	3 / 2.9 / 2.8	0 / 0.0 / 0.0	0 / 0.0 / 0.0	6 / 5.7 / 9.8	105 / 100.0%
3 workers in trade and public catering	19 / 18.8 / 4.8	5 / 5.0 / 3.9	8 / 7.9 / 7.3	2 / 2.0 / 14.3	0 / 0.0 / 0.0	3 / 3.0 / 4.9	101 / 100.0%
4 workers in enterprises with more than 50 workers	78 / 15.0 / 19.7	37 / 7.1 / 28.7	10 / 1.9 / 9.2	1 / 0.2 / 7.1	0 / 0.0 / 0.0	14 / 2.7 / 23.0	520 / 100.0%
5 technical intelligentsia (engineers)	24 / 27.0 / 6.1	9 / 10.1 / 7.0	7 / 7.9 / 6.4	1 / 1.1 / 7.1	1 / 1.1 / 14.3	2 / 2.2 / 3.3	89 / 100.0%
6 office employees in offices and institutions	146 / 44.4 / 37.0	20 / 6.1 / 15.5	13 / 4.0 / 11.9	3 / 0.9 / 21.4	2 / 0.6 / 14.3	6 / 1.8 / 9.8	329 / 100.0%

TABLE 6.8 (Continued)

Occupation of father	Occupation of mother					
	0	1	2	3	4	5
7 medical personnel	1 / 3.1% / 0.4	1 / 3.1 / 0.2	1 / 3.1 / 1.0	2 / 6.3 / 0.9	1 / 3.1 / 0.3	1 / 3.1 / 5.0
8 intelligentsia in the humanities (teachers, journalists, etc.)	7 / 8.0% / 2.6	1 / 1.1 / 0.2	3 / 3.4 / 2.9	6 / 6.9 / 2.7	5 / 5.7 / 1.5	4 / 4.6 / 20.0
9 leaders in trade unions, soviets, and other organizations	1 / 2.9% / 0.4	3 / 8.6 / 0.5	0 / 0.0 / 0.0	5 / 14.3 / 2.3	4 / 11.4 / 1.2	0 / 0.0 / 0.0
10 scientific workers	7 / 21.2% / 2.6	1 / 3.0 / 0.2	0 / 0.0 / 0.0	1 / 3.0 / 0.5	1 / 3.0 / 0.3	1 / 3.0 / 5.0
11 occupations not in above categories	9 / 14.5% / 3.4	18 / 29.0 / 3.1	1 / 1.6 / 1.0	6 / 9.7 / 2.7	5 / 8.1 / 1.5	0 / 0.0 / 0.0
Total	266 / 100.0%	588 / 100.0%	102 / 100.0%	222 / 100.0%	330 / 100.0%	20 / 100.0%

Occupation of mother

Occupation of father	6	7	8	9	10	11	Total
7 medical personnel	5 15.6 / 1.3	17 53.1 / 13.2	2 6.3 / 1.8	0 0.0 / 0.0	1 3.1 / 7.1	0 0.0 / 0.0	32 100.0%
8 intelligentsia in the humanities (teachers, journalists, etc.)	20 23.0 / 5.1	4 4.6 / 3.1	35 40.2 / 32.1	0 0.0 / 0.0	1 1.1 / 7.1	1 1.1 / 1.6	87 100.0%
9 leaders in trade unions, soviets, and other organizations	14 40.0 / 3.5	0 0.0 / 0.0	5 14.3 / 4.6	2 5.7 / 14.3	1 2.9 / 7.1	0 0.0 / 0.0	35 100.0%
10 scientific workers	6 18.2 / 1.5	1 3.0 / 0.8	7 21.2 / 6.4	0 0.0 / 0.0	8 24.2 / 57.1	0 0.0 / 0.0	33 100.0%
11 occupations not in above categories	6 9.7 / 1.5	5 8.1 / 3.9	1 1.6 / 0.9	1 1.6 / 7.1	0 0.0 / 0.0	10 16.1 / 16.4	62 100.0%
Total	395 100.0%	129 100.0%	109 100.0%	14 100.0%	14 100.0%	61 100.0%	2,250

aNumber of marriages between fathers in a given category and mothers in given category.

bPercentage of fathers in given category married to mothers in given category.

cPercentage of mothers in given category married to fathers in given category.

*We have corrected a number of computational and typographical errors in the original table.

Source: Titma 1970:174–75. Translated in *Social Stratification and Mobility in the USSR*, edited by Murray Yanowitch and Wesley A. Fisher, © 1973 International Arts & Sciences Press, Inc., White Plains, NY. Used by permission.

TABLE 6.9

Occupational Homogamy of Parents of Students in the Third Year of Higher Education: Estonian SSR, 1969

Occupation of parents	N	Percent of men married to women of the same group	Percent of women married to men of the same group	Ratio of actual number to expected
Agricultural personnel	272	73.1	67.8	5.57
Members of the agricultural intelligentsia	11	15.7	34.4	14.99
Workers in small enterprises	23	15.6	39.6	8.23
Workers in large enterprises	103	32.2	52.0	4.96
Service personnel	17	37.8	11.1	7.54
Personnel in managerial apparatus	17	10.0	36.9	6.63
Intelligentsia in humanities	66	47.5	41.2	9.06
Technical intelligentsia	12	8.1	37.5	7.79
Medical personnel	15	57.7	22.4	10.54
Personnel in trade	10	43.5	6.6	8.19
Office employees	24	31.2	9.2	3.66
Others	8	17.8	6.8	4.56

Source: Aimre and Titma 1971.256.

TABLE 6.10

Proportion of Spouses Employed in Manual Labor in Three Rural
Areas of the USSR: Krasnodar Territory, Kalinin Oblast, and the
Tatar ASSR, 1967
(percent of total number of couples, by socio-occupational groups)

Socio-occupational groups	Krasnodar Territory	Kalinin Oblast	Tatar ASSR
Higher-level managerial personnel	48.4	25.0	46
Middle-level managerial personnel	49.9	50.9	65
Higher-level specialists	34.5	34.3	27
Middle-level specialists	61.7	58.3	51
Employees	60.1	60.5	54
Machine operators	79.8	60.0	85
Skilled and low-skilled workers and collective farmers	83.8	86.4	91
Common laborers	83.4	87.4	96

N's for total samples of areas surveyed = 1,482 (Krasnodar Territory), 1,275 (Kalinin
Oblast), 2,113 (Tatar ASSR).
Source: Arutiunian 1971:319, translated in Yanowitch and Fisher 1973:336.

The Estonian data show much the same patterns for the manual worker
group and white-collar employees demonstrated by the census data on families
and the Kiev study of newlyweds. Both the 1966 and the 1969 Estonian figures
indicate a high degree of in-marriage not only within the manual/nonmanual
groups but also within specific occupational categories. Thus in 1969 57.7 percent of fathers in medicine were married to mothers in medicine (22.4 percent
of mothers), and 47.5 percent of fathers in the humanities were married to
mothers in the humanities (41.2 percent of mothers). Such groups not only have
a high proportion homogamous, but they also are considerably more likely to
choose spouses within the occupational category than to be expected were
marriages random (see Table 6.9).

Again, where the manual/nonmanual line is crossed, it most often is done
hypogamously—that is, male manual workers tend to marry female employees
more than male employees tend to marry female manual workers. Aggregating
the figures for 1966, whereas 35 percent of male manual workers crossed the
manual/nonmanual line to acquire a wife, only 18 percent of male white-collar
employees crossed it in the opposite direction. In contrast, while only 19 percent of female manual workers married male white-collar employees, fully 28

percent of female white-collar employees found husbands among manual workers. Again much of this is to be explained by the sexual division of labor: 43 percent of the mothers in the sample were in white-collar jobs as compared to only 34 percent of the fathers. In other words, the opportunities for male manual workers to find wives among their own class are more limited than those for male white-collar employees.

Table 6.11 lists the most common combinations of occupational groups in husband-wife pairs in the 1969 Estonian study. The most frequent combinations, as just discussed, are homogamous ones. The second most frequent combinations in marriages are either hypogamous unions between worker husbands and women who are employed in the service sector (trade and so on) or are office employees, or hypergamous unions within the nonmanual class, such as those between manager husbands and office employee wives. Examination of the ratio of actual to expected numbers of marriages shows the point made above: the fairly large number of marriages between worker husbands and employee wives is due primarily to the greater availability of wives from among the white-collar group. The ratio of actual to expected marriages between male workers in large enterprises and female office employees, for example, is 1.25, or in other words such marriages do not exceed very much what would be expected on the basis of random marriage. In contrast, the hypergamous union within the nonmanual class between male managerial personnel and female office employees is 3.11 times as frequent as would be the case were marriages random.

Not only are the marriages between male manual workers and female employees to a large extent explicable by the sexual distribution of occupations, but many such marriages also are heterogeneous in social class in name only. Most of the male workers in such marriages are highly skilled; the higher the skill of a worker, the more he is likely to be married to an employee. Thus in machine-building industries in Leningrad in 1965, 16.1 percent of those doing skilled hand labor as compared to only 5.3 percent of unskilled manual laborers were married to employees (Table 6.12). A similar pattern is observable in a second study of the Leningrad machine-building industry in the same year (Table 6.13), in a study of a telephone plant in Pskov in 1967 (Table 6.14), and in a study of Moscow residents (Iankova 1979: 116).

Conversely, most of the female employees married to workers are in low-skilled jobs in trade or the service sector that are low paying and of little prestige in the USSR. In the 1969 Estonian study, where a manual worker's wife was employed in the service sector or trade she was likely to have less education than her husband, a lower income, and a less interesting job. Only where a worker's wife was an office employee did the marriage differ significantly from those among manual workers; among half the couples of this sort the education of the wife was greater than her husband's and the child-rearing values of the couples tended to differ from those of homogamous worker couples. On the other hand, where the worker's wife was an office employee, her earnings were typically only half those of her husband (Aimre and Titma 1971: 259-61. Similar findings

TABLE 6.11

Most Frequent Combinations of Occupations of Husbands and Wives: Parents of Students in the Third Year of Higher Education, Estonian SSR, 1969

Occupation of husband	Occupation of wife	N	Percentage		Ratio of actual number to expected
			Husbands	Wives	
Agricultural personnel	Agricultural personnel	272	73.1	67.8	5.57
Workers in large enterprises	Workers in large enterprises	103	32.2	52.0	4.96
Intelligentsia in humanities	Intelligentsia in humanities	66	47.5	41.2	9.06
Workers in large enterprises	Service personnel	48	15.0	31.4	2.99
Managerial personnel	Office employees	45	26.5	17.0	3.11
Technical intelligentsia	Office employees	43	29.2	16.5	3.43
Workers in large enterprises	Office employees	34	10.6	13.1	1.25
Intelligentsia in humanities	Office employees	30	21.6	11.5	2.53
Workers in large enterprises	Personnel in trade	28	8.7	18.4	1.65
Workers in small enterprises	Service personnel	26	17.7	17.0	3.53
Office employees	Office employees	24	31.2	9.2	3.66
Workers in small enterprises	Workers in small enterprises	23	15.6	39.6	8.23
Managerial personnel	Intelligentsia in humanities	23	13.5	25.0	2.58
Technical intelligentsia	Intelligentsia in humanities	22	15.0	13.7	2.85

Source: Aimre and Titma 1971:258.

TABLE 6.12

Employment Status of Wives (Husbands) Depending on Socio-Occupational Status of Respondents: Survey of Machine-Building Industry, Leningrad, 1965 (percent)

Groups of respondents	Workers	Personnel with secondary specialized education	Personnel with higher education	Employees	Students	House-wives	Total
Unskilled personnel in manual labor	66.4	8.1	5.3	5.3	—	14.9	100
Personnel in nonmanual labor of medium skills	65.2	13.7	6.6	7.0	3.1	4.4	100
Personnel in skilled, primarily manual labor, employed on machines and mechanisms	61.5	15.3	5.4	13.0	1.0	3.8	100
Personnel in skilled, primarily manual, hand labor	52.9	17.3	6.3	16.1	1.7	5.7	100
Highly skilled personnel combining manual and mental work	47.9	14.8	6.2	24.9	—	6.2	100
Personnel in skilled mental work	27.9	22.1	31.5	10.7	2.9	4.9	100
Personnel in highly skilled scientific and technical work	10.5	23.2	53.8	6.3	3.1	3.1	100
Organizers of production collectives (from foremen to enterprise executives)	25.7	17.4	27.9	17.8	1.7	9.5	100
Total	51.2	16.3	12.6	12.7	1.7	5.5	100

Number of respondents in all groups together is 2,000 to 2,500.
Source: Shkaratan 1970a:445, translated in Yanowitch and Fisher 1973:307.

TABLE 6.13

Occupation of Wife (Husband) by Occupation of Respondent: Manual Workers in Machine-Building Industry, Leningrad, 1965 (percent)

Occupation of respondent	Worker	Technician	Other personnel with secondary education	Engineer	Other personnel with higher education	White-collar employee in other categories	Student	House-wife	Total
Unskilled auxiliary worker	62.3	15.5	4.2	1.3	2.8	5.6	1.3	7.0	100.0
Machine-operator	57.9	7.0	8.2	3.5	2.9	15.9	1.1	3.5	100.0
Highly skilled machine-operator	57.2	8.4	9.1	3.0	2.4	14.5	1.8	3.6	100.0
Metal-worker, craftsman	50.3	9.5	8.5	3.5	2.1	18.3	2.1	5.7	100.0
Adjuster of automatic lines	53.6	6.9	16.3	2.3	4.6	16.3	0.0	0.0	100.0
Constructor-designer	13.2	14.6	13.3	37.7	8.1	8.1	2.0	3.0	100.0

Number of respondents is unknown, but presumably study is connected to that done by Shkaratan (Shkaratan 1970). N therefore is probably 2,000 to 2,500.

Source: Trufanov 1973:95.

TABLE 6.14

Employment Status of Wives (Husbands) Depending on Socio-Occupational Status of Respondents: Survey of an Automatic Telephone Station Plant, Pskov, 1967 (percent)

Groups of respondents	Collective farmers	Workers in agriculture	Unskilled workers in city or in workers' settlement	Skilled workers in city or workers' settlement	Employees without specialized education	Personnel with secondary specialized education	Personnel with higher specialized education	Others	Number of respondents
Unskilled personnel in manual labor	–	–	23.0	26.8	38.6	7.7	3.9	–	26
Personnel in nonmanual labor	–	–	13.2	51.0	5.6	22.7	7.5	–	53
Personnel in skilled, primarily manual, hand labor	–	–	10.2	45.7	9.8	21.6	8.5	4.2	166
Personnel in skilled manual labor, employed on machines and mechanisms	1.2	1.2	13.4	61.0	8.6	14.6	–	–	82
Personnel in skilled mental work, and scientific and technical work	2.4	–	–	23.8	19.0	28.6	23.8	2.4	42
Executives of labor collectives	–	–	–	27.3	9.1	27.3	36.3	–	11

Source: Shkaratan 1970a:446, translated in Yanowitch and Fisher 1973:309.

were made in a 1971 replication. See Aimre 1977.) Most of the marriages mixed in social class therefore must be dismissed as in fact homogeneous marriages.

Although the stratification systems of the USSR and the East European countries have many things in common with those of the West, there is evidence that the existence of a workers' state has occasioned even more of an overlap between the manual and nonmanual classes as regards income and prestige than exists in industrial societies that are not state socialist. Indeed, it has been argued that this traditional divide is no longer very relevant to a depiction of social reality in Eastern Europe (Parkin 1971). The evidence on marriage patterns indicates that while the manual/nonmanual divide is still very significant and most marriages occur on either side of it, there are ostensibly a considerable number of marriages—primarily hypogamous—that do cross this boundary. While marriage patterns superficially show a blurring of class lines, examination of those marriages that straddle the manual/nonmanual divide negates the initial impression of much mixing of unequal groups. Such marriages tend to be relatively homogeneous as regards income, prestige, and education of the spouses and to be caused to a great degree by the sexual distribution of occupations. Were it not for the fact that women are more likely than men to be in nonmanual jobs in the Soviet Union, there would be little marriage across class lines.

This is not to say that marriages across class lines can all be explained in this fashion. As will be seen, the pattern of hypogamy among the lower strata of Soviet society is observable to some extent in education and income as well as in class and occupation.

MARRIAGE BETWEEN EDUCATIONAL GROUPS

There is something of a contradiction in Soviet sociological writings between attitudes toward intermarriage between class and occupational groups and those toward intermarriage between persons who differ in their levels of education. Marriage between different classes is considered to be something positive, to be evidence of the blurring of class lines, and proof of the freedom of mate-selection under socialism. Marriage between different educational groups, however, is not so readily approved. Since social factors are supposed to be eliminated as determinants of mate-selection and psychological factors to become the principle considerations in choosing a spouse, people's interests and values and therefore their education can be expected to play a greater role in mate-selection than in other, nonsocialist, socioeconomic formations. Thus the expectation is that there will be considerable homogamy in education in Soviet society, and such homogamy is hailed as demonstrating freedom of mate-selection from social restrictions (Baranov 1971: 80). It is anticipated that with the raising and equalization of the educational levels of the population, the range of possible spouses for an individual will become broader (Shliapentokh 1970: 144).

Whether or not one accepts this argument in favor of the marriage of those similar to each other in educational level, the fact remains that educational homogamy in the USSR is very considerable. The overriding impression from the data presented below is that men and women of a given educational level tend very strongly to marry each other rather than partners from differing educational levels. To some extent this is explained by the large proportion of couples who meet while studying (see Chapter 2), but of course such homogamy is also part and parcel of continuing social stratification in the Soviet Union. In bureaucratic state socialist societies, educational credentials are of enormous significance in obtaining interesting jobs, income, and prestige. It has been argued that education is more of a distinguishing characteristic in terms of inequality than class position or occupation in Eastern Europe (Markiewicz-Lagneau 1969). It is thus arguable that the continuing presence of educational homogamy in the Soviet Union is even stronger evidence of sharp lines between strata than homogamy among occupational groups.

Most of the information available on educational level of spouses comes from surveys of couples in the population who have been married for some time. The only information on education of spouses at the time of marriage is that obtainable from the study of brides and grooms in Kiev in 1970. In Table 6.15 are presented the educational levels of Kiev grooms by the educational level of their brides; in Table 6.16 are presented the ratios of actual to expected numbers of couples by educational level.

The major impression gained is of educational homogamy. The tables also show that men with some amount of higher education when marrying outside their group tend to marry women with less education than they; that is, there is also a pattern of hypergamy as regards the more educated men. For men with lesser educational attainment the tables show there also is a pattern of hypogamy: on the lower educational levels, when men marry outside their group they tend to marry women with more education than they.

The available information on the education levels of Soviet couples who have remained together for long periods of time does not show as great a prevalence of hypogamy as among newlyweds, even for those couples where the husband has comparatively little education. Perhaps this is because of an observed tendency for divorce rates to be particularly high among Soviet couples where the wife's education is greater than her husband's (Kuznetsova 1973).

A study of 1,211 already existing families in Leningrad in 1968 found that 565 couples were equal in education, in 417 cases the husband's education was higher than that of his wife, and in only 229 cases was the wife's education greater than her husband's (see Table 6.17). Younger couples were more likely to demonstrate a hypogamous pattern, but the gap between husband and wife in terms of average difference in number of years of study was less than among older couples. It would seem that over the years there has been growing educational homogamy together with a more even distribution of couples where the wife or husband has slightly more education.

TABLE 6.15

Educational Homogamy among Brides and Grooms: Kiev, 1970

Grooms		Brides				
	Elementary	Incomplete secondary	General secondary and specialized secondary	Incomplete higher, higher	Unknown	Total
	(As percentage of brides with given educational level)					
Elementary	66.7	5.8	1.2	0.3	—	1.1
Incomplete secondary	—	27.5	13.9	2.7	—	11.1
General secondary and specialized secondary	—	53.6	63.2	32.0	35.3	52.6
Incomplete higher, higher	33.3	13.1	20.7	64.7	17.6	33.6
Unknown	—	—	1.0	0.3	47.1	1.6
Total	100.0	100.0	100.0	100.0	100.0	100.0 (1,000)
	(As percentage of grooms with given educational level)					
Elementary	14.3	28.6	50.0	7.1	—	100.0
Incomplete secondary	—	17.1	75.9	7.0	—	100.0
General secondary and specialized secondary	—	7.0	73.4	18.3	1.3	100.0
Incomplete higher, higher	0.3	2.7	37.8	58.3	0.9	100.0
Unknown	—	—	40.0	6.7	53.3	100.0
Total	0.2	6.8	61.2	30.0	1.8	100.0

Source: Chuiko 1975:95.

TABLE 6.16

Ratio of Actual Number of Couples by Education to Expected
Number if Couples Married at Random: Kiev, 1970

	Brides			
Grooms	Elementary	Incomplete secondary	General secondary and specialized secondary	Incomplete higher, higher
Elementary	60.64	5.27	1.09	.27
Incomplete secondary	0.00	2.48	1.25	.24
General secondary and specialized secondary	0.00	1.02	1.20	.61
Incomplete higher, higher	.99	.39	.62	1.93

Source: Calculated on basis of Chuiko 1975:94–95.

Of interest in this Leningrad study is the large average difference in education where the wife has more education among the group 40 to 44 years of age. This group was 17 to 21 as of the end of the war in 1945 and therefore experienced the low sex ratios and consequent abnormal marriage market situation of the postwar years. Although direct information is lacking, it seems likely that this age group and that 22 to 26 years of age in 1945 had a larger percentage of cases in which the wife's education was higher than that of the husband's due to the favorable postwar market situation for men. A larger proportion of marriages directly after the war in which the women were more educated than the men seems probable also in view of the greater proportion of wives older than husbands in the immediate postwar years (see Chapter 5), and the greater opportunities of women in comparison to men to continue their schooling during the war years.

Other studies show a predominance of homogamy similar to that found in this Leningrad study. In a study of the parents of 4,824 students in grades three to ten in Leningrad schools in 1967-68, 78 percent of couples were in jobs requiring similar levels of education (Vasil'eva 1973: 23). Homogamy in educational levels also has been shown to be the rule among fathers and mothers of graduating students of secondary schools of Novosibirsk oblast in 1962 (Table 6.18).

In Table 6.19 are presented the ratios of actual to expected numbers of couples by educational level for the parents of applicants to Novosibirsk State University in 1970. Again homogamy is the rule, and again particularly for those with very little education. Unlike the case of newlyweds in Kiev, however, hypergamy is the second most prevalent pattern for couples regardless of educational level. These are couples who have stayed together long enough to have children sufficiently successful to be applying to a university. It may well be that the lack of educational hypogamy observed here is to some extent an effect of the instability of hypogamous marriages in the USSR.

The general picture that emerges is that men and women of similar education tend most of all to marry each other; among the more educated groups men are more likely than women to marry persons with less education than they; and among the less educated groups there is a tendency for women to be more likely than men to marry persons with less education than they, but such hypogamous unions do not seem to be very stable in spite of official ideological support of education and careers for women.

TABLE 6.17

Relative Education of Spouses: Leningrad, 1968

	Relative education			
Ages of spouses	Equal education	Husband more	Wife more	Total
18–24	49.0	30.2	20.8	100.0
25–29	49.0	34.7	16.3	100.0
65+	45.2	50.0	4.8	100.0
All husband/wife pairs	46.7	34.4	18.9	100.0
	(565)	(417)	(229)	(1,211)
Age of spouse answering questionnaire	Average difference in education in years of study			
18–24	0	2.9	2.8	
30–34	0	3.9	3.6	
40–44	0	4.6	4.2	
50–54	0	5.1	3.8	
65+	0	5.5	2.5	

Source: Baranov 1971:80–81.

TABLE 6.18

Educational Homogamy of Fathers and Mothers of Graduating Secondary-School Students: Novosibirsk Oblast, 1962 (percent)

Education of father	Education of mother					
	To 7th grade	7th grade	8–9th grades	Middle general and middle special	Higher	Total
To the 7th grade	65.2	8.7	8.7	17.4	–	100
7th grade	22.2	44.5	33.3	–	–	100
8–9th grades	25.0	25.0	50.0	–	–	100
Middle general and middle special	6.1	3.0	15.2	60.5	15.2	100
Higher	2.2	4.4	–	31.1	62.3	100

N = 300 in all probability but taken from total survey sample of 2,489.
Source: Shubkin 1966:201.

TABLE 6.19

Ratio of Actual Number of Couples by Education to Expected Number if Couples Married at Random: Parents of Applicants to Novosibirsk State University in 1970

Education of fathers	Education of mothers				
	Primary or less	Incomplete secondary	Secondary general	Secondary specialized	Higher education
Primary or less	4.63	.92	.57	.30	.08
Incomplete secondary	1.27	1.71	.58	.57	.18
Secondary general	.67	1.33	2.50	.61	.22
Secondary specialized	.28	.92	1.05	1.40	.52
Higher education	.14	.21	.67	.81	1.88

Source: Calculated on basis of Liss 1971:140, translated in Yanowitch and Fisher 1973:278.

TABLE 6.20

Average Monthly Income of Bride by Average Monthly Income of Groom: Couples Marrying in Kiev, 1970 (percent)

Grooms	Brides					
	Less than 50 rubles	50–100 rubles	100–150 rubles	Higher than 150 rubles	Unknown	Total
Less than 50 rubles	37.1	11.2	5.6	11.8	8.7	13.4
50–100 rubles	7.7	18.1	11.1	5.9	13.0	14.4
100–150 rubles	39.2	46.7	51.7	52.9	34.8	46.1
Higher than 150 rubles	11.2	19.4	25.2	29.4	18.8	19.7
Unknown	4.8	4.6	6.4	0.0	24.7	6.4
Total	100.0	100.0	100.0	100.0	100.0	100.0 (1,000)
			Brides			
Less than 50 rubles	39.5	44.8	9.7	1.5	4.5	100.0
50–100 rubles	7.6	67.4	18.1	0.7	6.2	100.0
100–150 rubles	12.1	54.5	26.2	2.0	5.2	100.0
Higher than 150 rubles	8.1	52.9	29.9	2.5	6.6	100.0
Unknown	10.9	39.1	23.4	—	26.6	100.0
Total	14.3	53.7	23.4	1.7	6.9	100.0 (1,000)

Source: Chuiko 1975:88.

MARRIAGE BETWEEN INCOME GROUPS

It may be argued how important divisions by income are in the stratification of Soviet society in comparison to divisions by occupation, education, or political power.* It is of interest, however, to see to what extent husbands and wives are similar in their earnings in a land where women are largely self-sufficient and where economic considerations in marriage are claimed to be a thing of the past.

Very few data exist concerning the relative income of Soviet spouses. The Kiev study of newlyweds indicates patterns not very different from those regarding occupation and education (Tables 6.20 and 6.21). The most prevalent combination generally was where both groom and bride were earning the same income. In the highest income levels grooms were more likely than brides to marry persons with incomes lower than theirs, while on the lowest income levels brides were more likely than grooms to marry persons with lower incomes. These extremes of the scale are affected, however, by the fact that a number of brides with high incomes were marrying grooms who were still studying or who were serving in the Soviet army and were therefore receiving very low stipends or wages below 50 rubles per month. Thus of those brides who were earning more

---

*Almost no empirical information is available concerning political power in relation to marriage patterns in the USSR. A study of civic and political activity in the Urals has found that those more active in community affairs tend to be married (Kogan 1972: 50-52).

TABLE 6.21

Ratio of Actual Number of Couples by Average Monthly Income to Expected Number if Couples Married at Random: Couples Marrying in Kiev, 1970

Grooms	Less than 50 rubles	50–100 rubles	100–150 rubles	Higher than 150 rubles
Less than 50 rubles	2.77	0.84	0.42	0.88
50–100 rubles	0.53	1.26	0.77	0.41
100–150 rubles	0.85	1.01	1.12	1.15
Higher than 150 rubles	0.57	0.98	1.28	1.49

Source: Calculated on the basis of Chuiko 1975:88. (See Table 6.20.)

than 150 rubles, over two-thirds were marrying grooms with incomes less than theirs, but some proportion of such marriages fairly shortly will become either homogamous or hypergamous in income. Taking this into account, the general picture is similar to that for education with marriages tending to be homogamous, but where not, hypergamous among the upper ends and hypogamous on the lower ends of the social scale.

Among couples married for some time the husband's wages tend clearly to be higher than the wife's. It is claimed that in approximately 73 percent of urban families the husband's wages are higher than his wife's, in 20 percent they are equal, and in only 7 percent are they lower than his wife's (Vasil'eva 1973: 15). While it is unclear how accurate these figures are for the country as a whole, they are in accord with studies done of the relative wages of husbands and wives among the families of workers in industrial enterprises (Kharchev 1974b). Thus it would seem that whatever the case upon entrance into marriage, with time the man earns more.

In view of the fact that the Soviet Union throughout so much of its history has had a shortage economy, monetary income may play less of a role in mate-selection than actual material possessions and housing (in this regard, see the discussion of fictitious marriages in Chapter 2). The only information that exists on differences in material well-being other than in money income prior to marriage is from the Kiev study and concerns housing. In Table 6.22 are presented the types of living conditions of brides and grooms and the number of occupied rooms of the families in which these brides and grooms were living prior to their marriages in 1970.

Judging by the table, in terms of housing men as a group tend to marry up. The living conditions of brides prior to marriage are somewhat better than those of grooms. With the data available it is not possible to make a more complete statement regarding homogamy or heterogamy in housing conditions. Grooms are more likely to have been living in dormitories and the number of rooms available to their families tend to have been somewhat fewer than those available to the families of brides. To some extent the explanation for this is to be found in the greater migration of men into urban areas such as Kiev, but to some extent these differences probably reflect the cross-class patterns of marriage already seen in relation to occupation, education, and ruble income.

A NOTE ON GEOGRAPHIC PROPINQUITY

Patterns of marriage between strata are known to be supported in the West by patterns of geographic settlement (see, for example, Peach 1974). The patterns of marriage between Soviet strata so far described also are partially maintained by geographic patterns. Few data exist concerning the residences of husbands and wives prior to marriage, but those that are available show the expected: there is a high degree of residential homogamy in the USSR.

TABLE 6.22

Living Conditions of Brides and Grooms Prior to Marriage:
Kiev, 1970
(percent)

Type of housing	Grooms	Brides
In separate one-family apartment	40.4	43.5
In communal apartment	14.7	12.8
In own house	10.2	14.0
In dormitory	28.5	20.3
Rent living space in private apartment	3.2	7.1
Unknown	3.0	2.3
Total	100.0	100.0
	(1,000)	(1,000)
Number of occupied rooms of families in which brides and grooms lived prior to marriage		
One room	10.4	10.4
Two rooms	32.6	32.3
Three rooms	16.0	20.8
Four or more rooms	2.9	3.6
Rent living space in private apartments or live in dormitories	31.7	27.4
Unknown	6.4	5.5
Total	100.0	100.0
	(1,000)	(1,000)

Source: Chuiko 1975:90.

As indicated above, the isolation of rural areas promotes homogeneous marriages among the peasantry. Thus until the early 1960s in rural Byelorussia the majority of spouses were born in the same village; only since that time has there been something of a greater geographic spread. In a study of 2,474 weddings from 1955 to 1968 in six village Soviets of Byelorussia, fully 36.26 percent of all weddings were between residents of the same village and 24.01 percent between residents of neighboring villages within the same village Soviet. In 15.92 percent of the cases the spouses came from the same raion and in 9.80 percent of the cases from the same oblast. Very few marriages seem to occur beyond the borders of a given oblast: only 5.86 percent of the rural marriages took place between residents of different oblasts within the Byelorussian republic,

TABLE 6.23

Distribution of Grooms and Brides by Place of Residence Prior to
Marriage: Couples Marrying in Kiev, 1970
(percent)

Place of residence prior to marriage	Brides Marrying grooms from Kiev	Grooms marrying brides from Kiev
Kiev	82.5	82.8
Urban settlements of Kiev Oblast	1.3	1.8
Rural areas of Kiev Oblast	4.5	2.5
Cities of the Ukrainian SSR	5.0	4.3
Cities of the USSR except Ukrainian SSR	3.1	4.5
Rural areas of USSR	3.1	2.5
Foreigners	—	0.6
Unknown	0.5	1.0
Total	100.0*	100.0

Source: Chuiko 1975:96.

and only 7.80 percent between residents of different republics (Institut Ekonomiki A.N. BSSR 1972: 177).

Similarly, most urban marriages do not encompass a very large geographic
range. Of couples marrying in Kiev in 1970, over 82 percent of both brides and
grooms whose spouses were from Kiev were also from Kiev themselves. In Table
6.23 are presented the places of residence prior to marriage of such grooms and
brides. There does not seem to be much difference between men and women in
the geographic distribution of such future spouses, with the exception that
foreigners marrying residents of Kiev in 1970 were all men (on this point see
the discussion of intercitizenship marriages in Chapter 7).

Those marrying at younger ages tend to be more residentially homogamous. Thus 9.2 percent of grooms in Kiev aged 15 to 19 had lived in the same
apartment house and 12.3 percent on the same street as their brides, compared
to only 1.9 percent and 0.0 percent of grooms aged 30 to 34 (Chuiko 1975: 99).
As in other societies younger people who have lived so close together prior to
marriage tend to be from the lower strata of society: 8.8 percent of Kiev grooms
with incomplete secondary education had lived in the same apartment house as
their future brides, compared to only 4.6 percent of those with incomplete higher
education (Chuiko 1975: 101).

It seems probable that while residential segregation of socioeconomic
groups exists in Soviet cities, such segregation is less prevalent than in the West.
More information on residential patterns presumably would go a long way toward

explaining the relative frequency of status homogamy and heterogamy in Soviet marriages.

The observation of overall status homogamy in Soviet marriages, followed in frequency by patterns of hypogamy among the lower strata and hypergamy among the upper, is in accord with the observations made throughout this study concerning the relatively greater value of men than of women on the Soviet marriage market that lingers in spite of the recent normalization of sex ratios. It perhaps would make more sense, for example, to speak of male mobility through marriage in the Soviet case rather than of female mobility, insofar as the largest group upwardly mobile through marriage are male manual workers rather than any group of women. While it is true that much of the hypogamy observable among the lower strata is explicable in terms of the sexual distribution of occupations and educational attainment, some of it is not, and the fact remains that women at these levels prefer to marry beneath them rather than not to marry at all. If data were available on the statuses of brides and grooms directly after World War II, they presumably would indicate even greater frequency of hypogamy than do data from the 1960s and 1970s.

To speak of upward male mobility through marriage assumes that couples in the Soviet Union do indeed derive their status from the occupation of the wife as well as from that of the husband. No attitudinal studies have been done on the point so it is difficult to judge the validity of such an assumption. It should be noted that few studies of the effect of a wife's status on that of her husband have been done in the West either (Safilios-Rothschild 1976).

Many of the observations made in this chapter do not differ very much from those made concerning U.S. society. Thus the same patterns of overall homogamy with hypogamy more frequent at the lower levels and hypergamy more frequent at the upper levels can be observed in the educational attainment of spouses in the United States (Carter and Glick 1976: 112-16). A large proportion of U.S. women also move down across the manual/nonmanual line in marriage. (Most studies on this point deal with social origins of wives rather than with their current occupations; for example, see Glenn et al. 1974: 691-93.) There is thus reason to believe that as regards status homogamy also, a marriage market operates in the USSR along principles similar to those reigning elsewhere.

Status considerations are certainly very much a part of Soviet patterns of mate-selection. None of the available information on marriages between occupational, educational, and income groups lends much credence to the notion that Soviet society is especially "open to social mobility and the possibility of establishing the most diverse ties, including marriage" (Kuznetsova 1973). Rather there are fairly clear boundaries between strata that marriages do not typically cross.

7

ETHNIC INTERMARRIAGE

As an ideological matter, marriages between nationalities are viewed with favor in the USSR since they show the extent to which Soviet mate-selection is free of considerations other than romantic love. Party and government leaders point to a growth in the number of mixed marriages with pride and note that they "number in the millions" (for example, see Brezhnev 1973: 41). Marriages between the many nationalities of the USSR are officially seen as demonstrating the growing "coming together," "internationalization," and "merging" of the many ethnic groups of the USSR. Such marriages are considered to be a "natural consequence of the comprehensive strengthening of economic and cultural ties among the peoples of the USSR, of migration, and of the elimination of racial, ethnic, and religious barriers in the sphere of marital and family relationships" (Kholmogorov 1970: 82-83).

The freedom of the Soviet population to marry across ethnic lines is favorably compared with the situation existing in czarist Russia. Until the beginning of the twentieth century, the Russian empire lent legal support to religious prohibitions against marriages between persons of different faiths. Religious intermarriage was forbidden under Orthodox canon law unless the non-Orthodox converted. Beginning with Peter the Great's permission to the Swedish prisoners who remained in Siberia after the Northern War to marry Orthodox women without undergoing conversion (ukaz of June 23, 1721), the czarist government gradually extended the right of intermarriage but kept it highly circumscribed in the interests of Orthodoxy and Christianity. Marriage remained primarily a religious matter until 1917, however, and ethnic inter-marriage was consequently highly discouraged (for the history of intermarriage laws before 1917, see Shein 1907; Achylova 1968: 45-69). Soviet freedom to enter into mixed marriages is favorably compared with the situation existing in the capitalist West (for example, see Abramzon 1962: 23; Achylova 1966; Kharchev 1964: 191-92; Gantskaia and Terent'eva 1975: 458-59).

Not only are Soviet laws concerning marriage free of restrictions on the contraction of marriage between members of different nationalities, but governmental and party authorities also actively attempt to thwart those who try to prevent such interethnic marriages. From time to time the Soviet press castigates the parents or other relatives of those who want to enter into such marriages for trying to force their children to follow what are considered to be outmoded ideas of limiting the pool of eligibles to those within their own particular ethnic group. Thus *Komsomolskaia pravda* censured a young Central Asian for giving in to the pressure of his parents to give up his Russian bride and for essentially abandoning his loved one to fend for herself and her child (Albogachiev 1970).

The present chapter examines the extent to which the Soviet population has accepted the official approval of marriages between nationalities, first in attitudes and then in actual behavior. After an attempt to explain the variations in the tendencies of different ethnic groups to intermarry, the discussion turns to the prevalence of different combinations of nationalities in intermarriages. Finally, examination is made of the prevalence of marriages between citizens of the USSR and those of other countries.

POPULAR VALUES CONCERNING
ETHNIC INTERMARRIAGE

A strong majority of the Soviet population has adopted the official view and is favorably disposed toward interethnic marriages. In surveys done of Latvians in Latvia from 1964 to 1969, some 77.3 percent of those surveyed approved of mixed marriages, while only 3 percent objected to such marriages and 19.7 percent declined to state their opinions (N = approximately 9,321; Kholmogorov 1970: 101). Attitudes elsewhere in the country are similar. Research in 1967 at multinationally staffed enterprises in Uzbekistan found that 84.5 percent approved of mixed marriages, 8.5 percent objected, and 7 percent declined to state their opinion (cited in Kholmogorov 1970: 100; no sample given). High levels of approval also have been found among Tatars in the Tatar ASSR (Arutiunian 1968, 1969, 1972, 1973; Drobizheva 1971; Guboglo 1972) and in West Siberia (Tomilov 1972); among Byelorussians, Ukrainians, and Chuvash in their respective republics (Drobizheva 1969); among residents of the Kirgiz SSR (Ismailov 1972); among Russians in the Tatar ASSR (Arutiunian 1968, 1969, 1972, 1973) and in the rural settlements of the Moscow region (Arutiunian 1971, as translated in Yanowitch and Fisher 1973: 132-33). Although it is not possible to generalize to absolute levels of response from samples of émigrés, it is of note that the Harvard Project on the Soviet Social System also found high levels of

TABLE 7.1

Attitudes toward Interethnic Marriages by Level of Education:
Tatars and Russians in Three Cities of the Tatar ASSR, 1967
(percent attributing significance to nationality in marriage)

Education	Kazan		Menzelinsk		Al'met'evsk	
	Tatars	Russians	Tatars	Russians	Tatars	Russians
Up to 4 classes	13.7	11.8	8.0	11.0	24.0	15.0
10–11 classes	9.0	10.0	2.0	0.0	12.0	7.0

N = approximately 4,231 for Kazan, 878 for Menzelinsk, and 2,002 for Al'met'evsk.
Source: Arutiunian 1973:288.

approval of interethnic marriages among Russian and Ukrainian displaced persons after World War II (Inkeles and Bauer 1959: 353).*

To some extent such popular approval is the direct result of exposure to the ideology. Thus those with more education are more likely to approve of interethnic marriages (see Table 7.1). In the available surveys, men are generally more likely than women to take a favorable view of interethnic marriages. Soviet researchers ascribe this to the higher educational level of the men interviewed. In surveys done in the late 1960s, for example, 88.3 percent of Latvian men as opposed to 68.2 percent of Latvian women approved of interethnic marriages (N = approximately 9,321; Kholmogorov 1970: 101). In the rural Tatar ASSR 74 percent of Tatar men as opposed to 66 percent of Tatar women were found to "have a positive attitude toward family contacts with persons of different nationality," while among Russians in the same rural areas the corresponding figures were 81 percent for Russian men and 72 percent for Russian women (N = 2,300; Drobizheva 1971: 8; Arutiunian 1973: 287). Since women typically have less experience with the outside world and are less likely to improve their "general cultural level," they are less likely to be exposed to the official ideology and consequently less likely to approve of mixed marriages.

Some direct evidence of the effect of mass media and consequent exposure to the official ideology can be seen in Table 7.2, which presents the percentage of Russians and Tatars in the rural Tatar ASSR who in 1967 felt that nationality was important both in contacts at work and in the family. Those who rarely or

---

*When the marriage involves the friends or children of the respondent, approval of interethnic marriage is weaker; but even in regard to such marriages approval of interethnic ties is quite strong (Ismailov 1972: 87).

practically never read newspapers, listened to the radio, went to the movies, or read Soviet fiction were less likely to approve of interethnic marriages (see also Drobizheva 1971: 11).

Similar to this effect of the mass media on attitudes toward intermarriage is the effect of knowledge of a second Soviet language. Members of the non-Russian nationalities who read and speak Russian have more contact with members of other nationalities and are more exposed to internationalist attitudes as portrayed in the more general Russian-language press. Thus 98.2 percent of Byelorussians in the Byelorussian SSR surveyed in 1965-66 who read newspapers in Russian or in Russian and their own nationality language were favorably disposed to interethnic marriages, as compared to only 80.2 percent who read newspapers mostly in Byelorussian (N = approximately 350); corresponding percentages of 87.1 percent and 77.1 percent were found to be true of Ukrainians in the Ukrainian SSR (N = approximately 33; Drobizheva 1969: 78). A clear relationship between knowledge of Russian of Tatars in both rural and urban areas of the Tatar ASSR and positive attitudes toward intermarriage has been found (Table 7.3).

In surveys of the Tatar ASSR, the relationship between knowledge of Russian among Tatars and favorable attitudes toward ethnic intermarriage was found to be specified by type of education. While 69 percent of those speaking only Tatar among rural Tatars in their autonomous republic responded that "nationality makes no difference: the most important thing is the person's individual qualities," 74 percent of those Tatars who know Russian but who had graduated from a Tatar school, and fully 82 percent of those Tatars knowing

TABLE 7.2

Ethnic Orientations by Nationality and Exposure to Mass Media: Russians and Tatars in Rural Areas of the Tatar ASSR, 1967 (percent attributing significance to nationality in contacts at work and in the family)

Type of media exposure	Russians		Tatars	
	Regularly do so	Rarely or not at all	Regularly do so	Rarely or not at all
Read newspapers	2	3	1	5
Listen to the radio	2	3	2	4.8
Go to the movies	2	3	1	4
Read fiction	2	2.8	0.6	3.6

Total N = approximately 2,300.
Source: Arutiunian 1973:292–93.

TABLE 7.3

Knowledge of Russian and Attitudes toward Interethnic Marriages: Tatars in Tatar ASSR, 1967 (percent)

Question: Do you approve of marriages of Tatars to Russians? What would be your attitude if one of your nearest relatives (son, daughter, brother, or sister) made such a marriage?

Knowledge of languages	Regard such a marriage as undesirable	Would prefer a person of my nationality, but would not object to such a marriage	Nationality makes no difference; the most important thing is the person's individual qualities	Find it difficult to say	No answer	N
Tatars in the Rural Areas of the Tatar ASSR						
Tatar	10.4	14.9	69.4	3.2	2.1	1,220
Tatar and Russian	4.4	10.7	75.0	4.8	5.1	252
Russian	3.6	5.4	80.4	3.6	7.0	52
Tatars in the City of Kazan						
Do not know Tatar	9.37	6.25	74.99	6.25	n.a.	approx. 1,468
Only speak Tatar	9.77	13.53	63.15	6.77	n.a.	
Read and speak Tatar	10.07	19.46	59.73	6.71	n.a.	
Read, write, and speak Tatar fluently	13.06	11.23	69.22	4.03	n.a.	
Regard as native language:						
Tatar	12.15	12.81	65.24	5.67	n.a.	
Russian	3.03	10.10	70.70	2.02	n.a.	

n.a.: Not available.

Source: Guboglo 1972:31, 34; Arutiunian 1969:133.

Russian who had graduated from a Russian school so answered (N = 1,220, 241, and 61 persons respectively; Arutiunian 1969: 134). The relationship between knowledge of a second Soviet language and type of education has been shown to apply to Russians as well. While 9 percent of Russians trained in Russian-language schools in Kazan had a negative attitude toward ethnic intermarriage, only 2 percent of those who had received their training in bilingual schools in Kazan felt negatively toward such marriages (Drobizheva 1971: 9).

Those who are more involved with the religions of their nationalities are less likely to approve of mixed marriages. Ukrainian émigrés surveyed after the war were more likely to feel that nationality was important in marriage if they were members of the Ukrainian Autocephalous Church, that is, members of a church that was specifically bound up with Ukrainian nationalism (Inkeles and Bauer 1959: 361). Among rural Tatars in the Tatar ASSR, 15 percent of those who celebrate religious festivals had a negative attitude toward interethnic marriages, while only 6 percent of those who did not celebrate religious festivals or were indifferent to them had such negative attitudes (Drobizheva 1971: 12). While 14 percent and 9 percent of Tatar religious believers and Russian religious believers respectively felt negatively concerning mixed marriages, only 5.7 percent of both Tatar and Russian nonbelievers felt negatively toward such marriages (rural Tatar ASSR; Arutiunian 1973: 292, 294).

The greater involvement of religious believers with their nationality and consequent greater negative attitudes toward interethnic marriage is paralleled by the greater dislike of ethnic intermarriage on the part of the old. The young are better educated, typically have been more exposed to the media and consequently to the official ideology, and are generally more favorably disposed to interethnic marriages (see Table 7.4).

The young also are more idealistic regarding the nature of the social world, and to some extent their favorable disposition toward interethnic marriages is a result of such idealism. Soviet youth have been shown to have very high levels of aspirations and expectations that are often crashed upon transition from school into the labor force (Shubkin 1965; Yanowitch and Dodge 1969; and others). In this connection it is of interest to note that Russians in the rural areas of the Tatar ASSR who are entering the labor force for the first time, those aged 18 to 27, are actually less favorably disposed than others to interethnic marriages. Many of them desire to leave the countryside but have difficulty doing so, and many undergo a crisis upon entering the job market and shift their frustrations so as to view mixed marriages more negatively (Drobizheva 1971: 7). There is some evidence of a general relationship between the disappointment of expectations in Soviet society and a negative attitude toward ethnically mixed marriages; those who are downwardly mobile also are more likely to feel negatively regarding interethnic marriages (see Table 7.5).

Studies on the relationship between socioeconomic status and attitudes toward interethnic marriage show a more or less curvilinear relationship. While the data are not uniformly consistent, it does seem to be the case that the most disapproval of interethnic marriage can be found at the two extremes of the social scale. Unskilled laborers and collective farmers, on the one hand, and members of the intelligentsia, on the other, are most likely to disapprove of such marriages. Typically the most support for interethnic marriage is to be found among skilled workers in factories and on farms. In Table 7.6 are presented the available data on attitudes toward interethnic marriage by socioeconomic status and nationality. While no breakdown by socioeconomic status was made in a study of Tatars in West Siberia (Tomilov 1972), a breakdown by size of settlement for this group is included in this table. Since it can be assumed that the intelligentsia is much more concentrated in a large city such as Tomsk than in the smaller cities in the region, it seems reasonable to suppose that the breakdown by size of settlement more or less corresponds to a distribution by socioeconomic groups.

TABLE 7.4

Attitudes toward Interethnic Marriages by Age and Nationality: Available Studies

Age	Tatars		Russians	
(percent who have a negative attitude toward ethnically mixed marriages; rural population of the Tatar ASSR surveyed in 1967)				
16–17	1.3	(75)	4.6	(43)
18–27	5.3	(581)	10.3	(222)
28–34	7.1	(595)	3.4	(296)
35–49	11.6	(1065)	7.7	(558)
50–59	5.9	(542)	7.4	(202)
Over 60	20.8	(149)	6.3	(95)

Percent agreeing that "marriages that are mixed in terms of nationality are undesirable" or no definite opinion concerning this question

	Russians (men only)*	
Up to 30	3	(39)
31–35	3	(31)
36–40	2	(44)
41–50	14	(36)
51–60	20	(40)

*Men in rural villages in the Lukhovitskii district of Moscow Oblast, late 1960s.
Source: Arutiunian 1973:285; 1971:187, as translated in Yanowitch and Fisher 1973:133.

TABLE 7.5

Change in Social Status and Attitude toward Mixed Marriages:
Tatars in Rural Areas of Tatar ASSR, 1967
(percent who have a negative attitude toward ethnically mixed
marriages)

Type of work at time of entrance into labor force	Type of work at time of survey	
	Non-manual	Manual
Monmanual	6.9	9.4
Manual	7.4	7.8

N = approximately 2,000.
Source: Arutiunian 1973:300.

The more negative attitude of those far down in the social scale toward
ethnic intermarriage is not surprising given the lesser experience with the social
world that such people have, their lesser education, the lesser likelihood that
they know a second Soviet language, and so on. Of more interest is the fact that
the upper intelligentsia also tends to disfavor ethnic intermarriage. While knowledge of Russian affects the extent to which laborers will have negative attitudes
toward mixed marriages, it does not seem to have any effect on the extent to
which professionals will have such negative attitudes (Arutiunian 1969: 134-35).
Such greater negative attitudes toward mixed marriages on the part of the intelligentsia are not the result of a lack of knowledge of other nationalities; on the
contrary, members of the intelligentsia are more likely to have relatives who are
in mixed marriages or to be in mixed marriages themselves than are other members of the population (Arutiunian 1973: 295. See also below on intermarriage
behavior.) It would seem that members of the intelligentsia are more conscious
of their own heritage and know more about their nationality's language, literature, and culture, and in their voiced attitudes, if not necessarily behavior, are
more ready to preserve it. In this connection it would appear that at least some
of the impression gained by Western observers of nationality dissatisfaction in
the USSR is derived from the somewhat unrepresentative attitudes of those
people with whom Westerners are most likely to come into contact; the intelligentsia. The materials in Table 7.6 provide some support for the notion that, at
least as regards the matter under discussion, it is those groups within the Soviet
population that are located in the middle reaches of the social hierarchy who are
most likely to support the official ideology.
    An interesting point that emerges from the data in Tables 7.1 through 7.6
is that in general Russians tend to favor interethnic marriages more than do the

TABLE 7.6

Attitude toward Interethnic Marriages by Socioeconomic Status and Nationality: Available Studies

Social Group	Percent who "consider nationality most important in marriage"		Number and Source
	Russians	Ukrainians	
Intelligentsia	5 (372)	15 (176)	N = 1,117 Russians and 743 Ukrainians, former Soviet citizens referring to pre-World War II era.
White-collar workers	6 (353)	10 (199)	Source: Inkeles and Bauer 1959:353.
Skilled workers	7 (123)	19 (80)	
Ordinary workers	10 (180)	20 (175)	
Collective farmers	17 (89)	22 (113)	

Percent agreeing that "marriages that are mixed in terms of nationality are undesirable" or no definite opinion concerning this question

	Russians (men only)*	Number and Source
Intelligentsia	10	N = ? (total sample including women equals 401).
White-collar employees	0	*Men in rural villages in the Lukhovitskii district of Moscow Oblast late 1960s.
Machine operators and other skilled manual laborers	8	Source: Arutiunian 1971:186, as translated in Yanowitch and Fisher 1973:132.
Unskilled manual labor	18	

Attitude toward mixed marriages (percent)

	Latvians		
	Approve	Decline to state	Object
Government employees	68.5	30.8	0.7
Physicians	81.9	11.2	6.8
Teachers	78.9	18.1	2.0
Agronomists	82.4	14.6	3.0
Farm equipment operators	90.5	5.3	4.2
Workers	78.5	18.5	3.0
Livestock hands	83.5	16.3	0.2
Field hands	76.0	22.5	1.5
Total	77.3	19.7	3.0

N = 9,321 Latvians surveyed in the Latvian SSR from 1964 to 1969.
Source: Kholmogorov 1970:101.

Percent who "regard nationality as without significance in marriage"

	Russians		Tatars	
White-collar workers	65	64	52	58
Skilled manual laborers	71	61	70	61
Unskilled manual laborers	69	57	67	56

N = 4,231 in Kazan (first set of percentages) and 2,002 in Al'met'evsk (second set of percentages). Figures refer to urban population of Tatar ASSR.
Source: Drobizheva 1971.

TABLE 7.6 (Continued)

Social Group	Percent who "regard nationality as without significance in marriage"	Number and Source
	Tatars	
Professional and paraprofessional		N = approximately 2,000 rural Tatars surveyed in 1967 in the Tatar ASSR. *Sources:* Arutiunian 1969:135; Arutiunian 1973:297; Drobizheva 1971:13.
Top executives	68	
Professionals with higher education	68	
Middle-level management	78	
Paraprofessionals	63	
Clerical workers	71	
Farm machinery operators	79	
Skilled manual workers (excluding farm machinery operators)	74	
Unskilled workers and collective farmers		
Regular	74	
Seasonal	72	

	Percent "favorably disposed to inter-ethnic marriages"	
	Rural population of Chuvash ASSR (88 percent Chuvash)	Rural population of Tatar ASSR (mostly Tatars and 34.5 percent Russians)

Percent who "have positive attitudes toward mixed marriage"

Intelligentsia	75.9	69.9
White-collar employees	82.2	71.4
Machine operators	81.6	78.8
Skilled manual workers	88.1	73.8
Unskilled manual workers	76.9	71.9

N = 500 for Chuvash ASSR and 2,000 for Tatar ASSR (approximately; although the survey of the Tatar ASSR is presumably the same as in the survey above, there is no way of determining the precise N's involved). Surveys in 1965–67.
Source: Drobizheva 1969:77.

Geographic location (roughly corresponds to social group)	Tatars	
Tomsk (large city)	66.8	(1,133)
Kolpashevo (medium-sized city)	86.1	(144)
Small urban settlements	84.0	(206)
Rural locales	66.0	(1,479)

N = 2,962 Tatars in West Siberia surveyed in 1969–70.
Source: Tomilov 1972:93.

Percent approving or indifferent to interethnic marriage

Social group	In general	Regarding colleagues and friends	Regarding own children
Workers	79.6	73.2	72.5
Peasants	84.7	61.0	57.5

N = 750 workers of various nationalities in enterprises in Frunze, Kirgiz SSR, and unknown for peasants interviewed.
Source: Ismailov 1972:87.

members of other nationalities. Such also has been shown to be the case in Latvia where 94.5 percent of Russians in the Valmiera district as compared to 85.2 percent of Latvians approved interethnic marriages (N = 1,889. Survey in the late 1960s. Kholmogorov 1970: 102.) In part this is because Russians can afford to do so. As the largest nationality group in the USSR, interethnic marriage threatens the Russians less than it does other smaller groups in the country. Also, since Soviet culture in general is primarily Russian culture, the fact of an interethnic marriage does not mean as great a loss of national identity on the part of Russians as it does on the part of other nationalities. An indication that the latter is the case is the choice of nationality of children of mixed marriages upon receiving passports at age 16. Evidence from the various parts of the USSR shows that while in certain nationality regions there is a tendency for the children of mixed marriages to choose the local nationality over being listed as Russian on their passports, that nonetheless in combinations of third nationalities with Russian the choice of Russian nationality is considerably more likely (Terent'eva 1969: 20-30; 1974). Russians also may be more exposed to the official ideology concerning mixed marriages.

THE RELATION OF ATTITUDES REGARDING ETHNIC INTERMARRIAGE TO MARITAL BEHAVIOR

As in many areas of family behavior throughout the world, there are major discrepancies between Soviet attitudes toward intermarriage—overwhelmingly favorable as has been seen—and the actual behavior of the Soviet population. The same rift between attitudes and behavior concerning intermarriage has been shown to be true of the U.S. population (for example, see Landis 1960). Nonetheless students of Soviet nationalities often try to deduce ethnic attitudes and ethnic consciousness from Soviet rates of intermarriage. If only one had more information concerning the extent to which members of a given Soviet nationality marry members of other nationalities, so the argument goes, one could use that information as an indication of the extent to which that particular ethnic group is conscious of its own national identity and possesses an ideology of non-assimilation. The underlying hypothesis is that members of a nationality who wish to retain their national identity consciously seek out partners from their own group; that is, ethnic consciousness is held to lead to high rates of endogamy. Differing rates of endogamy then are taken to measure differing degrees of nationalism, with nationalities with high rates of intermarriage seen as accommodating themselves to the Soviet system, while nationalities with low rates of intermarriage are seen as resisting pressures to become part of the Soviet melting pot and as potential sources of dissent. One exponent of this view that nationalism can be measured by intermarriage is Richard Pipes in his introduction to the *Handbook of Major Soviet Nationalities* (Pipes 1975: 3).

The premise that ethnic consciousness leads to endogamy is questionable, however, since there are so many other factors that affect marital behavior. Studies of intermarriage in the United States have found such social and demographic factors as the opportunity structure in a given area for finding members of other nationalities to marry and the sex ratio, size, and geographic concentration of a group to be enormously important in determining rates of endogamy—generally more important than a group's ideology of assimilation or ethnic consciousness (see, for example, Cohen 1974; Abramson 1973; Barron 1972; Merton 1941; Heer 1974; and others). How do the nationalities of the USSR differ in their rates of in-marriage and how are such differences to be explained? Available data on ethnic endogamy and exogamy in the USSR are presented below followed by an attempt to explain the differences between nationalities in the extent of their intermarriage.

Soviet authorities have published little information concerning intermarriage in the postwar period. Marital status by nationality was collected in the 1959 and 1970 censuses but was not published cross-tabulated by nationality of spouse. The nationalities of bride and groom are recorded at the time of registration of a marriage in the ZAGS offices. Since 1960 some cities have been exceptions to this rule (Gantskaia and Terent'eva 1975: 463), but it is unclear to what extent the data obtainable from such records are then collected. Nationality does not appear to be routinely a part of statistical reports on marriages and divorces (Chuiko 1975: 20; Skachkova 1975: 56).

Not since the 1920s have official statistics on marriages by nationality of groom and bride been published in the USSR, with the one exception of the publication of such statistics for Estonia for 1965 and 1968 (Ts. S.U. ESSR 1970: 26). Sociological and ethnographic studies done in various areas of the Soviet Union have filled certain gaps in knowledge regarding mixed marriages (Evstigneev 1971; Shkaratan 1970b; Ter-Sarkisiants 1973; Kholmogorov 1970; and others), but there have been few such studies on the Union republic level, let alone the all-Union level. Certainly there have been very little data until now that allow comparison of the situation for the major nationalities in different republics.

It is possible, however, to approximate the experience of the Soviet population regarding ethnic intermarriage fairly closely by use of several methods. In Table 7.7 are presented the numbers of ethnically mixed families per 1,000 families by Union republic in 1959 and 1970. These numbers are not the same thing as the number of mixed marriages per 1,000 marriages, but they approximate this since in order for a family to be ethnically heterogeneous, a mixed marriage must have occurred at some point in time even though now there may not be present a conjugal pair whose nationalities differ. (Presumably the number of families mixed because of the adoption of a child of different nationality is small.) It also has been possible to calculate the number of ethnically mixed families per 1,000 families in 1970 for the autonomous republics and autonomous oblasts (Table 7.8).

TABLE 7.7

Proportion of Ethnically Mixed Families: USSR and Union
Republics, 1959 and 1970
(number of ethnically mixed families per 1000 families)

	1959			1970		
	Total	Urban	Rural	Total	Urban	Rural
USSR	102	151	58	135	175	79
Latvian SSR	158	213	92	210	254	139
Ukrainian SSR	150	263	58	197	296	78
Kazakh SSR	144	175	119	207	238	171
Moldavian SSR	135	269	94	179	344	100
Kirgiz SSR	123	181	92	149	241	106
Byelorussian SSR	110	237	56	166	292	73
Estonian SSR	100	142	51	136	171	72
Tadzhik SSR	94	167	55	132	223	65
Georgian SSR	90	164	37	100	159	43
Turkmen SSR	85	149	25	121	200	34
RSFSR	83	108	56	107	125	77
Uzbek SSR	82	147	47	109	184	57
Azerbaidzhan SSR	71	118	20	78	128	20
Lithuanian SSR	59	104	30	85	149	46
Armenian SSR	32	50	14	37	45	26

Sources: Isupov 1964:38; Ts.S.U. 1974a:272–303.

As can be seen from the tables, the proportion of ethnically mixed families
is quite small. There has been an increase over the years, but as of 1970 mixed
families were still less than 14 percent of the total number of families in the
USSR. The largest proportions of such families are to be found in Latvia, Kazakhstan, and the Ukraine. Percentages of mixed families rose in those areas from
about 15 percent to 20 percent between 1959 and 1970. The smallest proportion of such families is consistently to be found in Armenia (3.2 to 3.7 percent).
Urban areas consistently have more mixed families than do rural ones, with over
17 percent of all urban families and a little less than 8 percent of rural families
mixed. The cities of Moldavia, the Ukraine, Byelorussia, and Latvia have the
highest proportions of heterogeneous families with from 25.4 percent to 34.4
percent of all families mixed. The rural areas of Azerbaidzhan and Armenia are
particularly homogeneous with only 2.0 to 2.6 percent of all families mixed. In
general these figures are not terribly different from the estimate of about a 15
percent intermarriage rate made by the Harvard Project on the Soviet Social
System (Inkeles and Bauer 1959: 97). Clearly opportunity for contact with

TABLE 7.8

Proportion of Ethnically Mixed Families:
Autonomous Republics and Oblasts, 1970
(number of ethnically mixed families per 1,000 families)

	Total	Urban	Rural
RSFSR			
Bashkir ASSR	159	202	115
Buryat ASSR	82	112	56
Daghestan ASSR	86	166	39
Kabardin-Balkar ASSR	116	160	67
Kalmyk ASSR	92	98	89
Karelian ASSR	332	322	356
Komi ASSR	311	337	261
Mari ASSR	79	116	52
Mordovian ASSR	102	166	64
Severo-Ossetian ASSR	147	180	84
Tatar ASSR	78	110	41
Tuva ASSR	74	121	40
Udmurt ASSR	123	145	93
Chechen-Ingush ASSR	86	133	43
Chuvash ASSR	92	184	37
Yakut ASSR	168	209	101
Adygey ASSR	119	150	96
Gorno-Altay AO	108	123	103
Evrey (Jewish) AO	201	198	209
Karachay-Cherkess AO	116	152	96
Khakass AO	153	145	165
Uzbek SSR			
Karakalpak ASSR	120	190	79
Georgian SSR			
Abkhaz ASSR	179	258	110
Adzhar (Ajar) ASSR	112	195	34
Yugo-Ossetian AO	133	182	104
Azerbaidzhan SSR			
Nakhichevan ASSR	24	58	12
Nagorno-Karabakh ASSR	29	52	15
Tadzhik SSR			
Gorno-Badakhshan AO	23	45	19

Source: Ts.S.U. 1974a:304–79.

members of other nationalities plays a great role in determining these proportions; Armenia as the Union republic with the most homogeneous population has the most homogeneous families.

The situation is not very different in the autonomous republics and oblasts (Table 7.8). Only three of these areas have more than 20 percent of their families mixed: the Jewish autonomous oblast (Birobidzhan) and the Komi and Karelian autonomous republics. The Karelian ASSR has fully 33.2 percent mixed families and more such families in the countryside than in urban areas. Taking these exceptions into account, the overall impression nonetheless is that virtually nowhere in the USSR has blending of ethnic groups occurred on any great scale.

Evidence regarding the generally low level of intermarriage is not the same as evidence regarding what is happening to particular nationalities, however. Some nationalities may be eroding through intermarriage faster than others and so may be principally responsible for those mixed families that exist while other nationalities continue to marry endogamously. It therefore is necessary to examine indications as to the endogamy of specific national groups.

Although the 1959 and 1970 censuses did not publish data on intermarriage, the number of people of a given nationality living in families consisting of only members of that nationality is calculable for the main nationalities for 1970 in Union and autonomous republics and in autonomous oblasts and national okrugs (on the basis of Ts. S.U. 1974a: 272-379). Unfortunately one does not know the proportion of a given nationality living in families nor the number of families by nationality composed of husband-wife pairs, and for many nationalities it is unclear what base population is intended. While for the most part simply sloppy presentation of statistics is to blame, it is clear that at least some purposeful censoring—not altering—of the census data was done in this case. Thus the number of all-Russian families is given for the RSFSR, but the number of other single-nationality families is given only for "territory of principal residence" of the nationality without indication as to what that territory might be (Ts. S.U. 1974a: 274-75). As a result the number of all-Jewish families, to take the most glaring example, is given as 16,785. This is clearly an impossible figure for the RSFSR as a whole in view of the fact that 807,915 Jews were listed as residing in the RSFSR as of the same census (Ts. S.U. 1973a: 12), and yet one that does not square with that given for Jews residing in their official territory, Birobidzhan. Nonetheless, much of the data concerning the number of members of a given nationality living in homogeneous families is usable to approximate figures on intermarriage.

Using the census data on numbers of people of a given nationality living in families consisting of only that nationality for those ethnic groups where the territory referred to and thus the total base population of the nationality living and not living in families was known, the proportion of members of a nationality who live only with people of their own ethnic group was computed. Since, however, nationalities differ as to the extent to which their members are likely to live in families to begin with, and the proportion of each nationality living in families of all kinds is unknown, the total population of each nationality was indirectly standardized on the basis of the tendency of the Soviet population as a whole in 1970 to live in families. In other words, the total population of each nationality group was multiplied by .8996, the proportion of the entire Soviet population living in families in 1970, to yield the expected number of a given nationality living in families of all sorts, had the tendency of the nationality to do so been the same as that of the Soviet population as a whole. Thus the proportion of Russians living in families who lived in all-Russian families in 1970 for the USSR as a whole was 776 per 1,000 standardized population; that is, if the tendency for Russians to live in families is assumed to be the same as for the USSR population as a whole, 77.6 percent of Russians who were living in families were living exclusively with other Russians.

The proportions so computed are presented for the 15 Union republic nationalities within the confines of their respective republics, and outside of them where possible, in Table 7.9. While these figures are not the same as the actual percentages of mixed marriages, they indicate quite accurately the extent to which members of a given nationality have experience and contact with ethnic intermarriage in their immediate families. As can be seen from the diagonal in Table 7.9, the proportions of the major nationalities within their own republics who live in homogeneous families are very high. Armenians in the Armenian SSR are particularly likely to know only other Armenians in their families. Over 90 percent of Azeri in Azerbaidzhan and the Central Asian nationalities (Turkmen, Uzbeks, Kirgiz, Tadzhiks, Kazakhs) within their respective republics have contact only with members of their own ethnic group within their families. At the other end of the scale, more than a quarter of Latvians are not living in families consisting only of Latvians, while Estonians and Ukrainians also are more likely than other groups to live in mixed families. To some extent the size of these differences is attributable to those effects of differential fertility and propensity to live in families generally for which the standardization discussed above could only partially control. It is clear, however, that the overwhelming majority of each of the major nationalities in the confines of its own republic has intimate family experience only with its own kind.

Again the opportunity to meet members of other nationalities plays a great role in the extent to which people's family members are likely to be of the same nationality. Members of the major nationalities are more likely to be in mixed families outside the boundaries of their own republics where obviously the chances of meeting people from other ethnic groups are greater. They also are more likely to be in mixed families in urban areas both within their respective republics and outside of them than in rural areas for the same reason (see Table 7.9). The same point regarding mixed marriages as such has been made by a number of Soviet ethnographers (for example, see Ter-Sarkisiants 1973: 121).

To the extent that these proportions living in homogeneous families reflect rates of intermarriage, it does not seem—with perhaps the exception of the Latvians—that there is much erosion of ethnic identity through mixed marriage

TABLE 7.9

Proportion Living in Ethnically Homogeneous Families: 15 Union Republic Nationalities in the Various Republics by Urban/Rural, 1970

(number of members of given nationality living in ethnically homogeneous families per 1,000 standardized* population of that nationality living in families)

Nationality	Armenian SSR	Turkmen SSR	Uzbek SSR	Azerbaidzhan SSR	Kirgiz SSR	Tadzhik SSR	Kazakh SSR	Georgian SSR	Lithuanian SSR	Moldavian SSR	RSFSR	Byelorussian SSR	Ukrainian SSR	Estonian SSR	Latvian SSR
Armenians	941							803							
Turkmen		939													
Uzbeks		828	930	859											
Azeri	916			927	856	842		920							
Kirgiz					925	822									
Tadzhiks						912									
Kazakhs		889					911								
Georgians								890							
Lithuanians									843						509
Moldavians										835					
Russians	440	693	710	698	730	689	701	576	559	484	816	339	474	635	609
Byelorussians									352			802		333	411
Ukrainians					406					589		205	782	250	
Estonians														767	
Latvians															747

222

URBAN POPULATION

Nationality	Armenian SSR	Azerbaidzhan SSR	Georgian SSR	Uzbek SSR	Turkmen SSR	Kazakh SSR	Tadzhik SSR	RSFSR	Lithuanian SSR	Estonian SSR	Kirgiz SSR	Latvian SSR	Byelorussian SSR	Ukrainian SSR	Moldavian SSR
Armenians	920	830	711												
Azeri	641	865	741												
Georgians			836												
Uzbeks				835	764		681				836				
Turkmen					833										
Kazakhs					885	809									
Tadzhiks							808								
Russians	439	695	573	719	700	710	698	796	554	652	741	603	348	466	494
Lithuanians									782			391			
Estonians										748					
Kirgiz							727				745				
Latvians												704			
Byelorussians									343	322		325	675		
Ukrainians										252	308		203	673	
Moldavians															562

TABLE 7.9 (Continued)

RURAL POPULATION

Nationality	Turkmen SSR	Armenian SSR	Azerbaidzhan SSR	Uzbek SSR	Kirgiz SSR	Kazakh SSR	Tadzhik SSR	Georgian SSR	Lithuanian SSR	Moldavian SSR	Byelorussian SSR	Ukrainian SSR	RSFSR	Latvian SSR	Estonian SSR
Turkmen	988														
Armenians		977	931					919							
Azeri		946	970					960							
Uzbeks	905			958	868		887								
Kirgiz					955		838								
Kazakhs	895					948									
Tadzhiks							948								
Georgians								930							
Lithuanians									894					594	
Moldavians										892					
Byelorussians									401		877			557	439
Ukrainians					508					689	212	875			241
Russians	541	444	729	632	709	682	559	589	584	451	301	521	853	631	492
Latvians														793	
Estonians															790

*Standardized on the basis of the proportion of the total USSR population living in families in 1970.
Source: Ts.S.U. 1974a:274–303.

among the major nationalities. Interestingly, the same thing is true for the titular nationalities of the autonomous republics and autonomous oblasts as well. In Table 7.10 are presented the proportions of the chief nationalities of the ASSRs and AOs who are living in homogeneous families. While it might have been expected that the smaller nationalities would be blending with other parts of the population, almost none of these groups seems threatened by large proportions of their populations living in mixed families. The two main exceptions are the Karelians in the Karelian ASSR, 44.5 percent of whom live in mixed families, and the Jews in the Jewish autonomous oblast (Birobidzhan), 31.3 percent of whom live in mixed families. It would seem that on the whole the government structure of the USSR with its division into nationality regions supports the continuation of ethnically homogeneous families through making it more likely that members of the nationality will reside together, and by providing cultural and social institutions through which members of the nationality can meet.

As regards more direct evidence on intermarriage as such, Chuiko's study on marriages and divorces in the Ukraine (Chuiko 1975) does give limited information on the extent of weddings between members of different nationalities in the 14 non-Russian Union republics. Based on statistical reports from ZAGS registration offices for 1969, it gives information on the extent of endogamy among the titular nationalities of the 14 republics (excluding the RSFSR). The data are given in the form of an index of endogamy, developed by the Ukrainian demographer M. V. Ptukha, which measures the extent to which nationality is a factor in the choice of a marital partner. The index measures the degree to which people are attracted to spouses of their own nationality in comparison to the probability of such attraction occurring were members of that nationality to marry randomly, and is computed according to the following formula:

$$s = \frac{AT - CL}{CL(T-C)(T-L)}$$

where L = the number of grooms of the titular nationality of the republic
  C = the number of brides of the titular nationality of the republic
  A = the factual number of marriages concluded between grooms from L and brides from C
  T = the total number of marriages of all sorts within the republic

This index varies from +1 (complete attraction or endogamy) to 0 (nationality is not a factor in marital choice) to -1 (complete repulsion or exogamy).*

---

*The rationale behind the index is as follows: the probability that a man will find himself a bride from the universe of C is equal to C/T, while the probability that a woman will find herself a groom from the universe L is equal to L/T. The probability that a bride and

In Table 7.11 are presented the indexes of endogamy expressed in percentage terms for each of the 14 nationalities within the confines of their own republics in 1969. Were nationality to play no role in marital choice—that is, were a single Soviet nationality to prevail as desired by the Soviet authorities—the index of endogamy for all 14 nationalities would approximate zero. As can be seen, however, such is far from the case. In all 14 nationalities there is a positive tendency to choose members of one's own nationality more than would be expected at random. Indeed, in the case of the Kirgiz the strength of endogamous behavior is almost total. In general the highest indexes of endogamy may be observed among the peoples of Central Asia. In second place are the peoples of the Caucasus with the exception of Armenia. For the peoples of the Baltic republics, rather high indicators of endogamy also are characteristic.

From the standpoint of current understanding of the extent to which nationality is a factor in marital choice, such an index is preferable to percentages of individuals marrying endogamously or percentages of marriages that are endogamous since it takes into account the opportunity to intermarry in a given region. From the standpoint of understanding to what extent a given nationality is eroding through intermarriage, however, percentages are more useful since it is possible to have a high preference for members of one's own nationality in the face of tremendous odds against that and still have a high percentage of people marrying out of the nationality. Neither the intermarriage rates as ordinarily reported in percentages for individuals and couples nor the raw data from which to compute them are provided by the Soviet source, and unfortunately there is no way to derive them from the above formula. With the help of two assumptions, however, it is possible to approximate them quite closely. Assume that the proportion of brides and grooms of a given nationality to all those marrying within a republic is approximately equal to the proportion of adults aged 16 to 59 of that nationality to all adults of all nationalities within that republic (call this proportion W); further assume that the number of grooms of the nationality approximately equals the number of brides of that nationality:

---

groom who are of the same nationality will marry each other equals $C/T \times L/T$ and the theoretical number of marriages equals $C/T \times L/T \times T$, or $C \times L/T$. This theoretical number of marriages is compared with the actual number of marriages A. The difference between these figures gives the extent to which nationality is taken into account in marital choice but does not yet give a quantitative characterization of attraction or repulsion insofar as it is an absolute figure and therefore has different weights for different universes of marriages T. Relative indicators are therefore computed that can serve as an indication of attraction. For this purpose the numerator is the difference between the factual and the theoretical number of marriages, and the denominator for men is $L - CL/T$ and for women $C - CL/T$. For both sexes the geometric mean of these two indicators is taken, yielding the formula in the text:

$$s = \sqrt{\frac{AT-CL}{L(T-C)} \cdot \frac{AT-CL}{C(T-L)}} = \frac{AT-CL}{\sqrt{CL(T-C) \cdot (T-L)}}$$

TABLE 7.10

Proportion Living in Ethnically Homogeneous Families: Titular
Nationalities of Autonomous Republics and Autonomous Oblasts
for which Data are Available, within Their Respective
Territories, 1970
(number of members of given nationality living in ethnically homogeneous families per 1,000 standardized* population of that
nationality living in families)

ASSR or AO and nationality		ASSR or AO and nationality	
RSFSR		RSFSR (continued)	
Bashkir ASSR		Chechen-Ingush ASSR	
Bashkirs	781	Chechens	.941
Buryat ASSR		Chuvash ASSR	
Buryats	902	Chuvash	871
Daghestan ASSR		Yakut ASSR	
Avars	884	Yakuts	831
Dargins	901	Adygey AO	
Kumyks	867	Adygey	884
Lezgins	843	Gorno-Altay AO	
Kabardin-Balkar ASSR		Altays	832
Kabardins	898	Evrey (Jewish) AO	
Balkars	858	Jews	687
Kalmyk ASSR		Karachay-Cherkass AO	
Kalmyks	905	Karachay	916
Karelian ASSR		Cherkass	757
Karelians	555	Khakass AO	
Komi ASSR		Khakass	780
Komi	721		
Mari ASSR		Uzbek SSR	
Mari	869		
Mordovian ASSR		Karakalpak ASSR	
Mordvins	817	Karakalpaks	884
Severo-Ossetian ASSR			
Ossetins	861	Georgian SSR	
Tatar ASSR			
Tatars	885	Abkhaz ASSR	
Tuva ASSR		Abkhazi	814
Tuvan	916	Yugo-Ossetian AO	
Udmurt ASSR		Ossetians	874
Udmurts	818		

*Standardized on the basis of the proportion of the total USSR population living in
families in 1970.
Source: Ts.S.U. 1974a:304–79.

227

TABLE 7.11

Nationality Endogamy in Marriages: 14 Titular Nationalities of the Non-Russian Union Republics within the Confines of Their Republics, 1969

Nationality	Index of endogamy*	Percent of individuals endogamous	Percent individuals intermarrying	Percent couples endogamous	Percent mixed couples
Kirgiz	95.4	97.0	3.0	94.3	5.7
Kazakhs	93.6	95.2	4.8	90.9	9.1
Turkmens	90.7	96.1	3.9	92.5	7.5
Azeri	89.8	96.8	3.2	93.7	6.3
Uzbeks	86.2	94.3	5.7	89.2	10.8
Georgians	80.5	93.5	6.5	87.9	12.1
Estonians	78.8	92.4	7.6	85.9	14.1
Tadzhiks	77.3	88.9	11.1	79.9	20.1
Lithuanians	68.2	93.1	6.9	87.0	13.0
Moldavians	62.0	85.4	14.6	74.6	25.4
Latvians	61.4	81.7	18.3	69.0	31.0
Byelorussians	39.0	87.1	12.9	77.2	22.8
Ukrainians	34.3	82.5	17.5	70.2	29.8
Armenians	33.4	92.7	7.3	86.5	13.5

*Chuiko 1975:76. See text for calculation of figures in other columns.

i.e., $\dfrac{C+L}{2T} \approx W$

and $\quad C \approx L$

then $\quad C \approx TW$

and $\quad A = \dfrac{Cs(T\text{-}C) + C^2}{T}$

$$\dfrac{TWs(T\text{-}TW) + T^2W^2}{T}$$

$$= TW(s\text{-}Ws+W)$$

It is possible to compute W on the basis of the 1970 census, and T is available from a separate publication (Ts. S.U. 1975a). The proportion of grooms (brides) of a given nationality marrying brides (grooms) of that same nationality then equals A/C, and the proportion of all couples involving a member of that nationality that are endogamous equals A/A + 2(C-A). The results of these computations are presented as percentages in Table 7.11. The estimates received by this method are presumably close to the actual percentages for 1969 since the assumptions on which they are based are not unreasonable, and the results square with the few other bits of knowledge that are available. Thus the estimated percentage of Estonians marrying other Estonians in 1969 equals 92.4 percent, while the actual percentage for 1968 equals 92.7 percent. (Calculated on the basis of Ts. S.U. ESSR 1970: 26. The figures for grooms and brides separately in 1968 are 92.4 percent and 92.9 percent, respectively.) The estimated percentage of Ukrainians marrying other Ukrainians in 1969 equals 82.5 percent, while the actual percentage for Ukrainian grooms is 83 percent (Boiarskii 1975: 244).

As can be seen from Table 7.11, nationality endogamy is overwhelmingly the rule among the 14 major nationalities. Presumably the reason the USSR has not published the percentages of individuals and couples who marry within their own nationality on such a countrywide basis is because these figures are so high. In terms of differences between the various nationalities, the Central Asian, Caucasian, and Baltic (with the exception of the Latvians) groups have particularly high rates of in-marriage. Whatever the propensity of a nationality to marry its own as measured by the index of endogamy, in no case (with perhaps the exception of the Latvians) does the continued existence of a nationality seem very threatened by intermarriage. At least as regards the 14 major Soviet nationalities, the strength of endogamy is quite impressive. In view of the general voiced approval of intermarriage (see above), there is a large gap between expressed ideals and behavior in this area.*

---

*There is evidence that even in labor camps "marriages" (not officially registered unions but considered by the prisoners as marriages) rarely cross ethnic lines (Solzhenitsyn 1975: 249).

This is not to say that there has been no increase in the extent of out-marriage of the major nationalities with time. In 1927 97.3 percent of Byelo-russian grooms and 95.1 percent of Byelorussian brides within their republic married other Byelorussians, as compared to an estimated 87.1 percent of such grooms and brides together in 1969. In the Ukrainian SSR 96.6 percent of Ukrainian grooms and 95.4 percent of Ukrainian brides married other Ukrainians in 1927, as compared to an estimated 82.5 percent of such grooms and brides together in 1969 (figures for 1927 calculated from Kommunisticheskaia Akademiia 1930: 41). It does not seem, however, that the percentage intermarrying for any of the principal nationalities is at present so high as to threaten erosion of these nationalities (again with the possible exception of the Latvians).

Causes of Nationality Variations in Endogamy Rates

How are the variations in endogamous behavior among the nationalities to be interpreted? If indeed endogamy is an indicator of nationalism, then one would have to say that while all 14 nationalities display ethnic consciousness, the Kirgiz are at the present time particularly nationalistic in comparison to, say, the Ukrainians. The problem is that there are a great many factors that can be seen to determine the differences in marital behavior among these various nationalities short of resorting to any explanation regarding ethnic conscious-ness. Below are a series of factors other than ethnic consciousness to be tested against the variations in the index of endogamy.

Size of Group

All other things being equal, a small group within a population will have to have strong norms of endogamy in order to preserve its own national identity. Where a nationality makes up a majority of the population the threat of people marrying out is not very great since on the basis of probability alone most mar-riages will be endogamous, and therefore the stress on such marrying within the group need not be as great. In other words, nationality need not be such a major factor to be considered in marital choice where partners have little opportunity to meet partners of other nationalities. One thus would expect that in those Union republics where the titular nationality makes up a large percentage of the population of the republic, the index of endogamy will be lower than for those nationalities that make up relatively small percentages of their republic. In deal-ing with the titular nationalities of the republics, one is in no instance dealing with a group that is so small that the possibility of marrying within the group is practically nil. Instead the opportunity for endogamy from a demographic stand-point is always there (this would not be so in a very small nationality). The opportunity for members of the nationality to meet also is there since all 14 nationalities have institutional resources at their disposal through which their members can become acquainted (again this is not necessarily so for the smaller nationalities). Depending on the extent to which there is a nonindigenous population, however, the threat of out-marriage may be sufficiently great so as to make a group that is a small percentage of its republic marry its own kind more than one would expect were marital behavior random. The first hypothesis to be tested is therefore:

1. Size of group X index of endogamy

   The smaller the percentage of its republic the titular nationality is, the higher its index of endogamy.

Sex Ratio

The worse the sex ratio in a given group, the more members of the disproportionately numerous sex are forced to look for partners within other groups. One would expect that those titular nationalities that have a deficit of males due to the effects of the war and other causes would be the nationalities with the least endogamy. The second hypothesis is therefore:

2. Sex ratio X index of endogamy

   The lower the ratio of males to females in a given nationality, the lower the index of endogamy for that nationality.

Percent Urban

Intermarriage is possible only if potential partners can meet. Thus endogamy is inversely correlated with the frequency of intergroup interaction. Another way of stating this is that geographic concentration of a group will lead to high rates of endogamy. It is clear that opportunities for meeting potential partners from other nationalities generally are greater in urban than in rural areas, since the frequency of interaction in cities and the ethnic mix in them is greater than in the countryside. One would expect that urban areas would have higher rates of out-marriage. The third hypothesis is therefore:

3. Percent urban X index of endogamy

   The more urban a given nationality, the lower its index of endogamy.

Bilingualism

When ethnic groups share a language in common, intermarriage among them is facilitated. Such a shared language may be either as a result of bilingualism or as a result of linguistic assimilation on the part of a given nationality. The fourth and fifth hypotheses are therefore:

4. Knowledge of a second Soviet language X index of endogamy

The greater the percentage of a nationality that speaks a second Soviet language in addition to its own native tongue, the lower the nationality's index of endogamy.

5. Native language X index of endogamy

The larger the proportion of a nationality that claims as its native language a language other than that characteristic of the nationality, the lower the nationality's index of endogamy.

Kin Control of Mating

Nationalities that traditionally have had mate selection systems in which kin controlled the transactions are less likely to have high rates of intermarriage than are nationalities that have well-developed self-selection romantic love systems. This is because third parties are less able to determine the presence of emotional attraction between a couple and are therefore more likely to be governed by external characteristics such as similarity of ethnic background. The main division among Soviet nationalities in this regard is between the Islamic and non-Islamic groups, with the former having greater kin control over mate selection. The sixth hypothesis is therefore:

6. Kin control X index of endogamy

Nationalities that traditionally have had much kin control over mate-selection are more likely to have high indexes of endogamy than those nationalities that traditionally have had self-selection systems.

Education

Those who are better educated are more likely to marry out of their own group than those who are less educated. Those who are highly educated typically meet in universities and higher educational institutions with people from other nationalities, and their values are likely to be universalistic. Studies in the United States have shown a small inverse relationship between education and endogamy (Abramson 1973; Cohen 1974; Laumann 1973 on homogeneity in ethnoreligious friendship). In addition, in the Soviet case those who are better educated also have been more thoroughly exposed to the ruling values of Soviet society, and it therefore can be predicted that those groups that are more highly educated also will tend to intermarry more. The seventh hypothesis is therefore:

7. Education X index of endogamy

The more educated a nationality, the lower its index of endogamy.

Existing Homogeneity of Families

There is evidence from studies in the United States that the endogamy of parents has an effect on the endogamy of their children (Cohen 1974: 121-26). That is to say, the children of intermarriages are more likely to intermarry than are the children of endogamous marriages. Presumably this is because those who are intermarried have less concern for maintaining their own ethnic identification; in part it is harder to express such identification in front of a spouse of differing nationality, in part there are competing identities. The opportunity structure is likely to be different for the children of mixed families from that for the children of homogeneous ones in the sense that they are likely to meet people of the opposite sex of more varying nationalities. One would expect that the general level of already existing endogamy of a group would affect its rate of endogamous marriage. Certainly persons who live in homogeneous families are likely to be surrounded by persons who are influencing them toward endogamy, and the extent to which a partner from another nationality will fit in with one's family to a great extent depends on the existing composition of one's family. As a general rule, it can be predicted that nationalities with primarily homogeneous families are less likely to have high rates of out-marriage than are groups that already have large numbers of mixed families. This leads to hypothesis eight:

8. Already existing homogeneity of families X index of endogamy

   The greater the percentage of ethnically homogeneous families within a nationality, the higher the index of endogamy for that nationality.

Methods

In order to test the above hypotheses, the variables were operationalized and correlated with the dependent variable, the index of endogamy for the titular nationalities within the borders of their own republics in 1969. The independent variables were operationalized as follows.

Size of Group

The size of a given nationality was taken to be the percentage of that nationality in the total population of the republic for which it is the main nationality according to the closest census to the year 1969, that of 1970 (Ts. S.U. 1973a: 12-15).

Sex Ratio

While ideally it would be desirable to have the sex ratios of the age groups from which brides and grooms in 1969 were drawn, it is not possible with any degree of accuracy to compute those ratios since the 1970 census does not provide sex ratios by age for individual nationalities. It therefore was necessary to use the number of males per 1,000 females of a given nationality within the confines of its republic (calculated on the basis of data in Ts. S.U. 1973a).

Percent Urban

It was not possible to compute the percent urban of a nationality by age. The percent urban of the total nationality, however, is available from the 1970 census and was used (Ts. S.U. 1973a).

Knowledge of a Second Soviet Language

This was taken to be simply the percentage of a given nationality within its own republic claiming to speak a second language of the peoples of the USSR, including in some cases the language of its own nationality and including Russian (as presented in tables in Katz et al. 1975, on the basis of the 1970 census).

Native Language

The percentage of a given nationality within its own republic that claimed as its native language in the 1970 census a language other than its own indigenous one was used (as presented in tables in Katz et al. 1975, on the basis of the 1970 census).

Kin Control of Mating

The basic division for present purposes is that between Moslem and non-Moslem nationalities. Following the procedure used by Mazur (1967), for statistical purposes this was made into a dummy variable with a value of one for cases where Islam was present as the main religion, and a value of zero for cases where it was not.

Already Existing Homogeneity of Families

It perhaps would be preferable to know the family background of those specific people who entered into endogamous marriages in 1969, but this information is not available. The closest indicator that can be computed is the percentage of members of a nationality within its republic who in 1970 were living in families where only members of that particular nationality were present. It therefore is a measure of how likely it is if you are a member of a given nationality that you will be living with or surrounded by persons only of your nationality (calculated on the basis of data in Ts. S.U. 1974a).

Educational Level

The number of members of the nationality within their republic with higher and complete and incomplete secondary school education per 1,000 population ten years of age and older, as given in the 1970 census, was used (Ts. S.U. 1973a).

The raw data for the correlations may be found in Table 7.12.

Results

Zero-sum correlations based on data for the 14 Soviet nationalities are presented in Table 7.13. As can be seen, each of the variables presented bears on the index of endogamy in the predicted direction. Particularly strongly correlated are religion, the percentage claiming as native language a language other than that of their nationality, and the proportion the nationality forms of its own republic. The smallest correlation to be observed is interestingly enough that between educational level and endogamy. While the direction of the correlation is as expected, the influence of education does not seem to be very great. This fits with what is known about intermarriage in other countries (Cohen 1974: 151-65). Despite the limitations of the data, the fact that all the correlations are in the predicted direction and generally of a fairly high order implies that differences in endogamy are determined to a great extent by factors other than ethnic consciousness or a sense of nationalism as such. Rather, such differences are primarily a result of the opportunity structure in different regions plus some sociological factors.

A multiple correlation of all eight variables with the index of endogamy shows that when taken together these factors seem to explain the bulk of all differences among the nationalities as regards endogamy. Adjusting for degrees of freedom, R^{-2} = .76957, or, in other words, these factors explain fully 77 percent of the variation in the index of endogamy. Only two of the variables included in the multiple correlation—kin control of mating and percentage claiming as native language a language other than that of their nationality—are significant at the .05 level, and in view of the small number of cases, any such multiple correlation must be viewed with caution. The remaining unexplained portion of the variation may be due to random factors, to settlement patterns within a given republic, or to the fact that it was not possible to operationalize all the variables discussed above in a fully satisfactory manner. No single one of the 14 nationalities is exceptional in the sense that its level of endogamy is significantly higher or lower than can be predicted on the basis of the variables included here. None of the residuals computed from the regression equation is particularly higher than one standard error of estimate. Thus there is little reason to suppose that any one particular nationality or group of nationalities is exceptional as regards the explanation of its endogamous behavior.

There is a certain amount of intercorrelation among the variables. The Islamic groups are groups with relatively high sex ratios and also rather high proportions of their populations living in unmixed families. To some extent both the high sex ratios and the high proportion of persons living in unmixed families are due to higher fertility. It therefore may be difficult to separate out precisely

TABLE 7.12

Correlates of Nationality Endogamy: Raw Data for Correlations

Nationality	Index of endogamy (Y)	Percent of republic (X_1)	Males per 1,000 females (X_2)	Percent urban (X_3)	Percent second Soviet language (X_4)	Percent other native language (X_5)	Religion (Kin control of mating) (X_6)	Higher and secondary education per 1,000 (X_7)	Percent living in nonmixed families (X_8)
Kirgiz	95.4	43.8	944	15	20.6	0.3	Islamic	407	92.4
Kazakhs	93.6	32.6	957	26	42.3	1.1	Islamic	403	91.6
Turkmens	90.7	65.6	987	32	15.3	0.7	Islamic	433	92.9
Azeri	89.8	73.8	979	41	16.4	1.1	Islamic	437	93.6
Uzbeks	86.2	65.5	984	23	15.4	1.1	Islamic	420	92.9
Georgians	80.5	66.8	895	43	20.8	0.6	Orthodox	578	88.6
Estonians	78.8	68.2	805	55	28.2	0.8	Protestant	462	77.9
Tadzhiks	77.3	56.2	1,010	26	22.6	0.6	Islamic	387	91.5
Lithuanians	68.2	80.1	881	46	35.5	0.5	Catholic	356	83.9
Moldavians	62.0	64.6	883	17	35.5	2.3	Orthodox	337	83.2
Latvians	61.4	56.8	805	52	45.6	1.9	Protestant	490	75.3
Byelorussians	39.0	81.0	830	37	56.7	9.9	Orthodox	401	80.4
Ukrainians	34.3	74.9	806	46	33.1	8.6	Orthodox	458	77.6
Armenians	33.4	88.6	959	63	24.5	0.2	Close to Orthodox	519	94.8

Sources: See text.

236

TABLE 7.13

Correlates of Nationality Endogamy: Zero-Order Correlation Coefficients

	X_1	X_2	X_3	X_4	X_5	X_6	X_7	X_8
X_1		-0.2423	0.6135	-0.0027	0.3160	-0.5660	0.1999	-0.1705
X_2			-0.4520	-0.6531	-0.5593	0.8145	-0.1567	0.9551
X_3				0.1462	0.0670	-0.6213	0.6193	-0.3552
X_4					0.6134	-0.5272	-0.2237	-0.6711
X_5						-0.3801	-0.1010	-0.5522
X_6							-0.2862	0.7252
X_7								0.0033
X_8								
Y	-0.6617	0.5327	-0.5255	-0.5161	-0.6535	0.7418	-0.1489	0.4853

Multiple correlation: $R^2 = .911373$ $\bar{R}^2 = .76957$

Standard error of estimate $= 10.5121$

$Y = 265.686 + .61439x_1 - .34987x_2 - .88716x_3 + .40968x_4 - 6.62631x_5 + 55.0508x_6 + .09406x_7 + .61475x_8$

T-ratio
(+3.206) (+1.003) (-1.774) (-1.647) (+.694) (-2.876) (+2.762) (+.942) (+.353)

Probability T-ratio
(.024) (.364) (.135) (.159) (.523) (.034) (.039) (.608) (.736)

237

how much effect a variable has in a given area. It seems safe to say that the populations of Central Asia with their greater kin control of mating also tend not to speak a second Soviet language, to be relatively rural, to be less educated, to have high sex ratios, to be smaller proportions of their republics, and that these factors—in particular the first two—in turn determine a relatively high rate of endogamy. That is to say, as a result of these factors these nationalities tend to choose their spouses from their own nationality much more greatly than one would expect on a random basis.

It is clear from the forgoing that most of the differences among Soviet nationalities in endogamy can be explained by sociodemographic factors. It would seem that nationalism or ethnic consciousness as such plays little role in explaining such differences. This is not to say that there is no relation between ethnic consciousness and marital behavior. It is possible, for example, that members of the various Soviet nationalities do marry out of a sense of ethnicity and that questions of nationality come up in the mate-selection process, but that Soviet nationalities do not differ in the extent to which this is likely to happen.

However, to a great extent ethnic consciousness and marital behavior are independent variables. To the extent that there is an association, it is more reasonable to suppose that endogamy leads to ethnic consciousness than that ethnic consciousness leads to endogamy. This direction of relationship is more likely since there are so many other factors that influence marital behavior besides simple ethnic consciousness. A relation between endogamy and ethnic consciousness as measured by attitudinal scales has been found for the United States, but the relationship is not particularly strong (Cohen 1974: 276). One must suppose that in both the USSR and the United States there is a tendency for endogamy to bring about a certain greater ethnic consciousness, but that people do not marry primarily out of a sense of ethnicity. It therefore is incorrect to suppose that one can take differences among the major nationalities of the USSR in their marital behavior as indicators of ethnic consciousness. Marital behavior is one of the factors determining or influencing ethnic consciousness, but in itself is not a particularly good indicator of such consciousness.

To the extent that the Soviet regime has provided the conditions for greater intermarriage, it has not done so directly. Given the extent to which sociodemographic factors determine rates of endogamy, it does not seem reasonable to suppose that any ideological push in favor of intermarriages or inculcation of a spirit of internationalism has had much effect. The varying rates of endogamy for the major Soviet nationalities are, however, the indirect result of the policies of the Soviet regime in the sense that by favoring urbanization and the migration of nationalities and by raising educational standards and increasing bilingualism, the regime also is indirectly fostering intermarriage.

A caveat is in order since the materials presented here concern only the major nationalities of the 14 Union republics. Each of these nationalities, by virtue of being the main nationality in its own area, has institutions through which members of the nationality can meet each other, and each is basically in the same cultural or political position. The situation of smaller nationalities within these republics may be somewhat different as may be the situation of those nationalities such as the Jews who do not really have a territory in any one part of the USSR.

The available data show rather high proportions of Jews intermarrying throughout the USSR. Table 7.14 shows those figures concerning the proportion of Jews living in all-Jewish families that can be calculated from the 1970 census (see above for method of computation). Table 7.15 presents all the available data on Jewish intermarriage collectable from various sources for different regions of the USSR in the postwar period. The percentage of Jewish individuals intermarrying varies from region to region but averages 30 to 40 percent of all Ashkenazic Jews marrying. Jewish men are more likely to intermarry than are Jewish women. At the same time the available evidence on the degree to which Jews marry within their own group in spite of great odds against doing so shows that the propensity of Jews to marry endogamously is very strong. Thus the index of endogamy for Jews in the Ukraine for 1969 was 66.3, higher than that for any other nationality group in the republic (the index for Ukrainians was 34.3; Russians 30.4; Byelorussians 7.3; Moldavians 44.3; Poles 21.1. Chuiko 1975: 73.)

While it may be that differences in Jewish endogamy from that of other nationalities result from discrimination by other Soviet citizens and/or from ethnic consciousness on the part of Jews as opposed to the sociodemographic factors discussed above, it is not possible to demonstrate that this is the case without more information on such factors as the residential patterns of Jews. Certainly many of the sociodemographic factors that have been examined for the major nationalities do affect the degree to which Soviet Jews intermarry.

TABLE 7.14

Proportion of Jews Living in All-Jewish Families: Areas for which Data are Available, by Urban/Rural, 1970
(number of Jews living in all-Jewish families per 1,000 standardized* population of Jews living in families)

	Total	Urban	Rural
Byelorussian SSR	768	777	303
Moldavian SSR	618	866	552
Jewish Autonomous Oblast (Birobidzhan)	687	701	560

*Standardized on the basis of the proportion of the total USSR population living in families in 1970.

Source: Ts.S.U. 1974a:282–83, 292–95, 340–41.

TABLE 7.15

Endogamous Marriages among Jews: Available Data, Postwar USSR (percent)

Region	Year	Current weddings			Couples in population			Source
			Per 100 Jewish			Per 100 Jewish		
		Per 100 couples	Grooms	Brides	Per 100 couples	Husbands	Wives	
Ukrainian SSR								
Total republic								
Urban	1959				89.7			Based on 5 percent sample in 1959 census. Naulko 1965:110.
Rural	1959				90.2			
Total republic	1969	49.8	66.8 (7,300 est.)	63.0				All marriages registered in the republic in course of year. Calculated on basis of index in Chuiko 1975:73; Boiarskii 1975:244.
Kharkov	1960	54.1 (897)	73.3 (662)	67.4 (720)				All marriages contracted in year. Kurman and Lebedinskii 1968:126–27.

Region / District	Year			Notes
Uzbek SSR				
Tashkent				
October District	1962	93.2	92.3 / 91.4	Based on analysis of 1,000 marriage certificates in region for all nationalities. District is primarily composed of Bukhara Jews. Khanazarov 1964:30.
Kuibyshev District	1962	63.9	66.3 / 68.9	Based on analysis of 1,000 marriage certificates in region for all nationalities. District is primarily composed of Ashkenazi Jews. Khanazarov 1964:30.
Lithuanian SSR				
Vilnius Novaya Vilna	1945–49	71.0	76.0	Marriages in district with total population circa 12.5 thousand. Newth 1968:68.
	1950–54	52.0	68.0	
	1955–59	77.0	92.0	
	1960–64	65.0	93.0	
Entire city	1960–68		Maximum of 81.4	Families of recipients of first passports. Calculated from Terent'eva 1969:20–30.

TABLE 7.15 (Continued)

Region	Year	Current weddings			Couples in population			Source
		Per 100 couples	Per 100 Jewish		Per 100 couples	Per 100 Jewish		
			Grooms	Brides		Husbands	Wives	
Estonian SSR								
Total republic	1965	26.0 (50)	37.1 (35)	46.4 (28)				All marriages registered in the republic in course of year. Calculated from Ts.S.U. ESSR 1970:26.
	1968	21.4 (70)	26.8 (56)	51.7 (29)				
Latvian SSR								
Total republic	1964–69					64.0 (164, both husbands and wives together)	65.2	Various surveys. Kholmogorov 1970:89.
Riga	1960–68	Maximum of 87.9						Families of recipients of first passport. Calculated from Terent'eva 1969: 20–30.
	1970	71.0	67.0	76.0				All marriages registered in year. Vitols 1972:34.

242

RSFSR

Dagestan ASSR					
Makhachkala	1959–68	56.7 (903)	72.5 (706)	72.2 (709)	All marriages recorded in city. Evstigneev 1971.
Kazakh SSR					
Kokchetav	1940–69			52.9	N's are a few hundred for each city. Evstigneev 1972:76–79.
Kustanai	1940–69			49.6	
Pavlodar	1940–69			48.1	
Tselinograd	1940–49			54.0	

243

Lack of opportunity to meet other Jews plays a great role in determining the high percentages of Jews out-marrying in such a region as the Estonian SSR, where the absolute number of Jews is small and they form a small proportion of the population. The fact that the majority of Jews are highly educated and speak Russian or another second Soviet language increases their opportunities for meeting members of other nationalities. Soviet Jewish intermarriage rates, moreover, are quite similar to those of Jews in the United States in recent years. It therefore would seem likely that ethnic consciousness plays no greater role in determining in-marriage among Soviet Jews than it does among other nationalities.

Whatever the case for Jews and other nonterritorial groups, however, it is clear that for the 14 major nationalities differences in endogamy are explicable in sociodemographic terms.

COMBINATIONS OF NATIONALITIES
IN ETHNICALLY MIXED MARRIAGES

The most prevalent combination of nationalities in Soviet mixed marriages is that between members of the titular nationality of a given area with Russians. The predominance of this combination is to be expected in view of the migration patterns of the population whereby most nationalities do not migrate to areas outside their own territory while Russians tend to disperse throughout the country (for discussion of migration patterns by nationality see Lewis et al. 1978). Thus over 32 percent of all mixed families in the Latvian and Estonian SSRs consist of Latvians with Russians and of Estonians with Russians, respectively. In the Armenian SSR 40 percent of all mixed families are composed of Armenians and Russians; in Azerbaidzhan 44 percent consist of Azeri and Russians; and in Georgia 26 percent are made up of Georgians and Russians. In Central Asia where Uzbeks constitute the chief nationality of the region as a whole, Uzbeks to some extent play the same role as Russians elsewhere, and marriages between the basic local nationality and Uzbeks come close to or exceed the number of marriages between Russians and the local nationality. Thus in the Turkmen SSR, Turkmen-Russian families constitute 11 percent of all interethnic families and Turkmen-Uzbek families comprise 8 percent of such mixed families. In the Tadzhik SSR, Tadzhik-Uzbek families actually exceed the number of Tadzhik-Russian families.

Since the basic local nationality is in almost all cases also the most numerous nationality in its own region, intermarriages of all sorts are most likely to be contracted with members of the basic local nationality. Thus 50 percent of mixed families in Latvia involve Latvians; 50 percent of mixed families in Estonia involve Estonians; 60 percent of mixed families in Lithuania involve Lithuanians; 50 percent of mixed families in Armenia involve Armenians; 60 percent of mixed families in Azerbaidzhan involve Azeri; approximately the same proportions of

60 percent of mixed families in Georgia involve Georgians; and some 30 to 40 percent of mixed families in Tadzhikistan and Turkmenistan involve Tadzhiks and Turkmen.

Another major variation is that of Russians with nationalities other than the basic local one. In a few republics, due to patterns of settlement, the main nationality of the region as a whole may substitute for Russians in this type of mixed family. In Tadzhikistan and Turkmenistan a common type of family is as a result that between Uzbeks and nationalities other than Tadzhiks and Turkmen. In Moldavia marriages between Ukrainians and nationalities other than Moldavians are similarly frequent. (The above figures are Soviet calculations on the basis of unpublished data of the 1970 census. Gantskaia and Terent'eva 1975: 465.)

In Table 7.16 are presented the percentages of these types of interethnic combinations in mixed marriages for capitals of seven of the Union republics and capitals of three of the autonomous republics in the RSFSR. The data are for the parents of recipients of first passports and therefore refer to marriages that have lasted at least long enough to have a child. The distribution of combinations in the table is not quite the same as that prevailing on entrance into marriage, but it seems likely that the combinations depicted are fairly close to those in current weddings since the data are similar to what is known from marriage registration figures.

As can be seen from Table 7.16, irrespective of geographic location Russian-Ukrainian marriages are a frequent combination. In part this is because Russians and Ukrainians as the most numerous nationalities in the country and the ones most likely to migrate are also close to each other in language, culture, and religion. For the last 20 to 25 years the actual number of Russian-Ukrainian marriages (both where the husband is Russian and the wife Ukrainian and vice versa) reportedly exceeds the expected number of marriages were mate-selection to occur without regard to nationality in such cities as Moscow, Kiev, Minsk, and Ashkhabad. Marriages between Byelorussians and Russians are similarly very close to the theoretically expected number in many areas as are Ukrainian-Byelorussian marriages (Gantskaia and Terent'eva 1975: 466-67). Evidently the three main Slavic nationalities tend to marry among themselves without much reference to ethnic heritage.

The frequency of Russian-Ukrainian-Byelorussian combinations is paralleled by the preference of other nationalities when intermarrying for staying within their general cultural group. Ethnic intermarriage is in particular much more likely to occur between persons having the same traditional religion than between those of different faiths. Moslems especially tend to marry only other Moslems. In part this is because Moslem law permits only men to intermarry while "the Moslem clergy instilled in the working people of the local nationalities the conviction that marriages with persons of other faiths were a gross violation of the *shariat* (Muslim religious law)" and "those who entered into such marriages were persecuted" Abramzon 1962: 42; cited in Dunn and Dunn 1973: 45). While

TABLE 7.16

Prevailing Combinations in Ethnically Mixed Marriages: Parents of Recipients of First Passports in Seven Capitals of Union Republics and Three Capitals of Autonomous Republics, 1960–69 (percent)

	Basic local nationality with Russians	Basic local nationality with other nationalities	Russians with Ukrainians	Russians with other nationalities	Other variants of inter-nationality marriages	Total
Kiev, Ukrainian SSR	72.2	15.5		9.8	1.5	100.0
Minsk, Byelorussian SSR	60.8	21.5	10.9	5.2	1.6	100.0
Kishinev, Moldavian SSR	21.0	19.6	35.1	13.7	10.6	100.0
Vilnius, Lithuanian SSR	14.3	17.0	17.0	36.0	15.7	100.0
Riga, Latvian SSR	25.2	12.3	22.8	27.6	12.1	100.0
Tallin, Estonian SSR	35.4	7.3	23.2	16.1	18.0	100.0
Ashkhabad, Turkmen SSR	10.3	10.1	29.2	33.2	16.3	100.0
Kazan, Tatar ASSR	33.2	11.0	25.8	28.0	2.0	100.0
Cheboksary, Chuvash ASSR	67.0	4.0	14.0	14.0	1.0	100.0
Saransh, Mordovian ASSR	52.2	3.4	24.4	17.8	2.2	100.0

Note: Figures may not add, presumably due to rounding.
Source: Terent'eva 1974:17.

other faiths are less strict regarding religious intermarriage, in Russia before the Revolution intermarriage could occur legally only between those of similar faiths, and the effect of such legal restrictions may have lingered into the Soviet period. It is difficult to distinguish, however, between the effect of religious barriers as such and the cultural and linguistic barriers that tend to accompany them.

As a result, marriages between Central Asians and Soviet citizens of European origin are quite infrequent (Sheehy 1975). Uzbeks, Tadzhiks, Kirgiz, Turkmen, and Kazakhs generally marry each other when they intermarry. To the extent that they do marry European Soviets, they are more likely to choose Tatars (also Moslems) than Slavs. This preference for marrying within religious lines is true even of Kazakhs in Kazakhstan who are more likely to know Russian, are less strongly attached to Islam than are other Central Asian groups, and in whose republic live a larger proportion of Europeans than in the regions to the south. Kazakhs do marry Europeans somewhat more than do other Central Asian nationalities, but they too choose Tatars over non-Moslem Europeans. Between 1935 and 1970, 4.9 percent of mixed marriages in Petropavlovsk (northern Kazakhstan) involved partners who were Kazakhs and Tatars, while only 1.9 percent of such marriages involved Kazakhs and Russians. Put in other terms, of the 773 Kazakhs who married Russians or Tatars during this period, 561 or over 70 percent married Tatars (Egurnev 1973: 30). So, too, in four cities of northern Kazakhstan between 1940 and 1969 some 50 percent of all mixed marriages occurred between Kazakhs and Tatars (see Table 7.17).

In another region in which religion is a major factor in determining combinations of nationalities in mixed marriages, Armenians are more likely to choose Russians and other nationalities close in faith to the Armenian Apostolic church than they are to choose Moslem Azeri as mates. In Table 7.18 are presented the expected and actual frequencies of several combinations of intermarriage in Armenia in 1967 and 1969. Although marriages between Armenians and Azeri are theoretically more probable than between Armenians and Russians, the actual frequency of Russian-Armenian marriages is far greater than that of Armenian-Azeri marriages. To some extent this is atrributable to the geographic distribution of Azeri in rural areas of Armenia, but religion clearly plays a major role (Ter-Sarkisiants 1973: 95).

Similarly, in the northwest regions of the country marriages of Byelorussians with Poles are as numerous as their theoretical probability in such cities as Minsk, Vilnius, and Moscow. To some extent these are marriages between Catholic Byelorussians and Catholic Poles. In similar manner marriages between Protestant Latvians and Estonians also are greater in comparison to their theoretical probability than are marriages between Latvians and Russians or Estonians and Russians. Catholic Lithuanians evidently are somewhat more likely to enter into marriages with Russians than are these two Protestant groups (Gantskaia and Terent'eva 1975: 459, 467).

A few ethnic combinations that cross religious lines reportedly are as great as their expected number. In particular, marriages between Russians and

TABLE 7.17

Marriages Involving Members of Other Nationalities as Percentage of Total Marriages Contracted by Kazakhs, 1940–69

Oblast center	Percentage of Kazakh men marrying non-Kazakhs				
	All	Tatars	Russians	Ukrainians	Byelorussians
Kokchetav	16.8	9.7	3.6	1.0	0.6
Kustanai	21.3	11.5	5.7	1.9	0.5
Pavlodar	13.2	5.2	4.5	1.7	0.8
Tselinograd	14.1	6.9	4.4	0.9	0.5
	Percentage of Kazakh women marrying non-Kazakhs				
Kokchetav	2.1	0.9	0.5	0.4	—
Kustanai	4.3	1.3	2.0	—	0.4
Pavlodar	1.4	0.4	0.3	0.1	0.1
Tselinograd	1.4	0.6	0.3	0.1	—

Sources: Evstigneev 1972; Sheehy 1975.

TABLE 7.18

Interethnic Marriages of Armenians: Armenian SSR, 1967–69

	Total				Urban				Rural			
	1967		1969		1967		1969		1967		1969	
	theoretical frequency	actual frequency	theoretical frequency	actual frequency	theoretical frequency	actual frequency	theoretical frequency	actual frequency	theoretical frequency	actual frequency	theoretical frequency	actual frequency
Armenian men with Azeri women	4.22	0.002	4.31	0.001	0.75	0.025	0.53	0.02	10.06	0.017	10.01	—
Azeri men with Armenian women	4.16	0.05	4.18	0.01	0.75	0.05	0.50	0.01	10.02	0.03	9.93	0.02
Armenian men with other nationalities of the Caucasus	0.36	0.25	0.33	0.27	0.35	0.35	0.44	0.72	0.20	0.05	0.15	0.09
Men of other nationalities of the Caucasus with Armenian women	0.30	0.14	0.17	0.08	0.36	0.20	0.19	0.06	0.18	0.03	0.15	0.11
Armenian men with Russian women	3.54	1.77	4.18	2.15	4.49	2.30	5.48	2.87	2.29	0.74	2.15	0.89
Russian men with Armenian women	1.98	0.21	2.11	0.18	2.42	0.28	2.64	0.27	1.19	0.03	1.18	0.02

Source: Ter-Sarkisiants 1973:94.

Tatars in a number of cities outside the Tatar ASSR are as frequent as their expected number (Gantskaia and Terent'eva 1975: 468). As might be expected, groups with similar cultural backgrounds but different religions who find themselves in regions of the country where they are both ethnically different from the main nationality and constitute a small minority also are highly likely to ignore religious lines. Thus Russian-Jewish and Ukrainian-Jewish marriages in Ashkhabad in the Turkmen republic have been evidently greater than their theoretical probability for several years (Gantskaia and Terent'eva 1975: 473). Obviously Russian-speaking Jews, cut off from contact with most other Jews and essentially similar in all respects to Russians and Ukrainians, in entering such unions are for all practical purposes marrying homogamously.

Different proportions of men and women from a given nationality enter into mixed marriages depending on the particular combination. Religious prohibition against Moslem women marrying outside their faith, but permitting such intermarriages to Moslem men, makes far more likely the participation of Moslem men in intermarriages with Europeans than the participation of Moslem women. The vast majority of marriages between Central Asians and Europeans involve a Central Asian man and a European woman, and marriages between Azeri and non-Moslems are very likely to involve male Azeri and female non-Moslems. Moslem Tatars similarly are far more likely to enter marriages with Russian women than Tatar women are likely to enter marriages with Russian men (Vasil'eva 1968: 14-15). From 1936 to 1970 approximately ten times as many Kazakh men as Kazakh women married Russians or Tatars in Petropavlovsk in north Kazakhstan (Egurnev 1973: 28-34; see also Table 7.17). Although the number of Moslem women marrying outside their nationality has been growing, it is still very small in comparison to the number of men (Sheehy 1975: 7).

Although other religions may not make this kind of distinction between the sexes in permitting intermarriage as a matter of religious law, it seems likely that as elsewhere in the world women are more closely tied to their family circles, more protected, and less likely in general to enter into mixed marriages, particularly with men of vastly different cultures or faiths. Men tend to move around the country more, have more access to other nationalities, and are as a consequence generally more likely to enter into mixed marriages than are women. Thus a common source of mixed marriages is where men demobilized from the Soviet army bring back wives of other nationalities to their home regions (Dzhumagulov 1960: 72).

In certain ethnic combinations both husband-wife variations are equally likely. It does not seem that Ukrainian men are consistently more involved in mixed marriages with Russians than are Ukrainian women, and the same holds true for Ukrainian-Byelorussian and Russian-Byelorussian marriages, although in Minsk marriages of Russian men with Byelorussian women are somewhat more common than the reverse. Not much difference in the proportions of men and women participating in marriages between Lithuanians and Russians, Latvians and Russians, and Estonians and Russians is observable when the theoretical probabilities of such marriages are taken into account (Gantskaia and Terent'eva 1975: 466-67).

In the United States, studies concerning black-white intermarriage have shown that marriages between black males and white women tend to predominate over those between white men and black women in most regions of the country (Monahan 197a, 197b, 1971; Heer 1966, 1974). The main theory advanced to explain this fact is that a trade-off is made on the U.S. marriage market whereby a black man wishing to marry a white woman compensates for his being black by providing higher educational and occupational attainment than his wife could expect to find from a husband of her own race, or in other words racial-caste hypogamous unions tend to be class hypergamous (Davis 1941; Merton 1941). The theory has received some empirical support when availability of partners is controlled (Heer 1974). To what extent does the same type of exchange or trade-off occur in the Soviet marriage market in marriages between nationalities? Although few data are available to test this question, some observations can be made.

While the relative prestige of Soviet nationalities is not known in detail, which nationalities are on the extreme ends of the scale are more or less clear. Thus within the European areas of the USSR there is a fair amount of evidence that it is preferable to be a Russian rather than a Jew. In addition to evidence of a general sort on Soviet popular and official anti-Semitism (see, for example, Korey 1973; Shaffer 1974), it is known that the children of Russian-Jewish marriages upon receiving their passports greatly prefer to identify themselves as Russians rather than as Jews (Terent'eva 1969). While to some extent such preference for Russian nationality is attributable to the general pull of the dominant nationality, from what is known regarding the position of Jews in the USSR, it seems reasonable to suppose that Jews are in a lower position relative to Russians in the Soviet stratification scheme. In like manner it seems clear that the less developed Central Asian nationalities are in an inferior position relative to Russians.

Assuming such relatively lower prestige for Jews and Central Asians, it is possible to suggest some reasons for male-female differences in nationality intermarriages in the Soviet Union. As has been seen (Chapter 2), in spite of greater female participation in the labor force, it is still primarily husbands who convey class status on their wives and not vice versa. In marriages between Russians and Jews the overwhelming majority of such marriages involve a Jewish husband and Russian wife. In view of the greater educational attainment of Jews in the USSR, it looks very much as if the Jewish husband's greater educational attainment is being traded for the Russian wife's higher nationality status. In other words, it seems likely that Russian-Jewish marriages are nationality-hypogamous/class-hypergamous. While the main reason why marriages between Central Asians and Russians involve Central Asian men almost exclusively may be found in Moslem religious law, it seems probable that such combinations are reinforced by trade-offs between Russian women's higher nationality status and Central Asian men's educational and occupational attainment. Armenian and Azeri men similarly are far more likely to enter into marriages with Russian women than vice versa, and it is arguable that trade-offs are being made in these marriages as well. The proportions of mixed marriages of Baltic, Ukrainian, and Byelorussian husbands with Russian wives are approximately equal to those of Russian husbands with wives of these nationalities, and this corresponds to the general impression of a rough equality of status between these nationalities.

Without more information on the relative educational and occupational attainment of spouses in mixed marriages and the relative prestige of nationalities, it is not possible to test directly the hypothesis that marriages between certain Soviet ethnic groups are nationality-hypogamous/class-hypergamous. Turning the matter around, however, if one makes the assumption that the Soviet marriage market does operate in this fashion it becomes possible to infer the relative status of nationalities from marriage patterns. Thus the predominance of Jewish husbands in Russian-Jewish marriages and of Central Asian husbands in Central-Asian-Russian marriages, and the relatively equal proportions of men and women of Ukrainian nationality in Ukrainian-Russian marriages can be seen as indicators of the relative status of these nationalities vis-à-vis the Russians and vis-à-vis each other. Given such an assumption, the marriage data available do not contradict already existing general impressions on the relative status of Soviet nationalities. Further work in this area may be warranted in view of the lack of other indications of the comparative prestige of the nationalities.

MARRIAGE BETWEEN CITIZENS OF THE USSR AND CITIZENS OF FOREIGN COUNTRIES

In accordance with the spirit of Soviet ideology, it might be expected that the freedom in mate-selection promoted within the USSR also would apply to love attachments between citizens of the USSR and those of other countries. This, however, is not the case. In many respects the Soviet marriage market as a whole is a closed market well protected from outside competition. For several years at the height of the Cold War it even was legally a closed market with a prohibition against the marriage of Soviet citizens to foreigners. More recently, while not precluded by statute, such marriages are strongly discouraged by government authorities.

An edict of February 15, 1947 (Vedomosti Verkhovnogo Soveta SSSR 1947) forbade marriages between Soviet citizens and foreigners. Prior to that time Soviet citizens could marry aliens, but marriage did not affect the citizenship of spouses, each retaining his or her original citizenship (such also is the case today). Some international marriages evidently took place in spite of the ban, and the law was rescinded as of November 26, 1953, in part as a result of pressure from the United Nations (*New York Times* 1954a; 1954b). It was not until the fall of 1955, however, that a U.S. citizen again married a Soviet (*New York Times* 1955).

In 1975 the Soviet Union became a signatory to the Final Act of the Conference on Security and Cooperation in Europe (CSCE). The CSCE Final Act commits the participating states to "examine favorably and on the basis of humanitarian considerations requests for exit and entry permits from persons who have decided to marry a citizen from another participating state." Moreover, once citizens of different states are married, participating states are to "enable them and the minor children of their marriage to transfer their permanent residence to a state in which either is normally a resident . . ." (Commission on Security and Cooperation in Europe 1977: 119).

While marriage to aliens before 1947 was not forbidden and since 1953 has again been legally possible, in both periods it has been subject to strong harassment by the Soviet authorities. Under Stalin Soviet spouses or would-be spouses were subject to arrest and exile or imprisonment, as were members of their family. Family members also were subject to harassment of various sorts such as loss of employment (Gilmore 1968: 69-70).

Since de-Stalinization less extreme methods have been used to discourage their marriages, but reportedly have included such things as beatings of the parties and induction into the army. For the most part, however, discouragement has taken the form of obstructing such marriages by not granting the necessary exit and entrance visas for the marriage to take place and by making it difficult for the Soviet spouse to leave the USSR after the marriage. Research by the author on Soviet-U.S. marriages has shown that Soviet performance in granting such visas has improved in recent years: waiting times in exit visa cases involving spouses of U.S. citizens have been greatly reduced since mid-1975, and there does not seem now to be obstruction of Soviet-U.S. marriages where the U.S. spouse has permission to be in the USSR for a sufficient period of time to complete the formalities and the Soviet spouse lives in an area open to travel by foreigners (based on data compiled by the author with the assistance of the Consular Section of the U.S. Embassy in Moscow and conveyed to the Commission on Security and Cooperation in Europe. See Commission on Security and Cooperation in Europe 1977: 119-22.) It is important to note in view of the above discussion of Soviet ideology regarding mate-selection that it is not the ZAGS registration authorities who generally are responsible for the obstruction of intercitizenship marriages, but rather those authorities controlling visas.

Marriages between Soviets and foreigners are discouraged for the same reasons that emigration from the USSR is discouraged. Such marriages are a conduit for a brain drain from the USSR, much as are marriages to persons of Jewish nationality who are granted the right to emigrate to Israel. (A current Soviet joke goes: Question: What is a Jewish wife? Radio Armenia answers: A means of transportation.) A child born to such a mixed union is likely to be lost to the Soviet labor force, and this thwarts the regime's desire for a larger population. In view of the stratified access of Soviet citizens to foreign nationals—it is primarily the educated, privileged, and powerful who by reason of their position in Soviet society are able to meet with foreigners—the marriage of Soviets to aliens poses a real threat that personnel the USSR needs will leave the country. Permitting such marriages also would allow intimate exposure to non-Soviet ways of life and the possibility of alternative ways of living, and thus threaten a society that tries to force conformity as much as possible. "To let Soviet citizens marry beyond the bounds of communist society is to grant them a license that is psychological as well as physical" (Wren 1975).

It should be noted, however, that the author's research on waiting times for visas in Soviet-U.S. marriage cases showed no consistent tendency on the part of Soviet authorities to obstruct such marriages to a greater or lesser degree depending on the personal characteristics of the spouses. Contrary to widely held opinions, the waiting time involved in obtaining an exit visa for Soviet men married to U.S. women is no greater than that for Soviet women married to U.S. men, nor is it longer for those who have been previously married or possess advanced degrees. The only personal characteristics of Soviet-U.S. spouses that do seem to affect the handling of their cases are the age spread between husband and wife and the place of birth of the U.S. spouse. Waiting times for couples vastly differing in age are longer, presumably because of Soviet authorities' suspicions that these are fictitious marriages (see Chapter 5), as they are for couples where the U.S. spouse was born in the USSR, presumably because of Soviet authorities' distaste for such émigré contacts (Fisher 1977b).

In select cases the Soviet authorities have been known to expedite marriages between Soviet citizens and foreigners where such unions have been advantageous to the USSR. The most recent example is the marriage of Christina Onassis, the Greek shipping millionaire, to Sergei Kauzov, a former official of the Soviet merchant marine (see New York Times 1978).

No surveys have sought to elicit Soviet popular attitudes toward marriage with foreigners. Those looking for ways to emigrate from the USSR look favorably on such marriages, of course, but it is likely that the more general population combines the liberal attitude toward interethnic marriage already discussed with fear of attendant harassment and Soviet patriotism and love of homeland to view such marriages ambivalently. Tamara Gilmore reports the following conversation with her mother upon returning from a date with her future U.S. husband during World War II:

> "Mama," I began, "I met a foreigner tonight . . ."
> "What sort of foreigner is he?"
> "An American."
> "An American?"
> "Oh, Mama, it's all right. The Americans are our allies now."
> "Is he nice?"
> "I think so. He seemed nice."
> "That's what counts," she said. "It doesn't matter whether he's an American or what." (Gilmore 1968: 29)

Often such marriages are viewed as tragic. George Feifer describes the attitude of a Russian librarian:

> Don't marry one of us, she keeps whispering. No matter what she promises or pleads, don't become involved with a Russian girl. Because it can't work: your outlooks would be too irreconcilably different. Even before you'd leave the country, the great burden would be on her. Like white hunters taking native wives, it's always an injustice. (Feifer 1976: 84)

Conversations of the author with several Soviet citizens have evinced the response that such marriages are "a tragedy." It is likely this attitude has deep historic roots: for example, the marriage of a hero in Russian epic poetry to a foreigner is generally tragic (Dunn 1978: 166-67).

The consequence of such discouragement of international marriages and of such attitudes is that the number of such marriages is quite small in spite of the fact that a rather large number of foreigners now live in or visit the Soviet Union. No official figures exist on the point for the USSR as a whole—it is unclear that data on marriages between Soviet citizens and foreigners are routinely collected—but an information pamphlet published by Novosti Press Agency in 1977 contains the statement that "over the last few years more than 8,000 Soviet citizens have married foreigners and have gone to live in 110 different countries with their wives or husbands" (USSR: 100 Questions and Answers 1977: 72). This means that about 2,500 such marriages occur per year, or about 1 percent of the total number of marriages annually in the Soviet Union. While no figures are available, it seems very likely that the vast majority of such marriages are to citizens of East European socialist states, the category of foreigners with the greatest access to Soviet citizens.

Certainly the number of marriages of Soviets to U.S. citizens is small. Data compiled by the author from the files of the U.S. Embassy in Moscow show that only 81 marriages took place between January 1, 1974 and March 1, 1977 (about 25 a year) where one spouse was a USSR citizen and the other a U.S. citizen at the time of the marriage. Although there has been some increase in the number of such marriages since, in view of the large populations of the two countries this form of international contact is so miniscule as to be virtually nonexistent.

More Soviet women become spouses of U.S. citizens than do Soviet men (see Table 7.19). It seems likely that this imbalance toward foreign men marrying Soviet women is typical of the marriage patterns between other nations and the USSR as well. Of grooms marrying brides from Kiev in 1970, 0.6 percent were foreigners, but no brides were foreigners (Chuiko 1975: 96). In spite of a certain equalization of the sexes in the initiation of courtship in the Soviet Union, men are still granted the prerogative of starting up acquaintances more than are women, and foreign men may have more access to Soviet women than do Soviet men to foreign women. Perhaps a more important factor has been the difference in value—actual or supposed—of Soviet men and women on the

TABLE 7.19

Sex and Nationality of Soviet Citizens Marrying United States Citizens, January 1, 1974 to March 1, 1977

Nationality	Male	Female	Total
Russian	12	26	38
Armenian	4	10	14
Ukrainian	4	5	9
Lithuanian	1	6	7
Estonian	0	4	4
Latvian	0	2	2
Jewish	1	1	2
Byelorussian	0	1	1
Turkmen	1	0	1
Montenegran	0	1	1
Nationality unknown	0	2	2
Total	23	58	81
Percent	28	72	100

Source: Compiled by author from data of United States Embassy, Moscow.

internal Soviet marriage market. In view of the tremendous shortage of them, the pressure on Soviet men not to marry out of the country is considerable; after all, there is a plethora of girls at home from which to choose. "They are utter male chauvinists. . . . If a woman wants to marry a foreigner, it can sometimes be worked out. But if a Russian man wants to, it usually leads to trouble" (West European diplomat, quoted in Wren 1975).

Many of the marriages between U.S. and Soviet citizens are to be explained by the contact between U.S. citizens whose ethnic backgrounds are connected to Soviet nationality groups and those nationalities. Thus Soviet Armenians are the second largest group after Russians to marry U.S. citizens (see Table 7.19), and they are marrying primarily U.S. citizens of Armenian extraction. Of the 81 U.S. spouses about whom information was available, 20 were born outside the United States. About half of the 13 marriages involving Soviet citizens from the Baltic republics were to U.S. citizens who had been born in the region, and it is likely that many of the remaining marriages were to U.S. citizens of Baltic origin. The U.S. spouses come primarily from the Northeast and West of the United States, which may reflect in part the geographic distribution of ethnic groups with backgrounds linked to the USSR in the United States.

While the occupations and educational levels of those entering into Soviet-U.S. marriages include all socioeconomic levels, there is some overrepresentation of professionals, as might be expected given the expense of travel to the Soviet

Union and the profile of most Soviet-U.S. contacts. Interestingly, however, only two of the 81 Soviets who married U.S. citizens from January 1, 1974 to March 1, 1977 were members of the Communist Party of the Soviet Union. As also might be expected given the general tendency for second and subsequent marriages to be more heterogamous than first ones, more than half of those couples for whom previous marital status is known for one or both spouses contained at least one partner for whom the marriage was a remarriage. Partly as a result of this, the median age at marriage in such Soviet-U.S. unions is high: in the 75 cases where age was known, the median age for U.S. men was 32, for Soviet men 28; for U.S. women it was 26, for Soviet women 27.

It is the small number of Soviet-U.S. marriages of whatever sort that is striking. In relation to marriage with foreigners, the Soviet marriage market most clearly does not correspond to the ideal institutionalized romantic love complex envisioned by Engels and the Soviet leaders. To the extent that it is a free market, it is so primarily only within the confines of the borders of the USSR. Restrictions against marriage with foreigners today are not absolute, but they remain extensive. To the extent that such restrictions are overcome, the ensuing marriages are subject to the same market pressures that exist for all Soviet marriages.

8

CONCLUSION

As evidence of the preceding chapters has shown, the Soviet population in its attitudes and views has for the most part adopted Marxist-Leninist ideology concerning mate-selection. Soviet surveys show substantial verbal agreement with the idea that romantic love exists, with the idea of love as the sole legitimate basis for marriage, and acceptance of freedom of courtship between class and ethnic groups. This acceptance of the ideology has an aspect to it that U.S. beliefs in love and freedom of courtship do not: since love as the basis for marriage is proclaimed to be already a reality in Soviet life, romantic love is taken more seriously as an attainable goal for the individual than if it were only presented as an ideal. Although there is recognition of the difference between romance on the motion picture screen—the Hollywood kheppiend (happy end) as it is called in Russian—and real life, the confusion between what ought to be and what is gives a deeper, more serious character to the Soviet population's belief in love and in courtship free of all other considerations than love than otherwise would be the case.

As has been seen, however, many considerations other than love alone enter into the process of mate-selection in the USSR. Official denial of a market structure to mate-selection notwithstanding, the empirical evidence shows the continuing importance of economic considerations and, indeed, of economic calculation in Soviet decisions to marry. This is particularly so for men. Throughout the Soviet Union men are more likely to enter into marriage where the relative differential in wages between men and women is greater. That is to say, men are considerably more likely to enter into marriage where they can expect their prospective wives to specialize in housework, thereby removing the burden from them and making marriage an economic gain for them. The same considerations affect women's decisions to marry, though to a lesser degree. That is to say, the larger the gap between the wages of men and women the more attractive marriage is to the latter since, although they may specialize in household production, they receive through their husbands more income than they would obtain were they to remain single. Becker's hypothesis regarding the effect of relative wage differentials on entrance into marriage generally has received confirmation for Soviet mate-selection.

This is an important finding since it implies that the equalization of women's participation in the labor force and of their wage levels, even in societies that have had extensive participation of women in the labor force for many years and ostensibly have accepted such participation, decreases the attractiveness of marriage to both men and women, but particularly to men. As has been seen, the differences in proportions married among the various regions and nationalities of the USSR, whereby in general the more economically and culturally advanced regions and nationalities have smaller proportions married, is mostly explicable by the differences in male/female wage differentials. That is to say, the more advanced regions and nationalities tend to have smaller wage differentials between men and women and, as a consequence of that, smaller proportions married. As the more backward regions and peoples of the USSR develop economically and culturally, to the extent that such development entails equalization of the position of women, there is likely to be a decrease in the proportion married. The Soviet Union, in other words, has not succeeded sufficiently in freeing marriage from economic considerations so as to enable the greater participation of women in the labor force to be without consequences for the desirability of marriage, let alone without effects on the marital relations of husbands and wives.

Because it has been so very difficult for women to marry at all due to extremely low sex ratios in the postwar period, women have been more ready than men to enter into marriage whether or not it was economically advantageous. Indeed, far more women than men (1,384,673 more according to the 1970 census, see Chapter 4) claim to be married. "Most opposition to marriage seems to be mostly male" (Kharchev 1973: 18). In Chapter 3 it was shown how with the normalization of sex ratios in recent years male rates of entrance into marriage have decreased. While the interpretation given there was that sociodemographic pressure on men to marry has lessened over time and that men have found nonparticipation in the marriage market to be less costly in terms of desirable mates foregone, an additional explanation is that as women's position has become more equal to that of men in Soviet society, the economic gain to marriage for men has grown less and men have been less willing to marry.

Other evidence for the continuing importance of monetary considerations in marriage was seen in the practice of fictitious marriages to obtain apartments, cars, and the like; in the continuance of kalym in Central Asia and in the bit of evidence available on the rise in the size of such bride-prices with the normalization of the sex ratio; and in the continuance of dowries in the immediate postwar period.

Considerations not directly monetary in character other than love or emotional attraction also continue to be important in Soviet mate-selection. As in other societies spouses tend to be homogamous in most social characteristics; the overwhelming majority of couples are similar in age, education, ethnic identity, and occupational level. Ethnic groups generally intermarry very little, and what crossing of the blue-collar/white collar line that exists in a fair number of Soviet marriages is due primarily to the unequal distribution of occupations by sex.

While it may be objected that much of the homogamy in marriages is due to geographic distribution and lack of opportunity to meet with persons in other social groups, and that this is not quite the same thing as saying that considerations other than love are taken into account in marrying, the evidence on those marriages between groups that do occur shows that there are trade-offs that demonstrate the presence of such considerations in mate-selection. Thus, for example, where the wife of a manual worker has a nonmanual job and more education than her husband, there is typically a trade-off whereby the husband compensates by earning considerably more money than his wife. Similarly, combinations of nationalities in ethnic intermarriages were seen to involve in all likelihood trade-offs between the occupational status of one partner and the ethnic identity of the other. As regards nonmonetary as well as monetary considerations, in other words, it seems clear that a marriage market is at work in Soviet mate-selection.

Confirmation of the usefulness of market conceptions of mate-selection does not mean that state socialism in the USSR has no consequences for mate-selection, but that rather than eliminating a market structure to marriage, it has affected the market itself. Thus the greater employment of women and the greater equalization of women's position in Soviet society has reduced the economic gain to marriage, but considerations of such economic gain are still there. In like manner, the reduction of inequality in Soviet society generally and a somewhat greater overlap between the positions of white-collar and blue-collar workers is reflected in the existence of a fair number of marriages that cross the manual/nonmanual line, but these marriages are still occurring within a market structure; that is to say, potential spouses are competing on a marriage market, but because in some of their characteristics they are relatively more equal than in the marriage markets of Western countries, the patterns of marriage that result differ somewhat from those to be found in the West. The same holds for interethnic marriages. To the extent that a rough equality in social standing among many of the nationalities of the USSR exists, when other factors such as education, a language in common, and the like pose no problem, interethnic marriages are likely to take place, but they take place in a market context. The nationality of the potential spouse is weighed as more or less desirable and is irrelevant only to the extent that the nationality of the potential spouse and that of the individual may be considered relatively equal.

That considerations other than love or emotional attraction continue to play a role in Soviet mate-selection is not surprising not only in view of the continuing stratification of Soviet society, but also in view of the continuing participation of parents in the decision to marry. Third parties are less able to judge the emotional relationship between two people and are more likely to use objective, visible criteria in evaluating a potential spouse. A discrepancy between the criteria used by potential spouses themselves and those used by their parents in mate-selection has been found to be the case in the United States, with parents preferring objective criteria such as career prospects in evaluating their children's choice (Bell and Buerkle 1962). As long as there is continued parental participation in the decision to marry, it seems likely that considerations other than love alone will have to play a major part in Soviet mate-selection.

In addition to confirmation of the usefulness of market conceptions of mate-selection, the present study has confirmed in general terms Goode's observation regarding the movement of family systems toward some kind of conjugal system for the peoples of the USSR, at least as regards mate-selection. As in other areas of the world, the various family systems of the Soviet Union have been converging from different starting points to a self-selection form of courtship, to similar proportions married, to similar patterns of age at marriage, to a reduced prevalence of bride-price and dowry systems, and so on. As with other societies, the changes in the patterns observable can in part be attributed to modernization, but in particular in the Soviet case to the ideological favoring of such changes.

To conclude that mate-selection in the USSR operates in essentially similar fashion to mate-selection elsewhere in the world, and in the West in particular, and that Soviet marriage patterns have much in common with Western patterns is not the same thing as saying that the cause of these similar patterns is the same. While such a distinction is clear in Goode's work, it has not been made often in studies of Soviet society that subscribe to some form of industrial society theory (Inkeles and Bauer 1959). The thesis that industrialization has the same consequences everywhere and that therefore Soviet society shares many characteristics in common with other industrial societies has been challenged as a vulgar form of Marxism that fails to distinguish between genotype and phenotype, between the origins of a pattern and the pattern itself (Goldthorpe 1964). It is arguable that at least some of the Soviet marriage patterns observed to be similar to those prevailing in the West are not in fact caused by the same factors that have shaped the Western patterns. This is basically what Soviet sociologists mean when they claim that the different "essence" or true nature of the socialist family must be distinguished from the "practice" or patterns that one observes at any given time. (This was Kharchev's position at the Twelfth International Family Seminar. See "Sem'ia Kak byt' schastlivym . . ." 1972.)

As a specific example of the point, examine an alternative explanation for the prevalence of homogamy in the USSR. While in a market system of courtship homogamy is the general result as persons find their level on the marriage market, homogamy also may be the general result of a nonmarket system that insists that every marriage be concluded solely out of love and without regard to other considerations. Even without resorting to discussions of the nature of emotional attraction, it can be seen why this should be so. If as in Soviet society there is a norm that calculation must not take place in selecting a mate, the social control involved in enforcement of this norm will encourage homogamy since friends, relatives, and other third parties cannot observe directly whether love exists between the parties but are forced to judge a given union on the basis of objective observable criteria. Where there is insistence on no calculation whatsoever, marriages between the highly educated and the uneducated, between the wealthy and the poor, between the old and the young, are suspect as having involved calculation, as being marriages of convenience. In such a system there is likely to be social condemnation of heterogamous marriages on the ground that they are, at least at first glance, less likely to be concluded out of love by one or both parties. A strong institutionalization of a romantic love complex and prescription of love as the basis for marriage, in other words, likely results in a sorting of partners similar to that prevailing in market systems.

Some of the homogamy observable in Soviet marriages does result in this fashion from the strong institutionalization of love as the only basis for marriage and the strong social control against calculation that accompanies it. There are indications that this is the case in the suspicions leveled against odd combinations in marriages and the attempt to prevent them (see, for example, Beliavskii and Finn 1973: 54-61) and in the justifications for homogamy in education (see Chapter 6). At least some marriages concluded in the USSR, while following patterns similar to those in the West, are not the result of the same factors.

The confirmation of the applicability of market theories of mate-selection and of the movement of family systems to some sort of conjugal system for the USSR would be more extensive and solid if one had better and more information than is available. Although much could be learned concerning Soviet courtship and marriage since World War II were it possible to gain access to the raw data of the censuses or conduct a more comprehensive survey in the Soviet Union on the topic than has been done so far, there is much that shall never be known simply because the information was never gathered. Thus precisely what the marital status of the population was after the war—how many were widowed, divorced, never married—will remain unknown. Despite the fact that often it has been possible only to speculate regarding certain aspects of marriage patterns and their causes, and despite the fact that often the data reviewed are frustratingly poor, the present study is more or less exhaustive of all the available material. It is to be hoped that in future censuses and sociological studies Soviet demographers and sociologists will provide more sophisticated data for their own use as well as for secondary analyses such as this one. Steps evidently are being taken in this direction (see Fisher and Khotin 1977).

In conclusion, a number of observations are in order regarding the consequences of such strong Soviet insistence on love as the only legitimate basis for marriage in view of the actual existence of a marriage market involving considerations other than love. A gap between expectations and ideals regarding marriage, on the one hand, and reality on the other, exists in both the USSR and the United States. It is arguable, however, that the gap in the United States has been closing with the dissemination of marriage-counseling literature and lesser insistence on romantic love in recent years. The same cannot be said for the Soviet Union. Insofar as lowering expectations regarding marriage reduces divorce, it can be predicted that ceteris paribus divorce rates in the Soviet Union, which are now generally second only to those of the United States, will continue to rise as more and more of the various Soviet family systems move to an even fuller institutionalization of a romantic love complex.

At the same time it should be noted that the Soviet denial of a marriage market well may improve certain aspects of marital adjustment. It has been found that a nonexchange orientation or lack of tit-for-tat attitude on the part of spouses is helpful to marital adjustment, particularly to that of men (Murstein et al. 1977). Insofar as Soviet couples may see love less as a series of reciprocal exchanges, they may experience greater satisfaction with their relationships.

The strong ideological denial of a marriage market combined with the actual existence of one also may help to explain why in recent years Soviet women have been observed to be relatively conservative as regards women's rights and in a sense desire to be unliberated (Sacks 1976: 172-74). In the United States the recent ideological denigration of marriage and new emphasis on women's roles outside the home has occurred in the context of a decline in the value of women on the U.S. marriage market due to a marriage squeeze. Because women tend to marry men older than themselves, the rising birthrate in the postwar baby boom has meant that U.S. women of marriageable age in the 1960s and 1970s have found it difficult to find partners. In other words, U.S. values regarding marriage have tended to change in response to pressures in the marriage market, as well as in response to the women's liberation movement. In contrast to the United States, the Soviet Union, with more fixed ideological conceptions to start with, has experienced an enormous rise in the value of women on its marriage market due to the normalization of the sex ratio since World War II.* As a consequence it is now in a far better position than ever before to implement ideals with regard to marriage. Not only have women in the Soviet Union had a longer experience of occupational employment outside the home, but also it is just recently that they have had the opportunity to be wives and mothers, that there has been sufficient demand for them to be wives and mothers. This has made the attractions of a home life much greater than formerly, and the entire push of the experience of women in the USSR in recent

---

*Strictly speaking, the Soviet Union also has experienced something of a marriage squeeze in the 1960s and 1970s due to a rise in births after the war until 1960. This fact has been noted by Perevedentsev (1971b). Such a squeeze has prolonged the higher demand for men than for women on the Soviet marriage market and will begin to reverse itself only around 1980. It seems clear, however, that the normalization of sex ratios since the war has been of far greater importance than any such squeeze to the market position of Soviet women and has greatly overshadowed it.

decades thus has been toward cultivation of their family roles rather than of their roles outside the home in the labor force. Since marriage and being a wife always has been fostered as a Soviet ideal together with participation in the economy, the changing market position of Soviet women has allowed them to implement that ideal rather than forced them to change their views on marriage. It is unfair to accuse Soviet women of backwardness on the issue of women's liberation since they are coming from a very different historical and sociodemographic experience.

The official denial of a market structure to mate-selection in the USSR when there is one very well may help to stabilize Soviet society politically. As with the declaration to the effect that with the abolishment of the private owner-ship of the means of production no one is—by definition—exploited, which while of doubtful truth serves to curb dissatisfaction, so too the proclamation that love has become the basis for marriage in the USSR serves to reduce the extent to which the mass of the population views itself as having inadequate access to the family groupings of those on the top of the society. If the kin ties among the elite are the result of love alone, it is difficult to argue that it is really power and fortunes that are being consolidated in the union of two family lines. While it is possible to protest against marriages when they clearly involve economic or political considerations, it is difficult to protest marriages supposedly based on love since romantic love typically has been considered a progressive value and something everyone is capable of; that is, it is difficult to find or create a counter-ideology to Marxism-Leninism that does not have a conservative cast to it as regards mate-selection as well as most other phenomena, particularly when the claim is made that Marxism-Leninism has been put into practice. The actual in-equalities that are perpetuated by the Soviet marriage market are in this manner arguably more legitimated than in any other marriage market and less subject to question.

In general the Soviet claim that love has become the basis of marriage in the USSR is similar to other phenomena in the Soviet Union whereby a kind of theatricality or showmanship—a "Potemkin Village effect," if you will—retards social change. This theatricality is most manifest in the case of fictitious mar-riages, where for the sake of having the marriage accepted as valid the couple must put on a show for the outside world to the effect that it is a true marriage; but it seems likely that such theatrical display is widespread in courtship since love is so strongly institutionalized as the only legitimate basis for marrying. Competing in fact on a marriage market but told that the existing social system fulfills the need for romantic love, the individual is caught in a web of inauthen-ticity. To borrow Stojanovic's phrase, like much of Soviet society, mate-selection too is caught "between ideals and reality" (Stojanovic 1975).

In the move from older systems of arranged marriages, Marxist-Leninist ideology clearly has been and is a major liberating force in mate-selection. As such it has vastly expanded the freedom of the Soviet citizen to choose in marry-ing. A revolutionary ideology in power, however, is no longer revolutionary. To the extent that love is enforced as the only possible basis for marriage, the Soviet system of mate-selection may in many ways be as restricting as one that is not a romantic love complex. Love so strongly institutionalized may no longer liberate the individual.

BIBLIOGRAPHY

Abramson, Harold J. *Ethnic Diversity in Catholic America*. New York: John Wiley and Sons, 1973.

Abramzon, S. M. "Otrazhenie protsessa sblizheniia natsii na semeino-bytovom uklade narodov Srednei Azii i Kazakhstana." *Sovetskaia etnografiia* 3 (1962): 18-34.

Achylova, R. "Iz istorii razvitiia mezhnatsional'nykh brakov." In *Problemy sblizheniia sotsialisticheskikh natsii v periode stroitel'stva kommunizma*. Frunze: "Mektep," 1966.

——. "Mezhnatsional'nye braki i sem'i v SSSR (Sotsiologicheskoe issledovanie na materialakh Kirgizii i Uzbekistana)." Candidate of Philosophical Sciences dissertation, Leningrad State University, 1968.

——. "Izmenenie polozheniia zhenshchin pri sotsialisme kak faktor formirovaniia novykh vzaimootnoshenii mezhdu suprugami v kirgizskikh sem'iakh." In Sovetskaia Sotsiologicheskaia Assotsiatsiia et al., *Dinamika izmeneniia polozheniia zhenshchiny i sem'ia*. Moscow:, 1972.

Agaev, M-B. Kh. "Razvitie brachno-semeinykh otnoshenii v usloviiakh stroitel'stva kommunizma (na materialakh Dagestanskoi ASSR)." Candidate of Philosophical Sciences dissertation abstract, Makhachkala, 1972.

Aimre, I. A. "Uroven' obrazovaniia v sotsial'nogomogennykh i geterogennykh sem'iakh." In P. Kenkmann et al., eds., *Sotsial'no-professional'naia orientatsiia molodezhi i kommunisti-cheskoe bospitanie v vuze*. Tartu: Tartu State University, 1977.

——, and Titma, M. "Problemy opredeleniia sotsial'nogo proiskhozhdeniia molodezhi." In Tartuskii Gosudarstvennyi Universitet, Materialy konferentsii "Kommunisicheskoe vospitanie studenchestva," Chast' I. Tartu: 1971.

Albogachiev, M. "Otstupil pered ten'iu." *Komsomol'skaia pravda*, September 5, 1970: 2.

Aleksandrov, V. A., et al., eds. *Narody evropeiskoi chasti SSSR*. I. Moscow: Nauka, 1974.

Alliluyeva, Svetlana. *Twenty Letters to a Friend*. New York: Harper and Row, 1967.

Allworth, Edward, ed. *Central Asia: A Century of Russian Rule*. New York: Columbia University Press, 1967.

Andrianov, N., and Belov, A. "New Rituals for Soviet People." *Pravda*, May 28, 1976: 3. Translated in *CDSP* 18, 21: 19.

Antonov, Anatolii I., ed. *Molodaia sem'ia*. Moscow: Statistika, 1977.

"Are Betrothals Necessary Today?" *Komosomolskaia pravda*, November 17, 1968: 2. Translated in *CDSP* 20, 46: 13.

Arutiunian, Iurii V. "Opyt sotsial'no-etnicheskogo issledovaniia (po materiialam Tatarskoi ASSR)." *Sovetskaia etnografiia* 4 (1968): 3-13.

———. "Konkretno-sotsiologicheskoe issledovanie natsional'nykh otnoshenii." *Voprosy filosofii* 12 (1969): 129-39.

———. *Sotsial'naia struktura sel'skogo naseleniia SSSR*. Moscow: Mysl', 1971.

———. "Sotsial'no-kul'turnye aspekty razvitiia i sblizheniia natsii v SSSR." *Sovetskaia etnografiia* 3 (1972): 3-19.

———. *Sotsial'noe i natsional'noe*. Moscow: Mysl', 1973.

Atarov, N. "Reflections of a Witness at the Registry Office." *Izvestiia*, July 20, 1972: 6. Translated in *CDSP* 24, August 16: 20.

Baldwin, Godfrey. "Estimates and Projections of the Population of the U.S.S.R. by Age and Sex: 1950 to 2000." U.S. Department of Commerce, Foreign Demographic Analysis Division, International Population Reports, series P-91, no. 23 (March 1973).

———. "Projections of the Population of the U.S.S.R. and Eight Subdivisions, by Age and Sex: 1973 to 2000." U.S. Department of Commerce, Foreign Demographic Analysis Division, International Population Reports, series P-91, no. 24 (June 1975).

Bangerskaia, T. "Who is Head of the House?" *Soviet Life* 12 (December 1975): 49-50.

Baranov, A. N. "Gorodskaia sem'ia i lichnost'." In *Sotsial'nye issledovaniia, vypusk 7 (Metodologicheskie problemy issledovaniia byta)*. Moscow: Nauka, 1971.

Barron, Milton L., ed. *The Blending American: Patterns of Intermarriage*. Chicago: Quadrangle, 1972.

Becker, Gary S. "A Theory of Marriage: Part I." *Journal of Political Economy* 81 (July-August 1973): 813-46.

———. "A Theory of Marriage: Part II. *Journal of Political Economy* 82, Part II (March–April): 511–26.

Beliavskii, Al'bert V., and Finn, Emil' A. *Liubov' i kodeks*. Moscow: Sovetskaia Rossiia, 1973.

Belitser, V. N., et al., eds. *Narody evropeiskoi chasti SSSR*. II. Moscow: Nauka, 1964.

Bell, R. R., and Buerkle, J. V. "The Daughter's Role During the 'Launching Stage'." *Marriage and Family Living* 24 (1962): 384-88.

Benet, Sula. *How to Live to be 100: The Life-Style of the People of the Caucasus*. New York: Dial Press, 1976.

Berg, A. "O liubvi, mashinakh i orakulakh." *Literaturnaia gazeta*, March 18, 1970: 12-13.

Billington, J. H. "Beneath the Panoply of Power, the Intelligentsia Hits Out at the Old Order." *Life*, November 10, 1967: 70.

Blum, Jerome. *Lord and Peasant in Russia*. Princeton, N.J.: Princeton University Press, 1972.

Boev, V., and Ugrinovich, D. "Ceremonies in Soviet Society." *Nauka i religiia* 3 (1975): 36-41. Translated in *Current Abstracts of the Soviet Press* 27: 12, 20.

Boiarskii, Aron Ia. *Naselenie i metody ego izucheniia*. Moscow: Statistika, 1975.

Brezhnev, Leonid I. *O piatidesiatiletii S.S.S.R.* Moscow: Politizdat, 1973.

Briman, M. "The Dance Hall: Light and Shadows." *Sovetskaia kul'tura* May 30, 1975: 5. Translated in *CDSP* 27: 7.

Bronson, D. W., and Severin, B. S. "Recent Trends in Consumption and Disposable Money Income in the USSR." In U.S. Congress, Joint Economic Committee, *New Directions in the Soviet Economy*, part II-B. Washington, D.C.: U.S. Government Printing Office, 1966.

——. "Soviet Consumer Welfare: The Brezhnev Era." In U.S. Congress, Joint Economic Committee, *Soviet Economic Prospects for the Seventies*. Washington, D.C.: U.S. Government Printing Office, 1973.

Burr, Wesley R. *Theory Construction and the Sociology of the Family*. New York: John Wiley and Sons, 1973.

Carter, Hugh, and Glick, Paul C. *Marriage and Divorce: A Social and Economic Study*. Cambridge, Mass.: Harvard University Press, 1970. Also rev. ed., 1976.

Chachin V. "Myl'nyi puzyr'." *Pravda*, December 6, 1971: 6.

Chapman, J. "Equal Pay for Equal Work?" In Dorothy Atkinson, Alexander Dallin, and Gail Warshofsky Lapidus, eds., *Women in Russia*. Stanford: Stanford University Press, 1977.

Chistova, K. V., and Bernshtam, T. A., eds. *Russkii narodnyi svadebnyi obriad*. Leningrad: Nauka, 1978.

Chojnacka, H. "Nuptiality Patterns in an Agrarian Society." *Population Studies* 30 (1976): 203-26.

Chuiko, Liubov' V. *Braki i razvody*. Moscow: Statistika, 1975.

Chumakova, Tamara E. *Sem'ia, moral', pravo*. Minsk: Nauka i Tekhnika, 1974.

Coale, Ansley J., Anderson, Barbara, and Härm, Erna. *Human Fertility in Russia since the Nineteenth Century*. Princeton, N.J.: Princeton University Press, 1979.

Cohen, Steven M. "Patterns of Interethnic Marriage and Friendship in the United States." Ph.D. dissertation, Columbia University, New York, 1974.

Commission on Security and Cooperation in Europe. *Report to the Congress of the United States on Implementation of the Final Act of the Conference on Security and Cooperation in Europe: Findings and Recommendations Two Years after Helsinki*. Washington, D.C.: 1977.

"Comrades Have Lovely Soviet Wedding; But Irked Party Finds It Was a Fraud." *New York Times*, March 10, 1958: 12.

Cuisenier, J., and Raguin, C. "De quelques transformations dans le système familial russe." *Revue français de sociologie* 8 (October-December 1967): 521-57.

Danilov, A. "Do You Want to Be Happy?" *Komosomolskaia pravda*, November 29, 1972: 2. Translated in *CDSP* 25, 8: 18.

Davis, K. "Intermarriage in caste societies." *American Anthropologist* 43 (1941): 376-95.

Demko, G. J. "Divorce in the USSR: Spatial and Legal Changes, 1940-1960." *Soviet Union* 1 (1974): 141-46.

Di Maio, Alfred J. *Soviet Urban Housing: Problems and Policies*. New York: Praeger, 1974.

Dobson, R. B. "Mobility and Stratification in the Soviet Union." *Annual Review of Sociology* 3 (1977): 297-329.

Drobizheva, L. M. "O sblizhenii urovnei kul'turnogo razvitiia soiuznykh respublik." *Istoriia SSSR* 3 (1969): 61-79.

——. "Sotsial'no-kul'turnye osobennosti lichnosti i natsional'nye ustanovki (po materiialam issledovanii v Tatarskoi ASSR)." *Sovetskaia etnografiia* 3 (1971): 3-15.

Dunn, Stephen P. "The Family as Reflected in Russian Folklore." In David L. Ransel, ed., *The Family in Imperial Russia: New Lines of Historical Research*. Urbana: University of Illinois Press, 1978.

——, and Dunn, Ethel. *The Peasants of Great Russia*. New York: Holt, Rinehart and Winston, 1967.

——. "Ethnic Intermarriage as an Indicator of Cultural Convergence in Soviet Central Asia." In E. Allworth, ed., *The Nationality Question in Soviet Central Asia*. New York: Praeger, 1973.

Dzhumagulov, A. *Sem'ia i brak u kirgizov Chuiskoi doliny*. Frunze: 1960.

Eason, W. "Demography." In Ellen Mickiewicz, ed., *Handbook of Soviet Social Science Data*. New York: Free Press, 1973.

Easterlin, Richard. *Population, Labor Force, and Long Swings in Economic Growth*. New York: National Bureau of Economic Research, 1968.

Egurnev, A.P. "Mezhnatsional'nye braki i ikh rol' v sblizhenii natsii i narodnostei SSSR." *Nauchnyi kommunism* 4 (1973): 28-34.

Elder, G. H., Jr. "Appearance and Education in Marriage Mobility." *American Sociological Review* 43 (August 1969): 510-33.

Elnett, Elaine. *Historic Origin and Social Development of Family Life in Russia*. New York: Columbia University Press, 1926.

Engels, Frederick. *The Origin of the Family, Private Property and the State*. New York: International Publishers, 1942.

Ermishin, P. "Ideal'nyi muzh ili razborchivaia nevesta?" *Literaturnaia gazeta*, June 16, 1976: 12.

Esenov, R. "Patrimonial Traditions," *Pravda*, October 15, 1975: 4. Translated in *CDSP* 27, 41: 26-27.

——. "After Paying the Bride-Price." *Pravda*, February 7, 1977: 4. Translated in *CDSP* 29, 6: 23.

Esenova, T. "Nenavistyi kalym." *Literaturnaia gazeta*, May 22, 1974.

Evstigneev, Iu. A. "Natsional'no-smeshannye braki v Makhachkale." *Sovetskaia etnografiia* 4 (1971): 80-85.

——. "Mezhetnicheskie braki v nekotoryky gorodakh Severnogo Kazakhstana." Vestnik Moskovskogo Universiteta, *Istoriia* 6 (1972): 76-79.

Fainburg, Z. I. "K voprosu ob eticheskoi motivatsii braka." In G. V. Osipov et al., eds., *Problemy braka, sem'i i demografii. Sotsial'nye issledovaniia, vypusk 4*. Moscow: Nauka, 1970.

——. "Vliianie emotsional'nykh otnoshenii v sem'e na ee stabilizatsiiu." Paper read at the XII International Seminar on Family Research, Moscow, 1972.

"The Family and Its Members." *Literaturnaia gazeta*, May 1, 1975: 12. Translated in *CDSP* 30, 18: 18.

Farkas, G. "Education, Wage Rates, and the Division of Labor between Husband and Wife." *Journal of Marriage and the Family* 38 (1976): 473-84.

"Farms Cultivate Love, Khrushchev Declares." *New York Times*, October 18, 1959: 22.

Fedorova, A. "'Bottoms Up!'—With a Bitter After-Taste." *Nauka i religiia* 7 (July 1975): 18-21. Translated in *CDSP* 27, 45: 14, 24.

Fedoseeva, E. "SM-120 Would Like to Make a Date with SZh-40." *Literaturnaia gazeta*, October 25, 1978: 13. Translated in *CDSP* 30, 44: 6, 20.

Feifer, George. *Moscow Farewell*. New York: Viking, 1976.

Feofanov, Iu. "Suprug dlia zhilploshchadi." *Izvestiia*, December 20, 1971: 6. Translated in *CDSP* 22, 51: 30.

Field, M. G. "Workers (and Mothers): Soviet Women Today." In Donald R. Brown, ed., *The Role and Status of Women in the Soviet Union*. New York: Teachers College Press, 1968.

Filippov, F. R., and Chetyrkin, Iu. K. "Brak kak forma sotsial'nykh peremeshchenii v sovetskom obshchestve." In *Problemy marksistskoi filosofii*. Sverdlovskii Gos. Ped. In-t., Uchenye zapiski, sbornik 110, 1970.

Filiukova, Lidiia F. *Sel'skaia sem'ia*. Minsk: Nauka i tekhnika, 1976.

"First Steps toward Family Service." *Nedelia* 52 (1977): 7. Translated in *CDSP* 30, 1: 13.

Fischer, George. *The Soviet System and Modern Society*. New York: Atherton, 1968.

Fisher, Wesley A. *The Moscow Gourmet*. Ann Arbor, Michigan: Ardis, 1974.

——. "Ethnic Consciousness and Intermarriage: Correlates of Endogamy among the Major Soviet Nationalities." *Soviet Studies* 3 (1977a): 395-408.

——. "Soviet-American Marriages." Paper read at the Annual Meeting of the National Council on Family Relations, San Diego, California, 1977b.

——, and Khotin, L. "Soviet Family Research." *Journal of Marriage and the Family* 39 (1977): 365-74.

Freiden, A. "The United States Marriage Market." *Journal of Political Economy* 82, part II (March-April 1974): S34-S53.

Gantskaia, O. A., and Terent'eva, L. N. "Sem'ia—mikrosreda etnicheskikh protsessov." In *Sovremennye etnicheskie protsessy v SSSR*. Moscow: Nauka, 1975.

Geiger, H. Kent. *The Family in Soviet Russia*. Cambridge, Mass.: Harvard University Press, 1968.

Gerschenkron, A. "Time Horizon in Russian Literature." *Slavic Review* 34 (1975): 692-715.

"Get Acquainted!" *Literaturnaia gazeta*, December 22, 1976: 13. Translated in *CDSP* 28, 52: 12-13.

Gilder, G. "In Defense of Monogamy." *Commentary* 58, 5 (November 1974): 31-36.

Gilmore, Tamara. *Me and My American Husband*. New York: Doubleday, 1968.

Glenn, N. D.; Ross, A. A.; and Tully, J. C. "Patterns of Intergenerational Mobility of Females through Marriage." *American Sociological Review* 39 (October 1974): 683-99.

Goldthorpe, J. "Social Stratification in Industrial Society." In P. Halmos, ed., *The Sociological Review Monograph*, no. 8 (October 1964).

Golod, S. I. "Molodaia sem'ia." In V. T. Lisovskii and V. A. Iadov, eds., *Molodezh' i sovremennost'*. Leningrad: Znanie, 1975.

Golofast, V. B. "Vybor supruga i motivy braka v SShA." In A. G. Kharchev and Z. A. Iankova, eds., *Metodologicheskie problemy issledovaniia byta. Sotsial'nye issledovaniia, vypusk 7*. Moscow: Nauka, 1971.

Goode, William J. *After Divorce*. Glencoe, Ill.: Free Press, 1956.

——. "The Theoretical Importance of Love." *American Sociological Review* 24 (February 1959): 38-47.

——. "Marital Satisfaction and Instability: Cross-Cultural Class Analysis of Divorce Rates." *International Social Science Journal* 14 (1962): 507-26.

——. *World Revolution and Family Patterns*. New York: Free Press, 1963.

——. *The Family*. Englewood Cliffs, N.J.: Prentice-Hall, 1964.

——. *Explorations in Social Theory*. New York: Oxford University Press, 1973.

——. "Comment: The Economics of Non-Monetary Variables." *Journal of Political Economy* 82, part II (March-April 1974): S27-S33.

Guboglo, M. N. "Sotsial'no-etnicheskie posledstviia dvuiazychiia." *Sovetskaia etnografiia* 2 (1972): 26-36.

Hajnal, J. "The Marriage Boom." *Population Index* 19 (April 1953): 80-101.

——. "European Marriage Patterns in Perspective." in D. V. Glass, ed., *Population and History*. Chicago: Aldine, 1965.

" 'He,' 'She' and 'They'." *Literaturnaia gazeta*, January 18, 1978: 12. Translated in *CDSP* 30, 5: 17.

Heer, D. M. "Negro-White Marriage in the United States." *Journal of Marriage and the Family* 28 (1966): 262-73.

——. "The Prevalence of Black-White Marriage in the United States, 1960 and 1970." *Journal of Marriage and the Family* 36 (1974): 246-59.

——. "Female Labor-Force Participation Rates and Fertility in the USSR: Statics and Dynamics of the Relationship." Unpublished manuscript, 1975.

Hollander, Paul. *Soviet and American Society: A Comparison*. New York: Oxford University Press, 1973.

Hough, J. "The Soviet System: Petrification of Pluralism?" *Problems of Communism* 2 (March-April 1972): 25-45.

Iankova, Zoia A. "Urban Family in the Developed Socialist Society." Paper read at the VIII World Congress of Sociology, Toronto, Canada, August 17-24, 1974.

——. *Gorodskaia sem'ia*. Moscow: Nauka, 1979.

Inkeles, Alex, and Bauer, Raymond. *The Soviet Citizen*. Cambridge, Mass.: Harvard University Press, 1959.

Institut Ekonomiki A. N. BSSR. *Nauchno-tekhnicheskii progress i sotsial'nye izmeneniia na sele: na materialakh Belorusskoi S.S.R.* Minsk: Nauka i tekhnika, 1972.

Institut International de Statistique. *Aperçu de la démographie des divers pays du monde*. La Haye, Holland: W. P. Van Stockum and Son, 1932.

Ismailov, A. I. "Nekotorye aspekty razvitiia mezhnatsional'nykh brakov v SSSR." *Izvestiia AN Kirgizskoi SSR* 4 (1972): 86-89.

Isupov, Arkadii A. *Natsional'nyi sostav naseleniia S.S.S.R.* Moscow: Statistika, 1964.

Iunina, L. "Tol'ko Romeo!" *Literaturnaia gazeta*, May 12, 1971: 13.

Iurkevich, Nikolai G. *Zakliuchenie braka po sovetskomu pravu*. Minsk: Nauka i Tekhnika, 1965.

——. *Sovetskaia sem'ia*. Minsk: Izdatel'stvo BGU im. V. I. Lenina, 1970a.

——. "Motivy zakliucheniia i stabil'nost' braka." In N. Solov'ev et al., eds., *Problemy byta, braka i sem'i*. Vilnius: Mintis, 1970b.

Ivanov, V. N. *Ugolovnoe zakonodatel'stvo Soiuza SSR i soiuznykh respublik: edinstvo i osobennosti*. Moscow: Iuridicheskaia literatura, 1973.

Juviler, P. H. "Marriage and Divorce." *Survey* 48 (1963): 114-16.

——. "Family Reforms on the Road to Communism." In P. H. Juviler and H. W. Morton, eds., *Soviet Policy-Making: Studies of Communism in Transition*. New York: Praeger, 1967.

——. "Women and Sex in Soviet Law." In Dorothey Atkinson et al., eds., *Women in Russia*. Stanford: Stanford University Press, 1977.

Kaiser, Robert G. *Russia: The People and the Power*. New York: Atheneum, 1976.

Kapto, A. "Ideino, vyrazitel'no." *Nauka i religiia* 12 (1975): 24-27.

Katz, Zev; Rogers, Rosemarie; and Harned, Frederic, eds. *Handbook of Major Soviet Nationalities*. New York: Free Press, 1975.

Khanazarov, K. Kh. "Mezhnatsional'nye braki—odna iz progressivnykh tendentsii sblizheniia sotsialisticheskikh natsii." *Obshchestivennyi nauki v Uzbekistane* 10 (1964): 26-31.

Kharchev, Anatolii G. *Marriage and Family Relations in the USSR*. Moscow: Novosti Press Publishing House, undated.

——. *Brak i sem'ia v SSSR: opyt sotsiologicheskogo issledovaniia* . Moscow: Mysl', 1964. Also 2d ed., 1979.

——. "Byt i sem'ia pri sotsialisme." *Voprosy filosofii* 3 (1967): 12-19.

——. "Nekotorye tendentsii razvitiia sem'i v SSSR i kapitalisticheskikh stranakh." In *Sotsiologiia i ideologiia*. Moscow: Nauka, 1969.

——. "Today's Family and Its Problems." *Zhurnalist*, November 1972: 58-61. Translated in *CDSP* 25, 1: 18, 1973.

——. "Nekotorye metodologicheskie problemy issledovaniia braka i sem'i." In A. G. Kharchev et al., eds., *Sem'ia kak ob'ekt filosofskogo i sotsiologicheskogo issledovaniia*. Leningrad: Nauka, 1974a.

——. "Women's Career Work and Family." Paper presented at the VIII World Congress of Sociology, Toronto, Canada, August 17-24, 1974b.

——, and Emel'ianova, K. L. "Brak: ideal i deistvitel'nost'." In *Problemy braka, sem'i i demografii. Sotsial'nye issledovaniia, vypusk 4*. Moscow: Nauka, 1970.

——, and Matskovskii, Mikhail S. *Sovremennaia sem'ia i ee problemy (Sotsial'no-demograficheskoe issledovanie)*. Moscow: Statistika, 1978.

Khitynov, Maksim B. "Osobennosti formirovaniia i razvitiia sotsialisticheskoi sem'i u ranee otstalykh narodov (po materialam Buriatskoi ASSR)." Candidate of Philosophical Sciences dissertation abstract, Alma-Ata, 1974.

Kholmogorov, Aleksandr I. *Internatsional'nye cherty sovetskikh natsii (na materialakh konkretno-sotsiologicheskikh issledovanii v Pribaltike)*. Moscow: Mysl', 1970.

Khorev, A. "Incompatible with Dignity." *Krasnaia zvezda*, March 15, 1979: 2. Translated in *CDSP* 31, 18: 19.

Khotsianov, Lev K. *Opyt izucheniia demograficheskikh sdvigov v sel'skom naselenii Moskovskoi i Riazanskoi oblastei za istekshee stoletie (1851-1960)*. Moscow: Gosudarstvennoe izdatel'stvo meditsinskoi literatury, 1963.

Kodeks o brake i sem'e RSFSR. Moscow: Iuridicheskaia literatura, 1975.

Koemets, E. "Üldharidusliku kooli õpilaste arvamusi abielust." In *Perekennaprobleemid: Uurimisrühma seminaritööde kogumik*. Tartu: 1972.

Kogan, Leonid N., ed. *Obshchestvenno-politicheskaia aktivnost' trudiashchikhsia.* Sverdlovsk: 1972.

Kohn, S. "The Vital Statistics of European Russia during the World War 1914-1917." In Stanislas Kohn and Alexander Neyendorff, *The Cost of the War to Russia.* New Haven: Yale University Press, 1932.

Kolokol'nikov, V. T. "Brachno-semeinye otnosheniia v srede kolkhoznogo krest'ianstva." *Sotsiologiche skie issledovaniia* 3 (1976): 78-87.

Kommunisticheskaia Akademiia. Komissiia po izucheniiu natsional'nogo voprosa. *Natsional'naia politika VKP(b) v tsifrakh.* Moscow: Izdatel'stvo Kommunisticheskoi Akademii, 1930.

Kon, I. S. "Sputnik zhizni." *Nedelia* 5 (1976): 16.

Kopchak, Valentina P. and Kopchak, Stepan I. *Naselenie Zakarpat'ia za 100 let.* Lvov: Vishcha Shkola, 1977.

Koppel, E. and Tiit, E. *"Ideal suprugi (supruga) i sem'i."* In Sovetskaia Sotsiologicheskaia Assotsiatsiia et al., *Dinamika izmeneniia polozheniia zhenshchiny i sem'ia.* Moscow: 1972.

Korchak-Chepurkovskii, Iu. A., and Chuiko, L. V. "Ob izmerenii ponizhaiushchego vliianiia nesootvetstviia mezhdu chislennostiami muzhchin i zhenshchin v brakosposobnom vozraste na uroven' brachnosti." In *Voprosy demografii.* Kiev: 1968.

Korey, William. *The Soviet Cage: Anti-Semitism in Russia.* New York: Viking, 1973.

Kotelevskaia, L. "Ne tol'ko bestaktnost'." *Izvestiia*, February 13, 1968: 3.

Kron, Aleksandr. "Bessonnitsa. Part I." *Novyi mir* 1 (1977): 7-80.

Krupianskaia, Vera Iu.; Budina, Oksana R.; Polishchuk, Ninel' S.; and Iukhneva, Natal'ia V. *Kul'tura i byt gorniakov i metallurgov Nizhnego Tagila (1917-1970).* Moscow: Nauka, 1974.

Krupskaia, Nadezhda K. *On Education.* Moscow: Foreign Languages Publishing House, 1957.

Kulaeva, S. "Eshche raz o pomolvkakh i razmolvkakh." *Literaturnaia gazeta*, July 31, 1974:]2.

Kurganov, Ivan A. *Sem'ia v. SSSR: 1917-1967.* New York: 1967.

Kurkin, P. I. *Statistika dvizheniia naseleniia v Moskovskoi gubernii v 1883-1897 gg.* Moscow: 1902.

Kurman, Mikhail V., and Lebedinskii, Ivan V. *Naselenie bol'shogo sotsialisticheskogo goroda.* Moscow: Statistika, 1968.

Kushner, P. I., ed. *Selo Viriatino v proshlom i nastoiashchem: Opyt etnograficheskogo izucheniia russkoi kolkhoznoi derevni.* Moscow: 1958.

Kuvshinnikov, P. "Estestvennoe dvizhenie naseleniia RSFSR v 1920-1922 gg." *Vestnik statistiki* 21 (April-June 1925).

Kuznetsova, L. "Kogo my liubim." *Literaturnaia gazeta,* September 5, 1973: 13.

———. "Zhenikhi - smelee!" *Literaturnaia gazeta,* January 1, 1975: 12.

———. "The Single Man." *Nedelia,* August 6-12, 1979: 14-15. Translated in *CDSP* 31, 32: 1-3.

Lalaian, E. "Vaoits-dzor." *Azgagrakan handes* 13 (1906): 143.

Landis, J. T. "Religiousness, Family Relationships, and Family Values in Protestant, Catholic, and Jewish Families." *Marriage and Family Living* 22 (November 1960): 341-48.

Lane, David. *The End of Inequality? Stratification under State Socialism.* Baltimore, Md.: Penguin Books, 1971.

Lapidus, Gail W. *Women in Soviet Society: Equality, Development, and Social Change.* Berkeley: University of California Press, 1978.

Laptenok, Sergei D. *Moral' i sem'ia.* Minsk: Nauka i tekhnika, 1967.

Laumann, Edward O. *Bonds of Pluralism: The Form and Substance of Urban Networks.* New York: John Wiley and Sons, 1973.

Leonidova, B. "Ser'eznyi shag." *Izvestiia,* June 10, 1972: 5.

"Let It Be Like This Everywhere." *Pravda,* February 8, 1969: 3.

"Let's Get Acquainted." *Literaturnaia gazeta,* November 17, 1976: 13. Translated in *CDSP* 28, 47: 7.

Lewis, Robert A.; Rowland, Richard H.; and Clem, Ralph S. *Nationality and Population Change in Russia and the USSR: An Evaluation of Census Data, 1897-1970.* New York: Praeger, 1976.

Liegle, Ludwig. *Familienerziehung und sozialer Wandel in der Sowjetunion.* Heidelberg: Quelle and Meyer, 1970.

Liss, L. "Sotsial'naia obuslovlennost' vybora professii." In *Tartuskii Gosudarstvennyi Universitet, Materialy konferentsii "Kommunisticheskoe vospitanie studenchestva."* Tartu: 1971.

Lorince, G. "Brides for Sale." *New Statesman*, June 17, 1966: 169-70.

Lubrano, L.; Fisher, W.; Schwartz, J.; and Tomlinson, K. "Survey Research and Public Attitudes in the Soviet Union." In William Welsh, ed., *Survey Research and Public Attitudes in the USSR and Eastern Europe.* New York: Pergamon, forthcoming.

Luzbetak, Louis J. *Marriage and the Family in Caucasia.* Vienna-Modling: St. Gabriel's Mission Press, 1951.

Mace, David, and Mace, Vera. *The Soviet Family.* New York: Doubleday, 1963.

Madison, B. "Social Services to Women and Children: Problems and Priorities." In Dorothy Atkinson, et al., eds., *Women in Russia.* Stanford: Stanford University Press, 1977.

Malinovskii, L. "'Friendship' Correspondence Club." *Literaturnaia gazeta*, December 22, 1976: 13. Translated in *CDSP* 28, 52: 13.

Mandel, William M. *Soviet Women.* New York: Anchor, 1975.

Marcuse, Herbert. *Soviet Marxism.* New York: Vintage, 1961.

Markiewicz-Lagneau, Janina. *Éducation, égalité, et socialisme.* Paris: Éditions Anthropos, 1969.

"Marriage Insurance." *Turkmenskaia iskra*, November 22, 1977: 4. Translated in *CDSP* 29, 50: 18.

"Marriages Arranged by Electronic Matchmaker." *Pravda*, June 15, 1971: 3. Translated in *CDSP* 23, 24: 10.

Marx, Karl. *Capital: A Critique of Political Economy.* Translated from the 3d German ed. by S. Moore and E. Aveling. 2 vols. Chicago: C. H. Kerr, 1906.

Massell, Gregory J. *The Surrogate Proletariat: Moslem Women and Revolutionary Strategies in Soviet Central Asia: 1919-1929.* Princeton: Princeton University Press, 1974.

Matley, Ian. "Agricultural Development." In Edward Allworth, ed., *Central Asia: A Century of Russian Rule.* New York: Columbia University Press, 1967, pp. 266-308.

Matthews, Mervyn. *Soviet Government: A Selection of Official Documents on Internal Policies.* New York: Taplinger, 1974.

——. *Privilege in the Soviet Union: A Study of Elite Life-Styles under Communism.* London: George Allen and Unwin, 1978.

Mazur, D. P. "Fertility among Ethnic Groups in the USSR." *Demography* 4 (1967): 172-95.

——. "Correlates of Divorce in the USSR." *Demography* 6 (1969): 279-86.

——. "Relation of Marriage and Education to Fertility in the USSR." *Population Studies* 27 (1973): 105-16.

Meliksetian, A. "From Love to Divorce." *Zhurnalist* 1 (1978): 50-52. Translated in *CDSP* 30, 7: 3, 7.

Merton, R. K. "Intermarriage and the Social Structure: Fact and Theory." *Psychiatry* 4 (1941): 361-74.

Meyendorff, John. *Marriage: An Orthodox Perspective*. New York: St. Vladimir's Seminary Press, 1975.

Mickiewicz, Ellen, ed. *Handbook of Soviet Social Science Data*. New York: Free Press, 1973.

Monahan, T. P. "Are Interracial Marriages Really Less Stable?" *Social Forces* 48 (1970a): 461-73.

——. "Interracial Marriages in Pennsylvania and Philadelphia." *Demography* 7 (1970b): 287-99.

——. "Interracial Marriage in the United States: Some Data on Upstate New York." *International Journal of Sociology of the Family* 1 (1971): 94-105.

Morton, Henry W. "What Have the Soviet Leaders Done About the Housing Crisis?" In Henry W. Morton and Rudolf L. Tökes, eds., *Soviet Politics and Society in the 1970's*. New York: Free Press, 1974.

Murstein, B. I.; Cerreto, M.; and MacDonald, M. G. "A Theory and Investigation of the Effect of Exchange-Orientation on Marriage and Friendship." *Journal of Marriage and the Family* 39 (1977): 543-48.

Murtazakulov, I. "Make Atheistic Work Highly Militant." *Turkmenskaia iskra*, April 16, 1975: 2. Translated in *CDSP* 27, 38: 18.

Mushkina, E. "Great Expectations." *Zhurnalist* 12 (1978): 49-51. Translated in *CDSP* 31, 8: 12-130.

Narinyani, S. "A Rake's Progress." *Pravda*, June 21, 1952: 2. Translated in *CDSP* 4, 25: 25.

Narodnyi Kommissariat Zdravookhraneniia. *Trudy Kommissii po Obsledovaniiu Sanitarnykh Posledstvii Voiny 1914-1920 Godov*. Volume I. Moscow and Petrograd: 1923.

Naulko, Vsevolod I. *Etnichnii sklad naselennia Ukrains'koi RsR*. Kiev: Naukova dumka, 1965.

Nekhoroshkov, M. F. "Khristianstvo i brachno-semeinye otnosheniia." Candidate of Philosophical Sciences dissertation abstract, Kazan, 1971.

Newth, J. A. "Statistical Study of Intermarriage among Jews in Vilnius (Vilna)." *Bulletin on Soviet Jewish Affairs*, January 1968.

New York Times. February 4, 1954a: 3.

——. April 30, 1954b: 2.

——. October 11, 1955: 19.

——. December 10, 1977: 2.

——. August 2, 1978: 1.

Nikonov, Vladimir A. *Imia i obshchestvo*. Moscow: Nauka, 1974.

"Not Simply Love." *Sovetskaia kul'tura*, April 27, 1976: 6. Translated in *CDSP* 28, 18: 11.

Odinets, M. and Riaboshtan, I. "Svad'ba v dva tura." *Pravda*, March 18, 1968: 3.

Ofer, G., and Vinokur, A. "Earning Differentials by Sex in the Soviet Union: A First Look." Research report no. 120. Jerusalem: Hebrew University Department of Economics, 1979.

Orlova, Nina V. *Pravovoe regulirovanie braka v SSSR*. Moscow: Nauka, 1971.

Orwell, George. *1984*. New York: Harcourt, Brace, 1949.

Ostrovskii, Nikolai A. *Kak zakalialas' stal'*. Moscow: Molodaia gvardiia, 1936.

Ovchinnikova, I. "Potomu chto schastliv." *Izvestiia*, April 12, 1970: 4.

Parkin, Frank. *Class Inequality and Political Order: Social Stratification in Capitalist and Communist Societies*. New York: Praeger, 1971.

Peach, C. "Homogamy, Propinquity, and Segregation: A Re-Evaluation." *American Sociological Review* 39 (October 1974): 636-41.

Perevedentsev, V. I. "Budet li svad'ba?" *Literaturnaia gazeta*, February 24, 1971a: 13.

——. "Pora zhenit'sia." *Literaturnaia gazeta*, April 21, 1971b: 13.

——. "Speshit' li zamuzh?" *Literaturnaia gazeta*, August 30, 1972: 12.

——. "Brak i sem'ia." *Zhurnalist* 1 (1974): 91-96.

——. "Bachelor Cities." *Literaturnaia gazeta*, February 16, 1977: 13. Translated in *CDSP* 29, 7: 16.

Petrakova, E. I., comp. *Sbornik zakonodatel'nykh materialov o registratsii aktov grazhdanskogo sostoianiia v Ukrainskoi SSR*. Kiev: Izdatel'stvo Politicheskoi Literatury Ukrainy, 1972.

Petrogradskoe Stolichnoe Statisticheskoe Biuro. *Materialy po statistike Petrograda. Vypusk 1*. Petrograd: 1920.

Pipes, R. "Introduction: The Nationality Problem." In Z. Katz et al., eds., *Handbook of Major Soviet Nationalities*. New York: Free Press, 1975.

Powell, David E. *Antireligious Propaganda in the Soviet Union*. Cambridge, Mass.: MIT Press, 1975.

Pressat, R. "La Natalité et la nuptialité en Union Sovietique." *Population* 4 (1963): 877-86.

——. "La Population de L'U.R.S.S. Donées récentes." *Population* 27 (1972): 809-37.

Preston, S. H., and Richards, A. T. "The Influence of Women's Work Opportunities on Marriage Rates." *Demography* 12 (1975): 209-22.

Proletkin, V. "Kradenye nevesty." *Izvestiia*, March 16, 1968: 3.

Pushkareva, L. A. and Shmeleva, M. N. "Sovremennaia russkaia krestianskaia svad'ba." *Sovetskaia etnografiia* 3 (1959): 47-56.

Radzinskii, E. "Differing Faces of Loneliness." *Literaturnaia gazeta*, January 12, 1977: 13. Translated in *CDSP* 23, 3: 16.

Ransel, David L., ed. *The Family in Imperial Russia: New Lines of Historical Research*. Urbana: University of Illinois Press, 1978.

Rashin, Adolf G. *Naselenie Rossii za 100 let*. Moscow: Gosstatizdat, 1956.

Repin, I. *Dalekoe blizkoe*. 1887.

Riurikov, Iu. "Tol'ko li liubov'?" *Literaturnaia gazeta*, July 17, 1974: 13.

——. "Love and Family Today." *Molodoi Kommunist* 10 (1975): 89-97. Translated in *CDSP* 28, 15: 1-3.

Roshchin, Mikhail. "Valentin i Valentina." *Teatr* (1971): 157-86.

Rubin, Z. "Do American Women Marry Up?" *American Sociological Review* 33 (October 1968): 750-56.

Rubinov, A. "Happiness Is So Possible." *Literaturnaia gazeta*, March 8, 1978: 12. Translated in *CDSP* 30, 10: 14-15.

Rudnev, V. A. "O bytovykh prazdnikakh i ritualakh." In *Sovetskii etiket*. Leningrad: Znanie, 1971.

Sacks, Michael P. *Women's Work in Soviet Russia: Continuity in the Midst of Change*. New York: Praeger, 1976.

Safilios-Rothschild, C. "Family and Stratification: Some Macrosociological Observations and Hypotheses." *Journal of Marriage. and the Family* 37 (1976): 855-60.

Saikowski, C. "Boy Meets Girl as Moscow Laughs." *Christian Science Monitor*, December 12, 1970.

Santos, F. P. "The Economics of Marital Status." In Cynthia B. Lloyd, ed., *Sex, Discrimination, and the Division of Labor*. New York: Columbia University Press, 1975.

Sawhill, I. V. "Economic Perspectives on the Family." *Daedalus* (Spring 1977): 115-26.

Schlesinger, Rudolf, ed. *The Family in the U.S.S.R. Changing Attitudes in Soviet Russia: Documents and Readings*. London: Routledge and Kegan Paul, 1949.

Semenov, V. E. "Obrazy braka i liubvi v molodezhnykh zhurnalakh (Opyt kontent-analiza)." In *Molodezh': Obrazovanie, vospitanie, professional'naia deiatel'-nost'*. Leningrad: Nauka, 1973.

Semenov, Vladimir. "Dva stikhotvoreniia." *Novyi mir* 7 (1958): 137-38.

"Sem'ia: kak byt' schastlivym . . ." *Literaturnaia gazeta*, May 17, 1972: 13.

Sergienko, E. "A Conversation Not Only about Betrothals." *Nauka i religiia* 12 (1976): 41-44. Translated in *CDSP* 29, 11: 11.

Shabad, T. "Moscow Rabbi Says Visitors Abet Black Market." *New York Times*, October 5, 1962: 4.

Shaffer, Harry G. *The Soviet Treatment of Jews*. New York: Praeger, 1974.

Shakhot'ko, Liudmila P. *Rozhdaemost' v Belorussii*. Minsk: Nauka i tekhnika, 1975.

Shatunovskii, I. "Kak ishchut prostakov." *Pravda*, August 17, 1969: 6.

Sheehy, A. "Intermarriage in Central Asia and Kazakhstan." Radio Liberty Research Paper 149/75, 1975.

Shein, V. P. *K istorii voprosa o smeshannykh brakakh*. St. Petersburg: Senatskaia tipografiia, 1907.

Shkaratan, Ovsei I. *Problemy sotsial'noi struktury rabochego klassa*. Moscow: Mysl', 1970a.

———. "Etno-sotsial'naia struktura gorodskogo naseleniia Tatarskoi ASSR (po materialam sotsiologicheskogo obsledovaniia)." *Sovetskaia etnografiia* 3 (1970b): 3-16.

Shliapentokh, Vladimir E. *Sotsiologiia dlia vsekh*. Moscow: Sovetskaia Rossiia, 1970.

———. "Zankomstva i svad'by." *Literaturnaia gazeta*, June 9, 1971: 12.

———. "Their Own Problems and Others'." *Literaturnaia gazeta*, November 30, 1977: 12. Translated in *CDSP* 29, 48: 15-16.

Shtan'ko, N. "Anatolii i Marta." *Izvestiia*, December 17, 1967: 5.

Shubkin, V. N. "Molodezh' vstupaet v zhizn'. *Voprosy filosofii* 5 (1965): 57-70.

Simirenko, A. "Soviet and American Sociology in the 1970's." *Studies in Comparative Communism* 6 (1973): 27-50.

"60,000,000 semei." *Literaturnaia gazeta*, July 1, 1970: 11.

Skachkova, N. P. "Mezhnatsional'naia sem'ia kak faktor sblizheniia sotsialisticheskikh natsii." *Izvestiia AN Kazakhskoi SSR, Seriia obshchestvennykh nauk* 6 (1975): 55-63.

Sklar, June. "East European Nuptiality: A Comparative Historical Study of Patterns and Causes." Ph.D. dissertation, University of California at Berkeley, 1970.

———. "The Role of Marriage Behaviour in the Demographic Transition: The Case of Eastern Europe around 1900." *Population Studies* 28 (1974): 231-48.

Smith, Hedrick. *The Russians*. New York: Quadrangle, 1976.

Soloukhin, V. "Kaplia rosy" (Okonchanie). *Znamia* 2 (1960).

Solov'ev, Nikolai Ia. "Kto nravitsia devushkam . . ." *Literaturnaia gazeta*, December 19, 1973: 13.

——. "Pomolvki i razmolvki." *Literaturnaia gazeta*, July 17, 1974: 13.

——. *Brak i sem'ia segodnia*. Vilnius: Mintis, 1977.

Solzhenitsyn, Aleksandr. *Cancer Ward*. New York: Dial Press, 1968.

——. *The Gulag Archipelago, 1918-1956: An Experiment in Literary Investigation. III-IV*. New York: Harper & Row, 1975.

Soviet Life March 1973: 20.

Spiridonov, L. I., and Gilinskii, Ia. I., eds. *Chelovek kakob'ekt sotsiologicheskogo issledovaniia*. Leningrad: Izdatel'stvo Leningradskogo universiteta, 1977.

Statisticheskii spravochnik g. Moskvy i Moskovskoi gub. 1927 g. Moscow: Izdanie moskovskogo statischeskogo otdela, 1928.

Stepin, D. "Concerning Ordinary Events." *Nauka i religiia* 7 (July 1975): 13-16. Translated in *CDSP* 27, 45: 13-14.

Stites, Richard. *The Women's Liberation Movement in Russia: Feminism, Nihilism, and Bolshevism 1860-1930*. Princeton: Princeton University Press, 1978.

Stojanovic, Svetozar. *Between Ideals and Reality: A Critique of Socialism and Its Future*. New York: Oxford University Press, 1975.

Stone, L. "Marriage among the English Nobility in the 16th and 17th Centuries." *Comparative Studies in Society and History* 3 (1961): 182-206.

Svetlanova, E. "Muzh dlia Galochki." *Literaturnaia gazeta*, January 8, 1969: 12. Translated in *CDSP* 1, 9: 13-14.

Swafford, M. "Sex Differences in Soviet Earnings." *American Sociological Review* 43 (1978): 657, 673.

Sysenko, V. A. "Brak i sem'ia v usloviiakh krupnogo goroda (Na materialakh g. Moskvy)." In *Nekotorye sotsial'no-demograficheskie problemy narodonaseleniia, Vypusk 3*. Moscow: Moscow State University, 1971.

Tamimov, M. B. "Polovozrastnaia struktura, brachnost', i razmer sem'i narodov Srednei Azii i Kazakhstana." In *Problemy narodonaseleniia*. Moscow University, 1970.

Tavit, A. "Abiellumisvanusega seotud probleeme Eesti NSV-s." In A. Blumfeldt et al., eds., *Perekonna-probleemid II*. Tartu: Tartu State University, 1975.

Terent'eva, L. N. "Opredelenie svoei natsional'noi prinadlezhnosti podrostkami v natsional'nosmeshanykh sem'iakh." *Sovetskaia etnografiia* 3 (1969): 20-30.

——. "Formirovanie etnicheskogo samosoznaniia v natsional'no-smeshanykh sem'iakh v SSSR." Paper presented at the Eighth International Sociological Congress, Toronto, Canada. Moscow: 1974.

Ter-Sarkisiants, Alla E. *Sovremennaia sem'ia u armian*. Moscow: Nauka, 1972.

——. "O natsional'nom aspekte brakov v Armianskoi SSR (po materiialam zagsov)." *Sovetskaia etnografiia* 4 (1973): 89-95.

Titma, M. Kh. "Rol' sotsial'nogo proiskhozhdeniia v formirovanii tsennostei professii." *Uchenye zapiski Tartuskogo Gosudarstvennogo Universiteta, Trudy po filosofii* 15 (1970): 156-204.

Tol'ts, M. "Metodika postroeniia tablits brachnosti kholostiakov." In *Demograficheskaia situatsiia v SSSR*. Moscow: Statistika, 1976.

Tomilov, N. A. "Sovremennye etnicheskie protsessy u Tatar gorodov zapadnoi Sibiri." *Sovetskaia etnografiia* 6 (1972): 87-97.

Trufanov, Ivan P. *Problemy byta gorodskogo naseleniia SSSR*. Leningrad: Izdatel'stvo Leningradskogo Universiteta, 1973.

Ts. S.U. Azerbaidzhanskoi SSR. *Azerbaidzhan v tsifrakh: kratkii statisticheskii sbornik*. Baku: Azerbaidzhanskoe Gosudarstvennoe Izdatel'stvo, 1964.

Ts. S.U. ESSR (Tsentral'noe Statisticheskoe Upravlenie Estonskoi SSR). *Narodnoe khoziaistvo Estonskoi SSR v 1968 godu. Statisticheskii ezhegodnik*. Tallin: Statistika, 1969.

——. *Narodnoe knoziaistvo Estonskoi SSR v 1969 godu. Statisticheskii ezhegodnik*. Tallin: Statistika, 1970.

——. *Narodnoe khoziaistvo Estonskoi SSR v 1970 godu. Statisticheskii ezhegodnik*. Tallin: Statistika, 1971.

Ts. S.U. Latviiskoi SSR (Tsentral'noe Statisticheskoe Upravlenie Latviiskoi SSR). *Ekonomika i kul'tura sovetskoi Latvii. Statisticheskii sbornik*. Riga: Statistika, 1966.

——. *Narodnoe khoziaistvo Latviiskoi SSR v 1970 godu*. Riga: Statistika, 1972.

Ts. S.U. Litovskoi SSR (Tsentral'noe Statisticheskoe Upravlenie Litovskoi SSR). *Ekonomika i kul'tura Litovskoi SSR v 1968 godu.* Vilnius: Statistika, 1969.

———. *Ekonomika i kul'tura Litovskoi SSR v 1969 godu.* Vilnius: Statistika, 1970.

———. *Ekonomika i kul'tura Litovskoi SSR v 1970 godu.* Vilnius: Statistika, 1971.

———. *Ekonomika i kul'tura Litovskoi SSR v 1971 godu.* Vilnius: Statistika, 1972.

———. *Ekonomika i kul'tura Litovskoi SSR v 1972 godu.* Vilnius: Statistika, 1973.

Ts. S.U. RSFSR (Tsentral'noe Statisticheskoe Upravlenie RSFSR). *Estestvennoe dvizhenie naseleniia RSFSR za 1926 goda.* Moscow: Izdanie Ts. S.U. RSFSR, 1928.

Ts. S.U. SSSR (Tsentral'noe Statisticheskoe Upravlenie). *Estestvennoe dvizhenie naseleniia SSSR 1923-25.* Moscow: Izdanie Ts. S.U. SSSR, 1928.

———. *Vsesoiuznaia perepis' naseleniia 1926 goda.* Volume LI. Moscow: Gosstatizdat, 1931.

———. *Narodnoe knoziaistvo SSSR v 1960 godu.* Moscow: Statistika, 1961.

———. *Itogi vsesoiuznoi perepisi naseleniia 1959 goda. SSSR.* Moscow: Gosstatizdat, 1962a.

———. *Itogi vsesoiuznoi perepisi naseleniia 1959 goda. Estonskaia SSR.* Moscow: Gosstatizdat, 1962b.

———. *Itogi vsesoiuznoi perepisi naseleniia 1959 goda. Kazakhskaia SSR.* Moscow: Gosstatizdat, 1962c.

———. *Itogi vsesoiuznoi perepisi naseleniia 1959 goda. Latviiskaia SSR.* Moscow: Gosstatizdat, 1962d.

———. *Itogi vsesoiuznoi perepisi naseleniia 1959 goda. Moldavskaia SSR.* Moscow: Gosstatizdat, 1962e.

———. *Itogi vsesoiuznoi perepisi naseleniia 1959 goda. Uzbekskaia SSR.* Moscow: Gosstatizdat, 1962f.

———. *Itogi vsesoiuznoi perepisi naseleniia 1959 goda. Armianskaia SSR.* Moscow: Gosstatizdat, 1963a.

——. *Itogi vsesoiuznoi perepisi naseleniia 1959 goda. Azerbaidzhanskaia SSR.* Moscow: Gosstatizdat, 1963b.

——. *Itogi vsesoiuznoi perepisi naseleniia 1959 goda. Belorusskaia SSR.* Moscow: Gosstatizdat, 1963c.

——. *Itogi vsesoiuznoi perepisi naseleniia 1959 goda. Gruzinskaia SSR.* Moscow: Gosstatizdat, 1963d.

——. *Itogi vsesoiuznoi perepisi naseleniia 1959 goda. Kirgizskaia SSR.* Moscow: Gosstatizdat, 1963e.

——. *Itogi vsesoiuznoi perepisi naseleniia 1959 goda. Litovskaia SSR.* Moscow: Gosstatizdat, 1963f.

——. *Itogi vsesoiuznoi perepisi naseleniia 1959 goda. RSFSR.* Moscow: Gosstatizdat, 1963g.

——. *Itogi vsesoiuznoi perepisi naseleniia 1959 goda. Tadzhikskaia SSR.* Moscow: Gosstatizdat, 1963h.

——. *Itogi vsesoiuznoi perepisi naseleniia 1959 goda. Turkmenskaia SSR.* Moscow: Gosstatizdat, 1963i.

——. *Itogi vsesoiuznoi perepisi naseleniia 1959 goda. Ukrainskaia SSR.* Moscow: Gosstatizdat, 1963j.

——. *Narodnoe khoziaistvo SSSR v 1962 godu.* Moscow: Statistika, 1963k.

——. *Narodnoe khoziaistvo SSSR v 1964 godu.* Moscow: Statistika, 1965.

——. *Narodnoe khoziaistvo SSSR v 1965 godu.* Moscow: Statistika, 1966.

——. *Itogi vsesoiuznoi perepisi naseleniia 1970 goda. Volume 2: Pol, vozrast i sostoianie v brake naseleniia SSSR, soiuznykh i avtonomnykh respublik, kraev i oblastei.* Moscow: Statistika, 1972.

——. *Itogi vsesoiuznoi perepisi naseleniia 1970 goda. Volume 4: Natsional'nyi sostav naseleniia SSSR.* Moscow: Statistika, 1973a.

——. *Itogi vsesoiuznoi perepisi naseleniia 1970 goda. Volume 5: Raspredelenie naseleniia SSSR, soiuznykh i avtonomnykh respublik, kraev i oblastei po obshchestvennym gruppam, istochnikam sredstv sushchestvovaniia i otrasliam narodnogo khoziaistva.* Moscow: Statistika, 1973b.

——. *Narodnoe khoziaistvo SSSR v 1972 godu.* Moscow: Statistika, 1973c.

——. *Itogi vsesoiuznoi perepisi, naseleniia 1970 godu. Volume 3: Uroven'obrazovaniia naseleniia SSSR, soiuznykh i avtonomnykh respublik, kraev i oblastei.* Moscow: Statistika, 1973d.

——. *Itogi vsesoiuznoi perepisi naseleniia 1970 goda. Volume 7: Migratsiia naseleniia, chislo i sostav semei v SSSR, soiuznykh i avtonomnykh respublikakh, kraiakh i oblastiakh.* Moscow: Statistika, 1974a.

——. *Narodnoe khoziaistvo SSSR v 1973 godu.* Moscow: Statistika, 1974b.

——. *Naselenie SSSR (chislennost' sostav, i dvizhenie naseleniia) 1973. Statisticheskii sbornik.* Moscow: Statistika, 1975a.

——. *Zhenshchiny v SSSR: Statisticheskii sbornik.* Moscow: Statistika, 1975b.

Ts. S.U. Ukrainskoi SSR (Tsentral'noe Statisticheskoe Upravlenie Ukrainskoi SSR). *Narodne gospodarstvo Ukrains'koi RSR v 1970 rotsi. Statistichnii Shchorichnik.* Kiev: Statistika, 1971.

Tsentral'nyi Statisticheskii Komitet. *Dvizhenie naseleniia v evropeiskoi Rossii za 1894 goda. Statistika Rossiiskoi Imperii, volume 47.* St. Petersburg: 1894.

——. *Dvizhenie naseleniia v evropeiskoi Rossii za 1895 goda. Statistika Rossiiskoi Imperii, volume 49.* St. Petersburg: 1895.

——. *Dvizhenia naseleniia v evropeiskoi Rossii za 1896 goda. Statistika Rossiiskoi Imperii, volume 50.* St. Petersburg: 1896.

——. *Dvizhenie naseleniia v evropeiskoi Rossii za 1897 goda. Statistika Rossiiskoi Imperii, volume 56.* St. Petersburg: 1897.

——. *Dvizhenie naseleniia v evropeiskoi Rossii za 1898 goda. Statistika Rossiiskoi Imperii, volume 58.* St. Petersburg: 1898.

——. *Dvizhenie naseleniia v evropeiskoi Rossii za 1899 goda. Statistika Rossiiskoi Imperii, volume 62.* St. Petersburg: 1899.

——. *Dvizhenie naseleniia v evropeiskoi Rossii za 1900 goda. Statistika Rossiiskoi Imperii, volume 63.* St. Petersburg: 1900.

——. *Obshchii svod po Imperii resul'tatov razrabotki dannykh pervoi vseobshchei perepisi naseleniia. Volume I.* St. Petersburg: 1905.

——. *Ezhegodnik Rossii, 1906 g.* St. Petersburg: 1907.

——. *Ezhegodnik Rossii, 1907 g.* St. Petersburg: 1908.

——. *Ezhegodnik Rossii, 1908 g.* St. Petersburg: 1909.

——. *Dvizhenie naseleniia v evropeiskoi Rossii za 1910 goda. Statistika Rossiiskoi Imperii, volume 93.* St. Petersburg: 1910a.

———. *Ezhegodnik Rossii, 1909g.* St. Petersburg: 1910b.

———. *Statisticheskii Ezhegodnik Rossii 1914 g.* Petrograd: Izdanie Tsentral'nogo Statisticheskogo Komiteta, 1915.

Ugolovnoe zakonodatel'stvo Soiuza SSR i soiuznykh respublik. Moscow: Gosiurizdat, 1963.

Ulianova, L. "A Tree in the Yard." *Komsomol'skaia pravda*, March 7, 1979: 2. Translated in *CDSP* 31, 22: 15-16.

"Under the Impact of a New Way of Life." *Pravda*, July 27, 1975: 3. Translated in *CDSP* 27, 30: 21-22.

United Nations, Department of Economic and Social Affairs. *Demographic Yearbook. 1968.*

———. *Demographic Yearbook. 1969.*

———. *Demographic Yearbook. 1970.*

———. *Demographic Yearbook. 1971.*

———. *Demographic Yearbook. 1972.*

———. *Demographic Yearbook. 1973.*

———. *Demographic Yearbook. 1977.*

Urusova, A. "Traditsii nastoiashchie i mnimye." *Izvestiia*, October 20, 1973: 5.

U.S. Bureau of the Census. *Census of Population: 1970, Marital Status, Final Report PC(2)-4C.* Washington, D.C.: U.S. Government Printing Office, 1972.

USSR: 100 Questions and Answers. Moscow: Novosti Press Agency Publishing House, 1977.

Valkenier, Elizabeth. "The Peredvizhniki School of Painters against Its Social and Cultural Background." Ph.D. dissertation, Columbia University, 1975.

Van'kaev, Iu. K. "Geterogennye braki v Kalmytskoi ASSR." In G. A. Slesarev et al., eds., *Izmeneniia sotsial'noi struktur sotsialisticheskogo obshchestva.* Moscow: Institute of Sociological Research, 1976.

Vardanian, R. A., and Karavaeva, S. V. "Brachnost' naseleniia v Armianskoi SSR." In M. A. Adonts and L. M. Davtian, eds., *Materialy vsesoiuznoi nauchnoi konferentsii po problemam narodonaseleniia Zakavkaz'ia.* Ereven: 1968.

Vasil'eva, Evelina K. "Etnodemograficheskaia kharakteristika semeinoi struktury naseleniia Kazani v 1967 g." *Sovetskaia etnografiia* 5, 1968: 13-24.

——. *Sotsial'no-professional'nyi uroven' gorodskoi molodezhi.* Leningrad: Izdatel'stvo Leningradskogo Universiteta, 1973.

Vasil'evskaia, N. S. "Opyt konkretno-sotsiologicheskogo issledovaniia otnosheniia k religii v sovremennoi gorodskoi sem'e." *Voprosy nauchnogo ateisma* 13 (1972): 383-403. Moscow: Mysl'. Translated in *Soviet Sociology* 13, 3: 57-79.

Vedomosti Verkhovnogo Soveta SSSR. Number 10, 1947.

Velikanova, L. "Zhenshchiny stali molozhe!" *Literaturnaia gazeta*, September 22, 1971: 13.

Verb, Lidiia Ia. "Kul'tura vzaimotnoshenii muzhchiny i zhenshchiny." In *Sovetskii etiket.* Leningrad: Znanie, 1971.

——. *S glazu na glaz.* Leningrad: Lenizdat, 1975.

Vestnik statistiki. Number 8, 1963.

——. Number 1, 1965.

——. Number 11, 1967.

——. Number 2, 1969.

——. Number 6, 1970.

——. Number 2, 1971a.

——. Number 12, 1971b.

——. Number 12, 1973.

——. Number 12, 1974.

——. Number 11, 1975a.

——. Number 12, 1975b.

——. Number 11, 1976.

——. Number 12, 1977.

——. Number 11, 1978.

Vishnevskii, A. G. "Liubov' po rashchetu?" *Komsomolskaia pravda*, August 8, 1975a: 4.

——. "Rannii brak?" *Literaturnaia gazeta*, March 26, 1975b: 9.

——, ed. *Brachnost', rozhdaemost', smertnost' v Rossii i v SSSR*. Moscow: Statistika, 1977.

Vitols, Y. "Za kogo vykhodiat zamuzh i na kom zheniatsia rizhane." *Nauka i tekhnika* 2 (February 1972): 32-35.

Voina, V. "Razvodov ne budet." *Literaturnaia gazeta*, June 3, 1970: 13.

Vorozheikin, Evgenii M. *Semeinye pravootnosheniia v SSSR*. Moscow: Iuridicheskaia literatura, 1972.

Vyzhutovich, V. "The Hundred-Meter Strip." *Komsomolskaia pravda*, July 13, 1975: 2-3. Translated in *CDSP* 27, 33: 6.

Wädekin, K. E. "Soviet Rural Society. A descriptive stratification analysis." *Soviet Studies* 22 (April 1971): 512-38.

"Waiting Line for the Wedding." *Current Digest of the Soviet Press* 28, 42 (1976): 18-19.

Wallace, Sir Donald Mackenzie. *Russia*. London: 1912.

Wolfe, Thomas W. *Soviet Power and Europe 1945-1970*. Baltimore and London: Johns Hopkins University Press, 1970.

Wren, C. S. "Spassky Marriage Poses Moscow Test on Rights." *New York Times*, September 9, 1975: 3.

——. "A Spring Day in Kiev Brings Joy to Newlyweds, Shoppers." *International Herald Tribune*, March 24, 1977: 4.

Yanowitch, M. and Dodge, N. "Social Class and Education: Soviet Findings and Reactions." *Comparative Education Review* (October 1968): 248-67.

——. "The Social Evaluation of Occupations in the Soviet Union." *Slavic Review* 28 (1969): 619-42.

Yanowitch, Murray, and Fisher, Wesley A., eds. *Social Stratification and Mobility in the USSR*. White Plains, N.Y.: International Arts and Sciences Press, 1973.

"The Young Marrieds." *New Statesman*, September 4, 1964: 304.

"The Young Women Are Leaving Krasavino." *Pravda*, March 26, 1975: 2. Translated in *CDSP* 27, 12: 22.

Zamiatin, Evgenii. *We*. New York: E. P. Dutton, 1924.

Zhirnova, G. V. "Traditsionnye mesta vstrech molodezhi v gorode: seredina XIX-nachalo XX v." In *Polevye issledovaniia Instituta Etnografii 1974*. Moscow: Nauka, 1975.

Zhukovitskii, L. "Love and Demography." *Literaturnaia gazeta*, May 4, 1977: 12. Translated in *CDSP* 29, 18: 1-4.

INDEX

Adzhubei, A. I., 11
age: attitudes toward interethnic marriage
    by, 209–10; belief in love by, 21
age at marriage: 6, 69, 78–79, 148–69,
    257; in Baltics, 148, 155; in Caucasus,
    148, 155; in Central Asia, 148, 155;
    comparative ages of spouses, 6, 131,
    159–69, 259–60; legal restrictions on,
    15, 148; long-term trend, 149–54;
    mean, 149–54, 155, 159–60; median,
    149–54, 155, 159–60; and military
    draft, 154; minimum, 148–49; and pro-
    portion married, 116–17, regional vari-
    ations in, 155–59, and sex ratios, 131;
    in Slavic areas, 148, 155; urban/rural
    differences, 155–59; in West, 154; (*see
    also* specific nationalities and republics)
anti-Semitism, 251
Armenian Apostolic church, 247
Armenians, 221, 226, 244, 247–49, 252,
    256; (*see also* Caucasians)
Armenian SSR: comparative ages of
    spouses in, 160, 169; criminal code,
    14, 15, 79, 83; marital status in, 122–
    25; mixed marriages in, 218–20, 221,
    244, 247–50
Ashkhabad, 245, 247, 250
Astrakhan, 45
Astrakhan province, 57
Azerbaidzhan SSR: criminal code, 15;
    family code, 12; marital status in, 122–
    25; marriage rates in, 70–71, 83; mixed
    marriages in, 218, 221, 244, 245
Azeri, 221, 244, 245, 247–50, 252; (*see
    also* Caucasians)
Autonomous Oblasts (AOs), 221–25
Autonomous Soviet Socialist Repub-
    lics (ASSRs), 221–25

Balts, 125, 226, 229, 252, 255–57; (*see
    also* individual nationalities)
Becker, G. S., 8–10, 112, 130, 131, 134,
    137, 138, 146, 170

Berg, A. I., 45–46
bigamy, 16, 89
bilingualism: and attitudes toward inter-
    ethnic marriage, 207–09; and inter-
    ethnic marriage, 231–32
Birobidzhan (*see* Jewish Autonomous
    Oblast)
Bolsheviks, 3
Brezhnev, L. I., 12
Briansk province, 57
bride-price, 38–39, 48–49, 259; and age
    at marriage, 155; in Caucasus, 40–41;
    in Central Asia, 40–41; legal restric-
    tions against, 13–14, 48; and sex ratio,
    49
Buryat ASSR, 26
Byelorussians, 205, 207, 230, 245, 247,
    250, 252; (*see also* Slavs)
Byelorussian SSR: attitudes toward ethnic
    intermarriage in, 205; courtship in, 25,
    41; criminal code, 16; divorce in, 95,
    100; family code, 12, 51; geographic
    propinquity in, 204; marital status in,
    122–25, 143; marriage rates in, 83, 95–
    96; mixed marriages in, 230; relative
    ages of brides and grooms in, 169

Catholics, 139, 247
Caucasians, 125, 226, 229; (*see also* indi-
    vidual nationalities)
Caucasus: marriage rates in, 83–89; rela-
    tive ages of spouses in, 160; weddings
    in, 60; (*see also* specific republics)
censuses: and number married, 112–16
Central Asia: land distribution in, 136;
    marriage rates in, 69–70, 79, 83;
    polygyny in, 113–16; relative ages of
    brides and grooms, 160; wedding
    rituals in, 55; (*see also* specific repub-
    lics)
Central Asians, 125, 221, 226, 229, 238,
    247, 251–52; (*see also* individual na-
    tionalities)

housing: as criterion of mate-selection, 46–47; intermarriage between persons with different housing conditions, 200; and kin control of mate-selection, 41; marriage rates and, 70–73; proportion married and, 138
How the Steel Was Tempered, 35

ideology, 10–11; belief in love and, 21–35; duration of courtship and, 51–52; (*see also* Marxism-Leninism)
illegitimacy: fictitious marriages and, 37–38; marriage rates and, 69; number married and, 113; and waiting time for marriage, 50
incestuous marriages, 15–16
income: as criterion of mate-selection, 32, 33, 46–47; and divorce, 137; marriage rates and, 70–72; and proportion married, 9, 137–38, 143–46, 258–59; relative wages of men and women, 8–10, 134, 138; (*see also* interclass marriage, stratification)
intercitizenship marriages: between citizens of the USSR and of foreign countries, 16, 37, 51, 252–57; between citizens of USSR and citizens of US, 252–57, *passim*; discouragement of, 252–54; and Helsinki accords, 253; legal restrictions on, 252–53; number of, 255; popular attitudes toward, 254–55; and sex of Soviet spouses, 255–56; and sex ratios, 255–56
interclass marriages, 52–53, 171–79, 203; between persons of different class origins, 173–76; between persons of different educational levels, 191–97, 259–60; between persons of different income levels, 199–201; between persons of different occupations, 176–91, 259–60, 260; between persons with different housing conditions, 200; between social classes in the United States, 203; in rural areas, 179; (*see also* education, income, geographic propinquity, prestige, social classes, social mobility, socio-economic status, stratification)
interethnic marriages, 52, 204–52, 259–60, 260; and attitudes in US on, 216, 238; and bilingualism, 231–32, 234, 235, 238; combinations of nationalities in, 244–52; and education, 232, 234–

35, 238; and ethnic consciousness, 216–44, *passim*; and existing homogeneity of families, 232–33, 234–35; information on, 217; and kin control of mating, 232, 234, 235, 238; in labor camps, 229; legal restrictions on, 204–205; official attitudes towards, 204–205; popular values regarding, 205–16, 229–30; proportions of men and women in, 250–52; and religion, 245–50; and sex ratio, 231, 233–34; size of nationality, 230–31, 233, 235, 238; in US, 217, 232, 251; and urbanization, 231, 234; (*see also* intercitizenship marriages, interracial marriages, interreligious marriages)
interracial marriages, 5; in US, 16; (*see also* interethnic marriages)
interreligious marriages, 5, 245–50; (*see also* interethnic marriages)
Iunost, 34
Iurkevich, N.G., 4
Izvestiia, 15, 38

Jewish Autonomous Oblast, 220, 225
Jews, 43, 139, 143, 220, 225–27, 238–44, 250, 251–52, 253–54; (*see also* interethnic marriages, religion)

Kalinin Oblast, 179
Kalmyk ASSR, 176
Kalym (*see* bride-price)
Karelian ASSR, 220, 225–27
Karelians, 225–27
Kauzov, S., 254
Kazakhs, 247, 250; (*see also* Central Asians)
Kazakh SSR: criminal code, 14, 15; marital status in, 122–25; marriage rates in, 70; mixed marriages in, 218, 221, 245–47; number married in, 116
Kazan, 209
Kharchev, A. G., 4, 6, 10, 21, 41, 42, 261
Khrushchev, N. S., 11, 45, 69, 76
Kiev, 38, 41, 42, 52, 60–61, 175, 176, 185, 192, 195, 198–200, 202, 245, 255
Kirgiz, 226, 230, 247 (*see also* Central Asians)
Kirgiz SSR: belief in love in, 25; courtship in, 42–43, 51; criminal code, 14, 15; criterion of mate-selection in, 32; marital status in, 122–25, 143;

in US, 11, 69; wars and, 62–63, 76–78
marriage squeeze, 263
Marx, K., 1–4, 5, 6–7
Marxism, 14, 261
Marxism-Leninism, 7, 10, 16–17, 206, 253, 258, 264–65; (see also ideology)
mass media, 10–11; and attitudes toward ethnic intermarriage, 207; coverage of spouses of public figures, 11–12
matchmaking, 43–48; in Baltics, 40; in Byelorussia, 40; and duration of courtship, 51–52; in pre-revolutionary Russia, 38–40; in Ukraine, 40; (see also computer matchmaking, courtship)
mate-selection; attitudes toward, 20–38; calculation in, 7–8, 10, 14, 35–38, 51; under capitalism, 1–2, 3–5, 13; under communism, 3–8; criteria for, 20–38, 46–47,160–69, 261; economic variables in, 1–19 passim; Soviet sociologists on, 3–8; (see also bride-price, computer matchmaking, courtship, dowries, engagement, love, market theory of mate-selection, marriage advertisements, marriage bureaus, matchmaking, wedding rituals, ZAGS)
Mazur, D. P., 146
military service: marriage and, 12, 51, 61–63, 69–70, 79, 83, 154
Minsk, 21, 25, 29, 32, 37, 52, 245, 250
"Model Charter of the Collective Farms," 136–37
Moldavians, 125, 245
Moldavian SSR: family code, 12; criminal code, 16; marital status in, 122–25, 143; marriage rates in, 83; mixed marriages in, 218, 245; number married in, 83
Moscow, 21, 25, 46, 48, 52, 57, 63, 103, 176, 186, 245
Moscow province, 55, 66, 205
Moskovskii komsomolets, 47
Moslems, 139, 143, 155, 232, 245, 247, 250; (see also Central Asians)

names of husband and wife, 12–13
nationality: of children in mixed marriages, 216; as criterion of mate-selection, 32; prestige of, 251–52; proportions married and, 138–46; size of and inter-ethnic marriage, 230–31; variation in marital status, 125–29; (see also individual nationalities, interethnic marriages)
Nedelia, 47
nepotism: legal restrictions on, 20
Novosibirsk oblast, 194–95
Novosti Press Agency, 255

obshchina, 136
occupation: belief in love and, 21, 29; of bride and groom, 170–91 passim; as criterion of mate-selection, 32, 34; (see also interclass marriages, social classes, stratification)
Onassis, C., 254
Orel, 176
Orwell, G., 17
Ostrovskii, N. A., 35

Palaces of Weddings, 25, 50, 52, 55–59; Leningrad, 21, 41, 55
Perevedentsev, V. I., 264
Perm, 25, 41
personality: as criterion in mate-selection, 31
Peter the Great, 204
Petropavlovsk, 247
physical appearance: as criterion of mate-selection, 31, 32, 33
Pipes, R., 216
Poles, 247
political attitudes: as criterion of mate-selection, 35
political power: as factor in mate-selection, 199; (see also Communist Party of the Soviet Union, elite, political attitudes, interclass marriages, social classes, stratification)
polygyny, 16, 113–16
Pravda, 15, 46, 60–61, 89
prestige: derived from spouse, 170–71, 251–52; of nationalities, 251–52; (see also interclass marriages, stratification)
prostitution, 1, 13–14, 29
Protestants, 1–2, 247; (see also interreligious marriages, religion)
Pskov, 186
Ptukha, M. V., 225
puberty, 154
Pukirev, V. V., 159

Ratser, R., 34
religion: as factor in intermarriage, 204–

in, 221, 244–45, 250

Ukrainian Autocephalous Church, 208–209

Ukrainians, 205, 207–209, 221, 229–30, 245, 250, 252; (see also Slavs)

Ukrainian SSR: age at marriage in, 155–59; attitudes toward interethnic marriage in, 205; criminal code, 16; divorce in, 95; family code, 12, 148; marital status in, 122–25; marriage rates in, 66, 69, 79, 83, 95–96, 100, 107–111; mixed marriages in, 218, 225, 230, 239; number married in, 116; relative ages of brides and grooms in, 160–61, 169; wedding rituals in, 60

Unequal Marriage, 34

Union Republics of USSR: criminal codes, 14, 16; data on marital status, 112; family codes of, 12, 148; intermarriage between social classes in, 172; marriage rates in, 79–89; mixed marriages in, 221–25; (see also specific republics)

United Nations, 253

United States, 8–9, 11, 16, 38, 69, 122, 130, 131, 135, 138, 146, 203, 261, 262, 263–64

United States Embassy, Moscow, 253, 255

urbanization: and interethnic marriage, 231; and proportion married, 137–38, 143

Uzbeks, 244, 247 (see also Central Asians)

Uzbek SSR: attitudes toward ethnic intermarriage in, 205; criminal code, 15; family code, 148; marital status in, 122–25; marriage rates in, 70; weddings in, 60

Valentin and Valentina, 34

Vilnius, 52, 95

Vilnius State University, 32

virginity of Moslem females, 139

Vladivostok, 46

Volgograd province, 55

Wallace, D. M., 21

wedding rituals, 20, 54–61; in Leningrad Palace of Weddings, 57–59; matchmaking and, 43; religious ceremonies and, 55–57, 103–107; in remarriages, 60; after revolution, 54–55; in pre-revolutionary Russia, 38–39; Russian Orthodoxy and, 54; size of parties and, 57, 60–61

widows, 78, 117

Winch, R., 5

women's employment, 1–2, 10–12, 146; as criterion of mate-selection, 34; and housing, 138; and intermarriage between classes, 175–79; and proportion married, 135–36, 146–47, 258–59; in rural areas, 135; in US, 11

women's liberation movement, 263–64; in US, 263–64

World War I, 63

World War II: and marriage between educational groups, 192–95; marriage rates and, 66, 69, 70, 73–76; proportion married and, 117; wedding rituals and, 55, 57, 60

Yaroslavl province, 55

ZAGS (Bureau of Registration of Acts of Civil Status), 15, 25, 35–36, 42, 51, 52–54, 55, 159, 217, 225, 253

Zamiatin, E. I., 17

Zhensovet, 15

ABOUT THE AUTHOR

WESLEY A. FISHER is Assistant Professor of Sociology, Columbia University. The recipient of Fulbright-Hays awards, he has twice participated in the exchange of scholars with the USSR Ministry of Higher Education and has lectured in the Soviet Union at the invitation of the Estonian Academy of Sciences. He is US Coordinator for Projects in Sociology, American Council of Learned Societies—USSR Academy of Sciences Commission in the Social Sciences and Humanities.

Dr. Fisher's previous books include *Social Stratification and Mobility in the USSR* and *The Moscow Gourmet: Dining Out in the Capital of the USSR*. His articles and reviews have appeared in the *Journal of Marriage and the Family*, *Soviet Studies*, *Contemporary Sociology*, and other journals.

Dr. Fisher holds a B.A. from Harvard University and a Certificate of the Russian Institute, M.Phil., and Ph.D. from Columbia University.

STUDIES OF THE
RUSSIAN INSTITUTE

ABRAM BERGSON, *Soviet National Income in 1937* (1953).

ERNEST J. SIMMONS, JR., ed., *Through the Glass of Soviet Literature: Views of Russian Society* (1953).

THAD PAUL ALTON, *Polish Postwar Economy* (1954).

DAVID GRANICK, *Management of the Industrial Firm in the USSR: A Study in Soviet Economic Planning* (1954).

ALLEN S. WHITING, *Soviet Policies in China, 1917-1924* (1954).

GEORGE S. N. LUCKYJ, *Literary Politics in the Soviet Ukraine, 1917-1934* (1956).

MICHAEL BORO PETROVICH, *The Emergence of Russian Panslavism, 1856-1870* (1956).

THOMAS TAYLOR HAMMOND, *Lenin on Trade Unions and Revolution, 1893-1917* (1956).

DAVID MARSHALL LANG, *The Last Years of the Georgian Monarchy, 1658-1832* (1957).

JAMES WILLIAM MORLEY, *The Japanese Thrust into Siberia, 1918* (1957).

ALEXANDER G. PARK, *Bolshevism in Turkestan, 1917-1927* (1957).

HERBERT MARCUSE, *Soviet Marxism: A Critical Analysis* (1958).

CHARLES B. MCLANE, *Soviet Policy and the Chinese Communists, 1931-1946* (1958).

OLIVER H. RADKEY, *The Agrarian Foes of Bolshevism: Promise and Defeat of the Russian Socialist Revolutionaries, February to October, 1917* (1958).

RALPH TALCOTT FISHER, JR., *Pattern for Soviet Youth: A Study of the Congresses of the Komsomol, 1918-1954* (1959).

RICHARD T. DE GEORGE, *Soviet Ethics and Morality* (University of Michigan, 1969).

JONATHAN FRANKEL, *Vladimir Akimov on the Dilemmas of Russian Marxism, 1895-1903* (Cambridge, 1969).

WILLIAM ZIMMERMAN, *Soviet Perspectives on International Relations, 1956-1967* (Princeton, 1969).

PAUL AVRICH, *Kronstadt, 1921* (Princeton, 1970).

EZRA MENDELSOHN, *Class Struggle in the Pale: The Formative Years of the Jewish Workers' Movement in Tsarist Russia* (Cambridge, 1970).

EDWARD J. BROWN, *The Proletarian Episode in Russian Literature* (Columbia, 1971).

REGINALD E. ZELNIK, *Labor and Society in Tsarist Russia: The Factory Workers of St. Petersburg, 1855-1870* (Stanford, 1971).

PATRICIA K. GRIMSTED, *Archives and Manuscript Repositories in the USSR: Moscow and Leningrad* (Princeton, 1972).

RONALD G. SUNY, *The Baku Commune, 1917-1918* (Princeton, 1972).

EDWARD J. BROWN, *Mayakovsky: A Poet in the Revolution* (Princeton, 1973).

MILTON EHRE, *Oblomov and his Creator: The Life and Art of Ivan Goncharov* (Princeton, 1973).

HENRY KRISCH, *German Politics under Soviet Occupation* (Columbia, 1974).

HENRY W. MORTON and RUDOLPH L. TÖKÉS, eds., *Soviet Politics and Society in the 1970's* (Free Press, 1974).

WILLIAM G. ROSENBERG, *Liberals in the Russian Revolution* (Princeton, 1974).

RICHARD G. ROBBINS, Jr., *Famine in Russia, 1891-1892* (Columbia, 1975).

VERA DUNHAM, *In Stalin's Time: Middleclass Values in Soviet Fiction* (Cambridge, 1976).

WALTER SABLINSKY, *The Road to Bloody Sunday* (Princeton, 1976).

ALFRED ERICH SENN, *The Emergence of Modern Lithuania* (1959).

ELLIOT R. GOODMAN, *The Soviet Design for a World State* (1960).

JOHN N. HAZARD, *Settling Disputes in Soviet Society: The Formative Years of Legal Institutions* (1960).

DAVID JORAVSKY, *Soviet Marxism and Natural Science, 1917-1932* (1961).

MAURICE FRIEDBERG, *Russian Classics in Soviet Jackets* (1962).

ALFRED J. RIEBER, *Stalin and the French Communist Party, 1941-1947* (1962).

THEODORE K. VON LAUE, *Sergei Witte and the Industrialization of Russia* (1962).

JOHN A. ARMSTRONG, *Ukrainian Nationalism* (1963).

OLIVER H. RADKEY, *The Sickle under the Hammer: The Russian Socialist Revolutionaries in the Early Months of Soviet Rule* (1963).

KERMIT E. MCKENZIE, *Comintern and World Revolution, 1928-1943: The Shaping of Doctrine* (1964).

HARVEY L. DYCK, *Weimar Germany and Soviet Russia, 1926-1933: A Study in Diplomatic Instability* (1966).

(Above titles published by Columbia University Press.)

HAROLD J. NOAH, *Financing Soviet Schools* (Teachers College, 1966).

JOHN M. THOMPSON, *Russia, Bolshevism, and the Versailles Peace* (Princeton, 1966).

PAUL AVRICH, *The Russian Anarchists* (Princeton, 1967).

LOREN R. GRAHAM, *The Soviet Academy of Sciences and the Communist Party, 1927-1932* (Princeton, 1967).

ROBERT A. MAGUIRE, *Red Virgin Soil: Soviet Literature in the 1920's* (Princeton, 1968).

T. H. RIGBY, *Communist Party Membership in the U.S.S.R., 1917-1967* (Princeton, 1968).

WILLIAM MILLS TODD III, *The Familiar Letters as a Literary Genre in the Age of Pushkin* (Princeton, 1976).

ELIZABETH VALKENIER, *Russian Realist Art. The State and Society: The Peredvizhniki and Their Tradition* (Ardis, 1977).

SUSAN SOLOMON, *The Soviet Agrarian Debate* (Westview, 1978).

SHEILA FITZPATRICK, ed., *Cultural Revolution in Russia, 1928-1931* (Indiana, 1978).

PETER SOLOMON, *Soviet Criminologists and Criminal Policy: Specialists in Policy-Making* (Columbia, 1978).

KENDALL E. BAILES, *Technology and Society under Lenin and Stalin: Origins of the Soviet Technical Intelligentsia, 1917-1941* (Princeton, 1978).

LEOPOLD H. HAIMSON, ed., *The Politics of Rural Russia, 1905-1914* (Indiana, 1979).

THEODORE H. FRIEDGUT, *Political Participation in the USSR* (Princeton, 1979).

SHEILA FITZPATRICK, *Education and Social Mobility in the Soviet Union, 1921-1934* (Cambridge, 1979).